THE MAYFLOWER DESCENDANT

VOLUME XXIV

ISBN 9781451529975

Prepared for publication by
Melinda Adams Mohnike

THE
MAYFLOWER DESCENDANT

1620   2020

A QUARTERLY MAGAZINE OF
PILGRIM GENEALOGY AND HISTORY

VOLUME XXIV

1922

PUBLISHED BY THE

MASSACHUSETTS SOCIETY OF
MAYFLOWER DESCENDANTS
BOSTON

INDEX OF SUBJECTS

Signed, Sealed & delivered
In presence of us

Nath.ll Thomas

Margaret Little

Bethiah Little

Bethiah Little

Thomas Little

Isaac Little

Caleb Little

Nath.ll Little

William Little

Lemuel Little

LIEUT. ISAAC LITTLE'S HEIRS

by a general Consent from time to time be made choice of, and assented unto. The Contents whereof followeth.

IN the Name of God, Amen. We whose Names are under-written, the Loyal Subjects of our dread Soveraign Lord King *James*, by the grace of God of Great Britain, France and Ireland, King, Defendor of the Faith, &c. Having undertaken for the glory of God, and advancement of the Christian Faith, and the Honour of our King and Countrey, a Voyage to plant the first Colony in the Northern parts of *Virginia*; Do by these Presents solemnly and mutually, in the presence of God and one another, Covenant and Combine our selves together into a Civil Body Politick, for our better ordering and preservation, and furtherance of the ends aforesaid: and by virtue hereof do enact, constitute and frame such just and equal Laws, Ordinances, Acts, Constitutions and Officers, from time to time, as shall be thought most meet and convenient for the general good of the Colony; unto which we promise all due submission and obedience. In witness whereof we have hereunto subscribed our Names at *Cape Cod*, the eleventh of *November*, in the Reign of our Soveraign Lord King *James*, of *England, France* and *Ireland* the eighteenth, and of *Scotland* the fifty fourth, *Anno Dom.* 1620.

This was the first Foundation of the Government of New-Plimouth.

John Carver.	Samuel Fuller.	Edward Tilly.
William Bradford.	Christopher Martin.	John Tilly.
Edward Winslow,	William Mullins.	Francis Cook.
William Brewster,	William White,	Thomas Rogers.
Isaac Allerton.	Richard Warren.	Thomas Tinker.
Miles Standish,	John Howland.	John Ridgdale.
John Alden, —	Steven Hopkins.	Edward Fuller.

John

"THE COMPACT" AND TWENTY-ONE OF ITS SIGNERS
FROM MORTON'S "NEW-ENGLANDS MEMORIALL."

WILLIAM BREWSTER'S AUTOGRAPH ON A LEASE OF SCROOBY MANOR HOUSE

quiet inioyed to her free from moleſtation during her
Naturall life in conſideration wherof

I giue & bequeath to my ſaid two ſons Joſeph & Anthony
all my other Lands whatſoeuer & wherſoeuer to them &
their ſeuerall heires in equall halfe.

Item I haue allready formerly giuen to my Daughter
Sarah Howett the ſum of one hundred Pounds

Item I haue allready formerly giuen to my Daughter
Elizabeth Bartlett Deceaſed the ſum of one hundred pounds

Item I haue allready formerly giuen to my Daughter
Abigall Winſlow the ſum of one hundred pounds

Item I giue & bequeath to my Daughter Bethiah one hundred pounds to be paid her by my Executrix

Item I giue & bequeath to my Daughter Lydia one
hundred pounds to be paid her by my Executrix

Item I giue to Mary Oſquitan which I haue brought
up thirty pounds to be paid her by my Executrix
All the ſaid Legacys to be paid them at their full age
or day of Marriage which ſhall firſt hapen

Item I giue & bequeath unto my welbeloued wife Sarah
all the reſidue & remainder of my moneys goods & other
Eſtate whatſoeuer for her comfort & ſuppoſt during her
Naturall life & wiſh that ſhe remaine therof at her deceaſe
to be equally Deuided amongſt my Daughters that is to
ſay to my Daughters Sarah Abigall Bethiah Lydia & the
Children of my Daughter Elizabeth deceaſed & in caſe
any other of my ſaid Daughters ſhall deceaſe before their
Mother then their Children to haue their Mothers part

Laſtly I nominate & appoint my welbeloued wife Sarah to
be ſole Executrix of this my Laſt Will & Teſtament

Signed ſealed & declared
by the aboueſaid Joſeph Waterman   JOSsh Waterman
to be his Laſt Will & Teſtament

In preſence of us

Elizabeth Thomas

Samuell Hills
& Iſaac Thomas

Memorand That on the 12 day of March — 1710
The abouenamed Mrs Elizabeth Thomas & Iſaac
Thomas made oath before me that they ſaw
the abouenamed Joſeph Waterman ſigne & ſeale
& heard him Declare the abouewritten inſtrument
to be his Laſt Will & Teſtament & that he then was
of a diſpoſing mind & Memory to their beſt judgment
Nathaniel Thomas Juſtice

JOSEPH WATERMAN'S WILL

THE MAYFLOWER DESCENDANT

Vol. XXIV · JANUARY, 1922 · No. 1

LIEUTENANT ISAAC LITTLE'S ESTATE
BY THE EDITOR

ISAAC LITTLE[3], son of Thomas Little and his wife Anna[2] Warren (*Richard*[1]), was born about 1646, and was taken by his parents from Plymouth to Marshfield, when they removed to the latter town.

Isaac Little[3] married Bethiah Thomas, daughter of Captain Nathaniel Thomas of Marshfield, and they had eleven children. Three daughters, Dorothy, Bethiah, and one unnamed, died in infancy. Six sons and two daughters, Thomas, Isaac, Charles, Nathaniel, William, Lemuel, Abigail, and Bethiah (second of the name), were baptized at Marshfield, 24 March, 1700, and these eight children survived their father, who died 24 November, 1699.

Isaac Little[3] was called Lieutenant in the record of his death, at Marshfield, and in his nuncupative will, but is called Esquire on his gravestone. The town record does not tell us how old he was, but according to the gravestone record he died aged about 53 years. His widow Bethiah died 23 September, 1718, and is called wife of Isaac Little, Esq., in her gravestone record, but her age is not given. Both Isaac and Bethiah were buried in the Winslow Cemetery, at Marshfield.

The son Thomas Little[4] married Mary Mayhew and left issue.

Isaac Little[4] married, first, Mary Otis, and second, widow Abigail (Cushing) Thomas, and left issue by each wife.

Charles Little[4] married Sarah[4] Warren (*James*[3], *Nathaniel*[2], *Richard*[1]) and left issue.

Nathaniel Little[4] died in Carolina, before 25 June, 1715, apparently unmarried.

William Little[4] married Hannah.

Lemuel Little[4] married Jane Sarson and left issue.

Abigail Little[4] married John Arbuthnot of Boston.

Bethiah Little[4] married Thomas Barker of Pembroke, Mass., and left issue.

Lieut. Isaac Little[3] made a nuncupative will, 18 November, 1699, six days before he died, but it was not approved by the probate court and was not recorded. The original document is still in the probate files, and we give an exhaustive abstract of it, in this article, because of its genealogical importance. It .mentions the widow, without giving her name, the "Eldest Son Thomas", sons Isaac, Charles, Nathaniel, William, "youngest Son Lemuel", "my Two Daughters", "my Loving Brother Maj[r] Nathaniel Thomas and my Broth[r] Ephraim Little". Ephraim Little[3] and his wife Mary witnessed this will.

The widow, Bethiah Little, was appointed administratrix, on 8 January, 1699/1700, but a settlement of the estate was not made until 29 March, 1712. This settlement was signed by widow Bethiah Little; by sons Thomas, Isaac, Charles, Nathaniel, William and Lemuel; and by daughters Abigail Little and Bethiah Little.

On 29 March, 1712, widow Bethiah, sons Thomas, Isaac, Charles and Nathaniel, and daughter Abigail Little, "all of full age", and sons William and Lemuel, and daughter Bethiah, all three under age, acknowledged the settlement.

On 7 March, 1712/13, William Little, having come of age, confirmed his acknowledgment. On 3 April, 1714, "Thomas Barker & the abovenamed Bethiah his wife" confirmed her acknowledgment. And on 3 May, 1718, Lemuel Little also confirmed his acknowledgment.

The original agreement for a settlement of the estate bears the autograph signatures of the widow Bethiah and the eight surviving children, Thomas, Isaac, Charles, Nathaniel, William, Lemuel, Abigail Little and Bethiah Little (the daughter). The page of this document with these nine interesting autographs is reproduced in the illustration facing the first page of this article. This illustration has been prepared at the expense of a member of the Massachusetts Society of Mayflower Descendants, Miss Susan Barker Willard, of Hingham, Mass., who is a descendant of Lieutenant Isaac Little[3], through his daughter Bethiah, the wife of Thomas Barker of Pembroke.

We here present exhaustive abstracts of all records, and original documents on file, relating to the settlement of Lieutenant Isaac Little's estate, found in the Plymouth County, Mass., Probate records.

[ISAAC LITTLE'S ESTATE]

[From unrecorded nuncupative will] "November 18th 1699. Wee the Subscribers being att ye house of Leiut Isaac Little of Marshfeild he being on his Death bed weak of Body but in his right mind, and of Sound Memory heard him declare this to be his last will and Testament . viz.

"First . . . . that all my houses and Lands in Marshfeild be by my Overseers Equally divided into Three parts; And my Eldest Son Thomas to have his first Choice, my Son Isaac to have his 2d choice, and my Son Charles to have ye 3d part.

"Also my Two sons Nathaniel and William to have all my Lands at Showamett to be divided Equally & Nathaniel to have his first Choice."

"my Youngest Son Lemuel shall have all my lands att Rochester and Middleborough, & Matakesitt."

"my Two Daughters Shall have Each of them one hundred Pounds out of my Moveable Estate."

"I Leave all ye rest of my Estate with my loving Wife to make her life Comfortable & for ye bringing up of my young Children; and ye remaindr to be divided Amongst my Children as my wife Shall see Cause wth ye advice of my Overseers."

"I . . . . Apoint my Loving Brother Majr Nathaniel Thomas and my Brothr Ephraim Little to see that this my Will be observed and prformd."

"Most of his Children being present he charged ym to take notice as they Would Answer it at ye great day that this was his Will; he also told his Son Thomas that he had done Considerably for him already; And So Charged them all to fear God & obey their Mother and to live in Love one wth Another &c

"Hee also added that If his wife Saw cause wth ye advice of ye Overseers shee might add more to his daughters Portions or to his Son Lemuels Portion"

"Hee also Gave a Charge to mind in ye Division of his Lands att Marshfeild yt his wife must have ye Improvemt of ye farm that he now dwels on. The Question was asked Do you Intend yr wife ye Improvement of it during her Natural life? He returned No but as long as shee bares my Name. Hee was told that his Son Lemuels Portion was farr short of his brothers to wch hee Answered I leave that wth my Wife wth ye Advice of my Overseers to add w^t they see Cause out of my Moveable Estate"

The will was witnessed by Ephraim Little; Mary Little (by a mark) "who subscribed to what is within written but is doubt-full Concerning ye Questions & Answers above written"; and "As to ye five Eldest Sons Portions is Testified as above or within writin by me Job Otis."

"m^r Ephraim Little made oath to ye whole of what is above & within written vizt that he heard him s^d Isaac Little verbally Declare what is herein written in his last sickness to be his mind & will & that he ye s^d Ephraim forthwith committed ye same or Caused it to be Committed to writing: Also Mary his wife made oath to ye same according as she hath subscribed and Job otis otis as he hath hereto subscribed. Before William Bradford Esq Judge &c In Plimouth ye Sixth day of march An^o Domini 1699 or 1700"

The will is endorsed: "The Will nuncupative of Isaac Little Esqr deceased"

[Plym. Co. Probate 1:314] On 8 January, 1699/1700, "Be-thyah Little Gentlewoman Relict & widdow of Isaac Little late of Marshfield . . . . Esqr" was appointed administratrix.

[From unrecorded bond] On 8 January, 1699/1700, Bethiah Little, as administratrix, with Nathaniel Thomas, Esq., and Ephraim Little as sureties, all three of Marshfield, gave a bond for £1000. The witnesses were Samuel Sprague and James Partridge.

[From original inventory] The inventory was taken by Samuel Sprague and Ephraim Little, 17 January, 1699/1700. No real estate was mentioned. "Negro Servants" were valued at £100; "Sloopes" £100. Debts were due from the estate to Job Randall; "m^r Heath"; John Foster; Thomas Howland; Josiah Sawyer; "Capt Winslow"; John Bonney; Joseph Nash; "Nath^ll Thomas, Esqr".

Bethiah Little, administratrix, made oath to the inventory 6 March, 1699/1700, before William Bradford, Judge of Probate. [Also recorded, 1:315.]

[From original document] "wheras Isaac Little late of Marshfield . . . . Esqr deceas^d dyed without any written will, but in his last sicknes declared his mind . . . . how he would have his lands & other Estate disposed To his Widow And Amongst his children, after his decease . . . . Wee Thomas Little, Isaac Little, Charles Little Nathaniel Little William Little, Lemuel Little, Abigail Little, & Bethiah Little Children of our honored father Isaac Little deceas^d as Afors^d being minded to Settle the s^d lands and Estate in Such manner as our hon^d father by his s^d Nuncupative Will declared Should be done; Do therfore with the advice and consent of our hon^d Mother Mrs Bethiah Little Relict & Widow of our s^d deceas^d father . . . . agree that the s^d lands And Estate Shall be settled . . . . As in this Instrument here following is declared"

"Thomas Little the Eldest Son Shall have all those housing lands & meadows . . . . that were our fathers . . . . in Marshfild afors^d which he ye s^d Thomas hath already Sold to John Jones & Gilbert Winslow"

"Isaac Little Shall have all the housing & lands & meadows . . . . that were our fathers . . . . in Marshfield Afors^d which he is now in the possesion of viz one fourth part of ye lands formerly Brewsters grant Except^g the use of one half ye beach near the north river lying on the Southerly side of the ditch, for ye possesors of ye lands s^d Thomas Little Sold, to lay their own wood on for Ever. & also all that tract of land lying Between ye lands of Benjamin Philips & ye lands Sold by Thomas Little To John Jones And Gilbert Winslow; And also Six Acres of Medow near the north river lying between the medows of Ephraim Little And the medows S^d Thomas Little hath Sold to s^d Jones & Winslow lying below That part of the medow Sold to s^d Jones & Winslow, Adjacent to s^d Norcutts Creck Also all that parcell of medow lying on the northerly part of South river containing Twelve Acres more or less As it was bought of Mr Samuel Little, & also all that parcell of medow lying on the Southward Side of the South river bought of s^d Samuel Little being Twelve Acres more or less"

"Charles Little & Lemuel Little Shall have all the farm both upland & medow with the Appurtenances . . . . in Marshfield Afors^d formerly purchased of Ralph Powel And Martha his wife which ye s^d Charles Little hath already Sold To John Kent for" £542 "the one half of which Sum The s^d Charles Little hath responded by bond To ye s^d Lemuel, And also all those lands & medows which was our fathers being in ye Township of Rochester & Midleburro & also all those lands And medows which were our fathers lying & being in The Majors Purchase, and att Indian head river now in The Township of Pembrook, all which s^d Tracts or Pcells of lands (Except^g Powels farm) to them & their Severall respective heirs, to be Equally devid^d between them for their part & portion of their fathers Estate"

"The s^d Nathaniel Little And William Little Shall have all their fathers land . . . . att Shewamett in The Township of

Swansey in ye County of Bristoll . . . . to be Equally divided between Them"

"the s^d Abigail Little Shall have four hundred pounds in mony & moveables out of her s^d fathers Estate wch She hath already received for her part & portion"

"the s^d Bethiah Little Shall have four hundred pounds in money & movables to be received (of her Mother The Adm^rx) out of the s^d Estate"·

"And whereas the s^d Thomas Little by This division of our fathers Estate hath only one Single Share Thereof if it Shall herafter happen that Any of the s^d children Who are now within Age Shall disturb or break this Afors^d Settlement or refuse as they come respectively of Age to ratify & Confirm ye Same That then the s^d Thomas Little Shall have the proportion of a double portion out of their or Any of their parts that Shall break this Settlement."

"And it is Agreed & concluded That o^r Moth^r Afors^d Shall have & hold her right of thirds . . . . in all ye s^d lands that were our fathers during her naturall life; And Such part of the monyes & moveables As is already Agre^d betw. Them And likewise three sixteenth of ye Sawmill att Matakesit in ye Town of Pembrook afors^d with the lands & Appurtenances to the same belonging"

"In Wittnes wherof we The s^d Mother & Children have herunto Sett our hands & Seals" 29 March, 1712.

The division was signed by Bethiah Little, Thomas Little, Isaac Little, Charles Little, Nathaniel Little, William Little, Lemuel Little, Abigail Little, and Bethiah Little (the daughter). The witnesses were Nathaniel Thomas, Jr., and William Shurtleff, Jr.

On 29 March, 1712, Bethiah Little, Thomas Little, Isaac Little, Charles Little, Nathaniel Little and Abigail Little, "all of full age" acknowledged the settlement, "And also William Little Lemuel Little & bethiah Little acknowleged the same to be their act & Deed", before Nathaniel Thomas, Judge of Probate.

On 7 March, 1712, "William Little being then of full age affirmed to this Instrument as his Free act & Deed before" Nathaniel Thomas, Judge of Probate.

On 3 April, 1714, "Thomas Barker & the abovenamed Bethiah his wife affirmed to this Instrument as their free act & Deed" before Nathaniel Thomas, Judge of Probate.

On 3 May, 1718, "Lemuel Little acknowledged the above written to be his act & Deed" before Nathaniel Thomas, Judge of Probate.

The document was endorsed: "The Settlement of the Estate of Isaac Little Esqr" [Also recorded, 3:283]

LITTLE — BARKER — ARBUTHNOT

By the Editor

We here present exhaustive abstracts of three deeds of land which are especially interesting to descendants of Lieutenant Isaac Little[3] (*Anna*[2] *Warren, Richard*[1]) of Marshfield, Mass., as they furnish important data about his wife and the two daughters who married, and thus supplement our article on "Lieutenant Isaac Little's Estate", printed in this issue.

The first deed, dated 8 September, 1718, proves that Isaac's widow, Bethiah (Thomas) Little, was living in Pembroke, Mass., only fifteen days before she died. It also shows that William Thomas, late of Marshfield, had been her brother; that her daughter Abigail Little[4] was still unmarried; and that her daughter Bethiah Little[4] was the wife of Thomas Barker of Pembroke.

The second deed, dated 26 September, 1721, proves that the daughter Abigail Little[4] had become the wife of John Arbuthnot of Boston, and that both John and Abigail were living on 13 January, 1726/7; also that Thomas and Bethiah (Little) Barker were living on 18 April, 1728, when they acknowledged the deed.

The third deed, dated 20 January, 1757, proves that Abigail (Little) Arbuthnot had become a widow and was still a resident of Boston. In this deed she calls herself a daughter of Isaac Little, Esqr., completing the proof that Abigail (Little) Arbuthnot and Bethiah (Little) Barker were daughters of Isaac and Bethiah (Thomas) Little.

These three deeds are on record in the Plymouth County, Mass., Registry of Deeds.

[Bethiah Little to Abigail Little and Bethiah Barker]

[Plym. Co. Deeds, 18:165] On 8 September, 1718, "Bethiah Little late of Marshfield . . . . & now of Pembroke . . . . For and in Consideration of the Good Will & Motherly affection that I have & bear towards my two Daughters Abigail Little & Bethiah Barker the Wife of Thomas Barker of s^d Pembroke & for their tender Care towards me & for their Trouble & Expense in my Support in Sickness & Health Have Given . . . . unto them ye s^d Abigail Little . . . . & Bethiah Barker . . . . the one moiety or Half to the s^d Thomas Barker & Bethiah his Wife . . . . & the other Half to the s^d Abigail Little . . . . of all that my Right Title & Interest in & unto ye personal Estate which by Law doth accrue to me of or belonging to my Broth^r William Thomas late of s^d Marshfield deceas^d and also all my Right & Interest in & unto all that Part of my s^d Brother William's Real Estate in the Township of Pembroke afores^d both in the Tract of Lands called the Maj^{rs} Purchase & in the Several Divisions of Lands of late the Town of Marshfields Commons, as also to the Several Divisions & allotments of ye late Division of s^d Marshfields Commons now in ye Township of s^d Marshfield, Together with all & Singular ye Profits Priviledges & appurten^{ces} to the Same belonging"

The deed was witnessed by Mary Barker & Deborah Howland.

It was acknowledged, 8 September, 1718, before Isaac Little, Justice of the Peace, and was recorded 10 February, 1724.

[JOHN AND ABIGAIL ARBUTHNOT, AND THOMAS AND BETHIAH BARKER, TO ISAAC LITTLE]

[Plym. Co. Deeds, 28: 194] On 26 September, 1721, "John Arbuthnot of Boston . . . . & Abigail his Wife & Thomas Barker of Pembroke . . . . & Bethiah his Wife" for £30, sold to "Isaac Little of Marshfield . . . . All that our one fourth Part of all those Several Tracts Rights Lots & Parcells of Lands . . . . in the Townships of Marshfield & Pembroke afores^d of late ye Estate & Lands belonging to m^r Willm Thomas late of s^d Marshfield Deceased (Excepting the Great Farm or Homestead whereon he dyed) being that fourth Part of s^d William Thomas his Estate given to us by Our Hon^d Mother Bethiah Little deceased Which did accrue to her from her s^d Brother Willm Thomas Deceased . . . . He ye said Isaac Little Yielding & Paying to ye administrators of ye s^d Willm Thomas one fourth Part of what the moveables or Chattels shall fall Short of Paying of ye just Debts & funeral Charges"

The deed was signed by the four grantors, and was witnessed by Sarah Little, John Stetson, and Abigail Knap (who signed by a mark).

It was acknowledged by John and Abigail Arbuthnot, at Boston, 13 January, 1726/7, and by Thomas and Bethiah Barker, in Plymouth County, 18 April, 1728.

The deed was not recorded until 24 April, 1734.

[Widow Abigail Arbuthnot to Gideon Hackett]

[Plym. Co. Deeds, 45: 177] On 20 January, 1757, "abigail Arbuthnott of Boston . . . . widow to John Arbuthnot of s^d Boston deceased", for £26, 13s., 4d., lawful money, sold to "Gideon Hackett of Middleborough . . . . Labourer . . . . A certain Lot of Land lying & being in Middleborough aforesaid being the ninety ninth Lot in the Purchase called the South Purchase in s^d Middleborough containing about forty five acres be the Same more or less and in the Right of my Father Isaac Little Esqr late of Marshfield deceas^d The Bounds of s^d Lot may fully appear on the Records of said Purchase Reference thereto being had."

The deed was witnessed by Benjamin Gott and Mary Speakman.

Abigail Arbuthnot acknowledged the deed, in Middlesex County, Mass., 20 January, 1757, before Samuel Brigham, Justice of the Peace, and it was recorded, at Plymouth, 23 May, 1759.

JOHN SARGEANT'S WILL

By the Editor

John Sargeant, of Barnstable and Malden, Mass., was married three times. His first marriage, to Deborah Hillier, and the births of his first two children, Joseph and John, were recorded at Barnstable*. There is no record of the birth of the daughter Mary, who married Nathan Tobey; and a son Jabez Sargeant, recorded at Malden, died unmarried.

The first wife, Deborah, died at Malden, and John Sargeant married, second, Mary Bense, who died in 1670, without issue.

John Sargeant married, third, Lydia Chipman², daughter of Elder John Chipman by his first wife, Hope² Howland (*John¹*), but the date and place of the marriage are unknown.

Elder John Chipman's second wife was John Sargeant's sister Ruth Sargeant, whose first husband had been Jonathan Winslow of Marshfield. Ruth (Sargeant) (Winslow) Chipman survived her second husband also, and her will, printed in our third volume, mentions many relatives, including her brother John Sargeant and some of his children and grandchildren.

* Mayflower Descendant, 12: 154.

John and Lydia (Chipman) Sargeant had eleven children, and seven of them, Hannah, Jonathan, William, Ruth, Samuel, Ebenezer and Mehitable, were recorded at Malden. The names of the other four daughters, Lydia, Deborah, Hope and Sarah, we learn from their father's will.

John Sargeant's first and second wives were not descended from Mayflower Passengers. The descendants, therefore, of his third wife only are eligible for membership in the Society of Mayflower Descendants.

For convenient reference, the fifteen children are here listed:
Children of John and Deborah (Hillier) Sargent:
Joseph Sargeant, married and left issue.
John Sargeant, married and left issue.
Mary Sargeant, married Nathan Tobey and died before her
    father, leaving two children: Seth Tobey and Deborah
    (Tobey) Ivory.
Jabez Sargeant, died without issue, before his father.
Children of John and Lydia (Chipman) Sargeant:
Hannah Sargeant.
Jonathan Sargeant, married twice and left issue by each wife.
William Sargeant, married and left issue.
Lydia Sargeant, married Joseph Waite and left issue.
Deborah Sargeant, married Thomas Waite and left issue.
Hope Sargeant.
Ruth Sargeant, died unmarried.
Samuel Sargeant, married and left issue.
Ebenezer Sargeant, married twice, but left no issue.
Sarah Sargeant, died unmarried.
Mehitable Sargeant.

An original document in the Middlesex County, Mass., Probate Files, giving the distribution of the estate of the son Jabez Sargeant (who, as already stated, died without issue) identifies the four children of John Sargeant by his first wife. It is dated 4 February, 1694/5, and bears the following endorsement: "Ordered yᵗ Abovesd Estate" amounting to £66, 19s., "be Equally dvided betwixt Joseph & John Serjeant & Seeth & Debora Toby the children of Nathan & Mary Toby only brothers & Sister of Jabez Serjeant deceased in the whole blood"

John Sargeant made his will, 20 May, 1708, and as he signed his name "Sargeant" that form has been used in this article.

We here print exhaustive abstracts of the original will and all other original documents or records in the Middlesex County, Mass., Probate Records, relating to the settlement of the estate.

[JOHN SARGEANT'S WILL]

[From original document] "John Sargeant Senr of malden" made his will 20 May, 1708. Bequests were as follows:

To "wife Lydiea ye use and benifit of ye east end of my dweling house from bottom to ye top: So long as she Remains a widow and in my name: and also ye use of all my houshold Goods So long as she Remains in my name Also I give unto my wife one fether bed and furniture belonging to it to be at her one dispose: further my will is y^t my Executors heeraftar named shall aford my wife from time to time two Good milch Cows and maintain them well both wintar and Sumar: and also to alow and deliver to her ten bushels of indian-Corn: and two bushals of Ry: and three bushals of malt: and ten pound of sheeps wool: and a hundred and fifty waite of fatt pork: and Eighty waite of fatt beef: yeerly and every yeer: So long as she Remains a widow 'and in my name And also foure bushels of apls and one barril of sider: and a sufficant suply of fier-wood laid at her dore: but If my wife seeath Cause to mary againe she shall have ye fether bed and furniture which I have Given her and leave my hous And my Executors shall only pay to her three-pounds p^r yeer in currant pay during her naturall life: Consarning ye Two Cows That ever was in my wifes possesion which I have kept for hur: my mind and will is y^t them two Cows shall Remaine hers and none of my children shall deprive her of them: And also the Red mantle and my silver Cup: I give Them to her:"

To "my son Joseph Sargeant forty shilings in currant pay to be paid him by my Executors within twelve months after my decease—The Reson why I give him no more now is because I have Given him a good Trade and a loome to work in he also had his share or more then his share in my son Jabiz his estate which was Considerable and ye Gratest part of my children had not aney part of It Also when he lived with me He Raised up Severall Cattle and I entertaind them:"

To "my son John Sargeant forty shilings in current pay to be paid within twelve months after my decease by my Executors: The Reson why I give him no more now Is because I have Given him a good trade and helped him set up his treade—he also had Considerable of his brothar Jabiz estate"

To "my son william Sargeant: Thre pounds in currant pay to be paid by my Executors within twelve months after my decease: Also . . . . my grate book Intitled Anitations on y^e

Scriptures: The Reson why I give him no more Is because he possess my brothar Samuel Sargeants estate:"

To "my son Samuell Sargeant a weavars trade with a loome to work in The Reson why I give him no more in this my will is because I have Given him Considrable In lands which may apeere by a deed of gift under my hand"

To "my daughtar hannah twelve pounds The Reson why I give her no more Is because I have Given her a good Trade"

"my daughtar lydiea waite have Resaived of me her portion which is fifteen pounds as apeers upon book"

"Also my daughtar deborah have Resaived of me her full share which is fifteen pounds as will apeere upon book"

To "my daughtar hope" £15.

To "my daughtar Ruth twelve pounds: yᵉ Reson I give her no more is because I have Given her a treade:"

To "my daughtar Sarah" £15.

To "my daughtar mehitteball" £15.

"my will Is yᵗ these legecies to my five daughtars shall be paid by my executors In Currant pay: That is to say my daughtar hannah shall have ten pounds paid her within two yeers aftar my decease"

"my daughtar hope shall have Ten pounds paid her within three yeers after my deces"

"my daughtar Ruth shall have Ten pounds paid her within foure yeers after my deceas"

"my daughtar Sarah shall have Ten pounds paid her within five yeers aftar my deseas"

"And my daughtar mehitebell Shall have ten pounds paid her within Six yeers after my deceas"

"Then . . . . my daughtar hannah shall have forty shilings more paid her which makes up her full share: within seven yeers aftar my deseace:"

"my daughtar hope shall have five pounds more paid her within Eight yeers aftar my decease"

"my daughtar Ruth shall have forty shilings more paid her within nine yeers aftar my deseace—my daughtar Sarah shall have five pounds more paid her within ten yeers aftar my deseace: And my daughtar mehiteball shall have five pounds more paid her within Eleven yeers aftar my desease:"

"If aney of my daughtars doe dye before they atain to yᵉ age of eighteen yeers there portion shall be equaly devided to and amongst the surviving sistars:"

"I Give to all my daughtars yᵗ are unmarried at yᵉ time of

my deseace my west chambar which is a convenant fiare Roome: for there use and benefit So long as they Continue unmarried and no longer and a free pasag to it:"

To "my two Granchildren: Seth Tobe and deborah Ivery: five shilings to each of Them: The Reson why I give them no more is because I have given ther mothar my daughtar mary a Considerabl Sum when she married: And sinc they have had There share of my Son Jabiz Sargeants estate which was Considerable and Severall of my Children was forst to be contented without aney part of it:"

To "my Son Jonathan Sargeant and Ebenezar Sargeant that land of mine that Lyeth in y^t lott Called mavricks lot and also y^t accre of Salt marsh y^t lyeth by dextars marsh neer wilkensons Creek and all other my lands which I have not alredy dis disposed of I give it to them . . . . To be equaly devided between Them: And also . . . . all my goods And Chattls y^t Is not allredy disposd of to be Equaly devided between them—The Reson why I Give These my two sons Jonathan and Ebenezar no more in this my will is because I have Given to them an estate In housing and lands as may Apeer by a deed of Gift:"

"Lastly I mak my Son Jonathan Sargeant and my Son Ebenezar Sargeant my Executors"

"If These my two Sons doe Exept: and doe administar on this estat . . . . It is well if they doe not then my will is y^t they shall not have Aney part or share in this my esteate: and must be satisfied with a deed of Gift which I have Given them"

"If my son Ebenezar Sargeant doe dy without Isue . . . . Then my will is y^t his part of my Estate shall be Equaly devided between my Son Jonathan Sargeant and my Son Samuell Sargeant And Then my son Jonathan and my son Samuell Shall fulfill all those obligations which my Son Ebenezar Is obliged to fulfill in this my will: equaly between them: both for mannar and time"

The will was witnessed by John Greenland, "Phinehas Upham Senr" and James Upham.

The will was probated, at Cambridge, "12th 9^m 1716", on the oaths of the three witnesses, and administration granted to the "decds Son Ebenezar" and "room is left for Jonathan being now Sick"

Notes on the will read "Eben^r accepts his Ex^r" and "& m^r Greenland say further y^t Jonathan accepts his Legecy & ye trust as Execut^r—at p^{r}sent sick" and "memorandum, Dea^s Greenland & Upham say y^t Joseph Sergeant was by them notifyed at

Sev^r^al times y^t^ they were cited this Day to prove this Will"
[Also recorded, 14:451.]

[From unrecorded document] On 9 November, 1716, at
Malden, "lidya Sargeant" assents to probating of will, as follows: "I should have gladly ben presant when my husbands will
is proved: butt I am well in yeers and very unwildey of body:
and canot well Apeer: butt I am willing y^t^ my late husbands
will may be proved .... And I doe sit down satisfied with y^t^
which my husband namly John Sargeant hath Given me upon
his last will"

[From unrecorded bond] On 17 March, 1717/18, Jonathan
Sargeant and Ebenezer "Sargnat", as executors, with Jonathan
Sprague as surety, all being yeomen, of Malden, gave a bond for
£300. .

PLYMOUTH, MASS., VITAL RECORDS

Transcribed by Miss Ethel A. Richardson

(Continued from Vol. XXIII, p. 188)

[p. 101] The Children of William Goodwin & Lydia Cushing his Wife
1   Simeon Samson Goodwin born July 23^d^ 1782.
2 . William Goodwin born November 22^d^ 1783.
3   a Son born April 1st 1785 lived ab^t^ 4 Hours.
4th Isaac Goodwin born June 28th 1786.
The Children of Joseph Faunce & Mercy his wife
1 Eleaz^r^ Faunce born Jan^ry^ 11th 1786
2 Joseph Faunce born Sep^t^ 15th 1787
The Children of Lemuel Morton, Azubah Cushman Morton his wife
1 Nathaniel Morton born May 27th 1789
2 Lemuel Morton born April 9th 1792
3 Elizabeth Cushman Morton born Novr 8th 1796
4 Mary Ellis Morton . born Sep^t^ 5th 1799
5 Nancy Morton born Feb^ry^ 5th 1801
[p. 102] The Chilldren of Bartlett Marshell & Ruth his wife
1 Ruth Marshell born Aug: 8th 1778
2 Bartlett Marshell born Aug: 11th 1780
3 Samuel Marshell born May 2nd 1783
The Children of William Davis & Rebecca his wife
William Davis born April 20th 1783 Dec^d^ March 28th 1824
Nathaniel Morton Davis born March 3 1785
Thomas Davis born*
Elizabeth Davis born*

* The dates were not entered.

The Children of Jonathan Farnam & Dorcas his wife
Sarah Barnes born March 4th 1785
Dorcas Farnum born Decr 18th 1786
The Children of Wendal Hall & Mary Ann, his Wife
1. Mary Wendal, born January 25th . 1830
Of Betsey his wife previous.
1. John Atwood born Sept 22d . 1828
[p. 103] The Chilldren of Joseph Robbins & Eliza his wife
1 Joseph Robbins born at Plimton Novr 4th 1779
2 Mercy Robbins born Augst 1st 1781
3 Lemuel Stephens Robbins born Janry 25th 1783 Deceasd April 1st
    1786
4 Betsey Robbins born Octr 21st 1785
Joseph Robbins the Father Abovesd born in Kingston Decr 12th 1757
The Children of Rosseter Cotton & Priscilla his wife
1   Thomas Jackson Cotton born Janry 17th 1785
2   Charles Cotton born Octobr 7th 1788
3   Polley Cotton born May 20th 1790 Decd Augst 26th 1791
4   Polley Cotton born March 9th 1792 Decd Sept 24th 1793
5   Rosseter Cotton born Janry 27th 1794 Deced Jan: 30th 1796
6   Sophia Cotton born May 18th 1796
7. Rosseter Mather Cotton born July 11th 1798
8   John Winslow Cotton born March 29th 1800
9   Rowland Edwin Cotton born Janry 4th 1802
10. William Cushing Cotton born April 17 . 1804 Decd Augt 23 1805
The Child of Corbin Barnes Junr & Phebe his wife
Lemuel Barnes born Janry 12th 1785
The Children of Edward Doten & Esther, his Wife
1. Edward was born October 1st 1800
2. Samuel   "   "   June 22d 1803
3. Esther   "   "   Octr 17th . 1806
4. Lewis   "   "   Febr 27th . 1813
5. Lemuel   "   "   Mar 26th 1816.*
6. Phebe   "   "   Novr 18th 1815.*
7. Hannah   ". ·   "   Octobr 15th 1819
8. John   "   "   Febr 27th 1823.
[p. 104] The Children of Joseph Bartlett ye 3rd or fourth & Lucy
    his wife
1 Joseph Bartlett born Novr 15th 1770
2 Zepheniah Holmes Bartlett born Febry 17th 1772
3 Lucy Bartlett born March 25th 1775
4 Bradford Bartlett born Decr 15th 1776
The Children of Thomas Burges Junr & Lydia his wife
1 William Burges born Febry 2nd 1782
2 Polley Burges ⎫ Twins born Aug: 19th 1784
3 Lydia Burges   ⎭

  * Sic.

The Children of Charles Faunce & Jerusha his Wife
1. Abigail Thomas, born . March 11th . 1839.
The Child of Sylvanus Donham Mary his wife
Sylvanus Donham, born Aug: 5th 1780
Children of Richard Bagnell 2d & Lydia his wife, viz
1. Susan Sampson, born October 7th . 1819.
2. Richard William born Decr 2d . 1822.
[p. 105] The Children . of Richard Bagnal & Bethiah his wife
1 Samuel West Bagnal born Augst 19th 1785 Deceasd Febry 14th 1786
2 Samuel West Bagnal born Sept 9th 1787.
3 Hannah Jackson Bagnal born May 11th 1790
4 Benjamin Bagnal born Sept 17 . 1792
5 Joseph . Bagnal born Mar: 5th 1795
6. Nancey Ellis Bagnal born Sep. 18th 1797 Deceasd
7. Nancey Ellis Bagnal . born Febry 11th 1799
8 Richard . Bagnal . born Janry 12th 1802
The Chilldren of Elkanah Bartlett & Sarah his wife
1 Elkanah Bartlett born Decr 29th 1769
2. David Bartlett born July 24th 1775
3 John Bartlett born July 30th 1777
4 Jonathan Bartlett born June 17th 1779 Deceasd Sept 1780
5 Jonathan Bartlett born Aug: 9th 1782
6 Salley Bartlett born Janry 10th 1786
7 Jenne . Bartlett born ⎫
8 Joanna Bartlett born ⎬ may 27th 1792
The Children of Zacheus Bartlett Junr & Hannah his wife
1 James Bartlett born Janry 28th 1785
2 William Bartlett born Febry 4th 1787
3 Hannah Bartlett borne Aug: 6th 1795
The Children of John S. Payne & Deborah his Wife
1. Reuben Church'll, born April 5th . 1815
                 Of Susan his wife.
1. Stephen Payne,   born Sept 16 . 183[*]
2. Hannah Sherman   " Augt 28 . 1836
3. John Sampson   " Mar: 7 . 1838.
[p. 106] The Child of Eleazer Holmes Junr & Polley his wife
1 Esther Holmes born Febry 9th 1786.
2 Eleazer Holmes Born
3 Mary Holmes Born
4 James Avery Holmes Born — by Elizabeth his wife
The Children of Jacob Albertson & Lydia his wife
1 A Son Still born June 25th 1778
2 Martha Albertson born Aug: 30th 1779
3 Joseph Ryder Albertson born Decr 4th 1781 Deceasd Sept 9th 1782
4. Lydia Gardner Albertson born Octr 19th 1783
5 Margaret Albertson . born July 28th 1785 Deceasd Octr 27th 1785

    *The last figure was omitted.

The Children of Asa Peirce & Eliza his Wife
1. Amanda Stephens, born August 1st . 1839.
The Children of Daniel Jackson & Rebecca his wife
1 Daniel Jackson born April 19th 1787
2 Rebecca Jackson born . Sept 22nd 1789
3 Abraham Jackson born Novr 29th 1791
4 Jacob Jackson born Janry 9th 1794
5 William Morton Jackson born Feb: 4th 1796
6 Thomas Taylor* Jackson born Sept 11th 1798
7 Isaac Carver Jackson born Decr 22d 1799
8 William Morton Jackson born may 30th 1802
[p. 107] The Chilldren of Jacob Albertson & Margaret his wife
1 Jacob Albertson born Janry 30th 1752
2 William Albertson born
3 Elizabeth Albertson born
4. Rufus Albertson born
The sd Jacob Albertson the Father of the family abovesd born in
    North Carrolina in the County of Pasquetank and was Drownd
    on a fishg Voyg from Plimo in the year
Said Margaret his wife Deceasd at Plimo
The Chilldren of Cornelus Cobb & Gase† his wife
1 Cornelus Cobb born Febry 10th 1775
2 Betse . Cobb . born May 6th 1777
3 Grace Cobb born May 31st 1781
4 Isaac E Cobb born Janry 19th 1789 deceased Jany 14 . 1821
The Chilldren of Joseph Holmes & Rebecca his wife
1 Joseph Holmes born Sept 8th 1770
2 Rebecca Holmes born Sept 28th 1772
3 Cornelus Holmes born June 15th‡ 1774
4 Ansell Holmes born Ap: 23rd 1777
5 Barter Holmes born Octr 19th 1779
[p. 108] The Children of James Clark Jun: & Lucy his wife
1 Jonathan Clark born March 19th 1785 Deceasd April 21st 1785
2 Bartlett Clark born Janry 29th 1786 Deceasd April 26th 1786
3 James Clark born March 15th 1787 Deceasd Augst 2nd 1804
4 Lucy Clark born Aug. 11 . 1788
5 Thankfull Clark born June 9th 1791
6 Sarah Clark born April 10th 1794
7 Rebecca Clark born June 24th 1796
8 Ezra Clark . born March 20th 1798
9 David Clark . born May 2nd 1800
10 Lewis Clark . born . June . 11th 1802

* "Taylor" is interlined, in a different hand and ink.

† Cornelius Cobb and Grace Eames, both of Plymouth, were married 15 May,
1774. See page 266 of this original volume of records.

‡ "5" was written over "4".

The Child of James Harlow Junr & Sarah his wife
James Harlow born Aug: 27th 1785
The Children of William Atwood & Harriet his wife.
1. Edward Winslow, born . December 22d . 1835.
2. Harriet Elizabeth, born, Feby 22 . 1839.
The Chilldren of Cornelus Morrey & Jerusha his wife
1 Elijah Morrey born Augst 27th 1784
2 Sarah Morrey born July 22nd 1786
3 Cornelus Morrey born March 14th 1789
4 William Morrey born Sep^t 11th 1791
5 Jerusha Morrey born July 22nd 1794
6 Josiah Morrey born June 22 . 1797
The Children of Wm Drew 3d and Ann his Wife
1. William Warren, born 1831 . January
2. Frederick Augustus, born 1833 . November, 16
3. Augusta Ann born 1837 . August . 10.
[p. 109] The Child of Joshua Thomas Esq: & Isabella his wife
1 John Boies Thomas born July 28th 1787
        See this family in page 110
The Children of James Reed & Lucy his wife
1 Betsey Reed born June 1st 1789
2 James Reed born Novr 24th 1791
3 Polley Reed born April 28th 1794
4 Ruth Reed born Octr 26th 1796
5 Lemuel Fish Reed born May 4th 1800
  2 Daughters of the above family there names were Ruth Reed both
    of them were born between Polley & Ruth above named one
    liv^d about 2 years the other about ten Days
8 Samuel Reed was born April 24th 1803
9 Hezekiah Bryant Reed born June 10th 1805
10 Henry Reed born March 1808
11 Salley Reed born June 7th 1811
The Children of Judah Dellano & Penelope his wife
1 Salome Dellano born   Deceas^d
2 Penelope Dellano born   Deceas^d
3 a Daughter born not named   Deceas^d
4 Elizabeth Dellano born April 4th 1786 tuesday half past 8 aClock
    A. M
5 Henry . Dellano born July 6th 1788 Sunday 53 minutes past 9
    aClock A. M
6 Judah Dellano born Feb^{ry} 26th 1792
7 Priscilla Dellano born Decr 11th 1793
The Chilldren of Seth Ryder & Hannah his wife
1 Seth Ryder born Sep^t 7th 1788
2. Hannah Ryder born Sep^t 7th 1788 Deceas^d were Twins
3. Hannah Ryder born Octr 23 1789
4. Mary Ryder born Sep^t 4th 1792

5. Esther Ryder born Septr 6th 1794
6 John Ryder born Octr 18th 1797
7. Nathaniel Ryder born April 30th 1801
[p. 110] The Children of Joshua Thomas Esqr & Isabela his wife
1 John Boyse Thomas born July 28th 1787
2 William Thomas born March 15th 1788
3 Joshua
The Chilldren of William Straffin & Susannah his wife
1 William Straffin born Jan^{ry} 10th 1770
2 George Straffin born March 9th 1771
3 Lucy Straffin born Jan^{ry} 11th 1773 Deceas^d Jan^{ry} 31st 1773
The Chilldren of Robert Finney & Lydia his wife
1 Lydia Finney born
2 Robert Finney born June 17th 1768
3. Clark Finney born
4 George Finney born March 2nd *
5. Josiah Finney born
6 Elkanah Finney born
7 Experiance Finney born April 6th*

(*To be continued*)

EDMUND WESTON'S ESTATE

By the Editor

EDMUND² WESTON (*Edmund¹*), of Plymouth and Plympton, Mass., was married, on 13 December, 1688†, to Rebecca³ Soule, a daughter of John² Soule (*George¹*) of Duxbury, by his first wife, Rebecca Simmons.

Edmund and Rebecca (Soule) Weston had six children. The first five were recorded at Plymouth and also at Plympton, but the sixth was recorded at Plympton only.

On the Plymouth town records, printed in our second volume, we find five children, as follows: Nathan Weston, born 8 February, 1688; Zachariah Weston, born 16 December, 1690; Rebecca Weston, born 31 July, 1693; John Weston, born 27 July, 1695; Edmund Weston, born 21 October, 1697.

On the Plympton records, printed in our third volume, we find the same five children recorded, and the same dates of birth, with the addition of a sixth child, Benjamin Weston, born 14 November, 1701.

* The year was not recorded.
† Mayflower Descendant, 13:204.

On the Plymouth records Nathan's birth is entered as on 8 February, 1688, but on the Plympton records this date appears as 1688/9. These two dates, however, are the same, as each, when changed to New Style dating, becomes 18 February, 1689.

Edmund[2] Weston died 23 September, 1727, in his sixty-seventh year, and his widow, Rebecca (Soule) Weston, died 18 November, 1732, in her seventy-sixth year, according to the records on their gravestones at Plympton.*

Especial attention is called to the dates here given, because of the errors in "The Descendants of Edmund Weston of Duxbury", printed in the forty-first volume of the New England Historical and Genealogical Register†, and also reprinted separately, the same year, in pamphlet form. This article states that Edmund[2] Weston "was born 1660", and died "Sept. 23, 1723, aged 76 years"; but the year of death and the age at death are both printed incorrectly. Other errors, relating to the births and deaths of some of the children, will be taken up later.

Edmund[2] Weston died intestate, 23 September, 1727, and on 7 November, 1727, his youngest son, Benjamin Weston, also of Plympton, Mass., was appointed administrator and gave a bond, and on the same date appraisers were appointed. An agreement of the heirs, not dated, was approved by the probate court, on 6 November, 1727, the day before the appointment of an administrator, according to the records.

The five sons all married and left issue; the daughter, Rebecca Weston, married Thomas Darling, of Middleborough, Mass., and left issue.

We here print exhaustive abstracts of all records, and original documents on file, found in the Plymouth County, Mass., Probate Records, relating to the settlement of the estate of Edmund[2] Weston.

[EDMUND WESTON'S ESTATE]

[Plym. Co. Prob. 5:318] On 7 November, 1727, "m^r Benjamin Western of Plympton" was appointed administrator of the estate of "your Father m^r Edmund Western late of Plympton . . . . dyed Intestate"

[From unrecorded bond] On 7 November, 1727, "Benjamin Weston" of Plympton, as administrator, with Thomas Darling, of Middleborough, and "Philip Dilano" of Duxbury, as sureties,

---

* Mayflower Descendant, 1:178, 245; 11:194, 195.

† Boston, 1887. For other serious errors in the same article see Mayflower Descendant, 15:186.

gave a bond for £1000. The witnesses were Thomas Southworth and "Cornelius Soul."

[From original warrant] On 7 November, 1727, James Soul and Samuel Samson of Middleborough and George Sampson, Jr., of Plympton were appointed to appraise the real and personal estate. [Also recorded, 5: 349.]

[From original inventory] The inventory was taken by "James Soul", Samuel Samson and George Sampson, Jr., and they and Benjamin Weston, the administrator, made oath to it, 17 November, 1727. The real estate was "his lands medows seder swamp and Buldings" £1207. The total amount of the inventory was £1368, 18s. [Also recorded, 5: 349.]

[5: 350] On 6 November, 1727, the estate was settled, as follows:

"Rebeckah Weston of Plympton . . . . Widdow of Edmund Weston Late of Plympton afores^d Deceas^d & Nathan Weston, Zachariah Weston, John Weston Edmund Weston & Benjamin Weston all of Plympton afores^d & Thomas Darling of middleboro in ye County afores^d & Rebeckah His wife all Children of ye s^d dec^d Edmund Weston . . . . for a final Settlement & Distribution of ye Estate of ye s^d deceas^d . . . . Have mutually agreed & Concluded . . . . that ye same Shall be Settled to & amongst us in manner & form following: viz:

"That ye s^d Rebeckah Weston ye widdow . . . . Shall Receive ye Sum of twenty Pounds out of ye moveable Estate and that the s^d widdow Shall be Provided for . . . . with all things necessary for Her Comfortable Subsistance both in Sickness & Health during Her natural Life by ye afores^d Benjamin Weston His Heirs Executors or administrators.

"That ye s^d Nathan Weston Shall Have ye Land Whereon He now dwells in Plympton which ye s^d deceas^d bought of moses Soul described & bounded as by a deed from s^d Soul may appear also halfe a Share of Cedar Swamp lying in South meadow Cedar Swamp in ye Sixth Lott which ye s^d deceased bought of Samuel Ransome: To Have . . . . as His Part & Portion of His S^d father^s Estate."

"That ye s^d Zachariah Weston Shall Have ye Land whereon He now dwells in Plympton afores^d Containing fourty Six acres lying in Donhams Neck being Part of a grant of ye Proprietors of fifty acres Reference being Had to ye s^d grant for ye bounds of ye s^d fourty Six acres: also all ye meadow lying on ye South East Side of ye meadow herein assigned to ye s^d Edmund Weston adjoyning to ye afores^d Land being all ye meadow that was formerly granted unto John Dunham Senr att ye afores^d Dunham^s Neck Excepting what is herein assigned to & Settled upon John, Edmund & Benjamin Weston . . . . to Him ye s^d Zachariah Weston . . . . as His Part & Portion of His s^d father^s Estate

"That ye s^d John Weston Shall Have one halfe of ye Homestead whereon ye Said Deceas^d dwelt in Plympton afores^d divided by a Line beginning at a Stake & Heap of Stones Standing by Winatuxet River near ye Head of ye Grist: mill Pond Thence north halfe a Point westerly Twenty Pole to a Stake & Heap of Stones Standing near a well Thence north East & by north Sixteen Pole to a Stone Sett in ye ground Thence East thirty two Pole & halfe to a Stake & Heap of Stones Thence North twelve Degrees East Eighty Six Pole to Red oak bush or Sapling Standing in or near ye Head Range of ye s^d Home Lott The s^d John Weston to Have all that Part of ye s^d Home Lott that lyeth on ye Easterly & Southerly Side of ye said dividing Line: also a Peice of meadow being Part of ye afores^d Grant to John Donham Senr lying in Donham^s [p. 351] Donham^s Neck & at ye Head of ye meadow herein Settled upon Benjamin Weston bounded as followeth (viz) beginning at a Stake at ye Head of s^d Benjamin^s meadow Standing by Colchester brooke Thence South west & by west 3 degrees Westerly to a Stake & heap of Stones Thence South & by East to a Swamp oak bush, thence South East & by South to a Swamp oak marked on four Sides, Thence East & by North to a Stake by Said brooke, Thence by ye s^d brooke to ye bound first mentioned . . . . to Him ye S^d John Weston . . . . as His full Part & Portion of His Said fathers Estate.

"That ye Said Edmund Weston Shall Have ye Land whereon He now dwe[lls] in Plympton afores^d which ye S^d deceas^d bought of James Soul Containing fifty acres (be it more or less) Reference being had to a Deed under ye Hand & Seal of ye s^d James Soul", dated 17 May, 1696, "on Record for ye Description & Bounds of ye s^d Land Together with a Peice of meadow being Part of ye afores^d Grant to John Donham Senr Lying in Donham^s Neck bounded as followeth (viz) beginning at a Stake Standing at ye Head of John Weston^s meadow by Colchester brooke, thence west & by South to a Swamp oak marked on four Sides thence South & by East to a Stake & Heap of Stones, thence near South East to a Small Red oak marked, thence South South East 3 degrees East, to a Stake & Heap of Stones thence North East 3 degrees North to a Stake by ye S^d brooke, thence by ye s^d brooke to ye bound first mentioned . . . . to Him ye s^d

Edmund Weston . . . . as His full Part & Portion of His Said father^e Estate.

"That ye S^d Benjamin Weston Shall Have ye other halfe of ye afore[s^d] Homestead whereon ye s^d deceas^d dwelt ye one halfe whereof is herei[n] before Settled upon John Weston: The s^d Benjamin to Have all that Part of ye s^d Homestead that lyeth on ye westerly & Northerly Side of ye afores^d Dividing Line also . . . . a Lott of Lan[d] Lying in middleborough in ye South Purchase Containing fourty five acres laid out in ye Right of John Soul it being in Number the Hundred & Seventy fourth Lott Reference being Had to ye Record of ye s^d Purchase for ye bounds of ye s^d Lott: also two acres of meadow which ye s^d deceas^d bought of Benjamin Soul lying on ye North side of Colchester brooke Reference being Had to a deed from ye Said Benjamin Soul on Record for ye bounds of ye s^d meadow: also a Peic[e] of meadow being Part of ye afores^d grant to John Donham Senr bounded as followeth (viz) beginning at a Crotched maple Tree marked on three Sides Standing by Colchester brooke att ye Head of moses Wrights meadow thence South halfe a Point East to a dry Spruce tree marked thence East halfe a Point north on Streight Line to a Stake & Heap of Stones, thence North East & by East three Degrees East to a Stake Standing by s^d Colchester Brooke thence by y[^{e}] S^d Brooke to ye bound first mentioned: Together with all ye Esta[te] both Real & Personal Either in Plympton or middleboro which ye s^d deceas^d Dyed Seised of not herein assigned to or Settled upon any other Person, together with all ye moveable Estate whatso Ever . . . . Excepting what is heretofore ordered & assigned to ye widow of ye s^d deceas^d and it is hereby agreed & Concluded that ye s^d Benjamin Westo[n] Shall Pay all Debts due from ye Estate . . . . and also Provide for, maintain & Support ye widow of ye s^d deceased with [p. 352] with all things necessary for Her Comfortable Subsistance both in Sickness & Health During Her natural Life to ye well & true Performance whereof ye s^d Benjamin Weston doth hereby Stand bound"

"Rebeckah ye wife of Thomas Darling Shall have a Lott of Land in ye South Purchase In middleboro laid out in ye Right of John Soul being ye most westerly Lott that was laid out In s^d Souls Right Reference being had to ye Records of ye s^d Purchase for a more Particular Demonstration thereof . . . . to Her ye s^d Rebeckah . . . . as Her full Part & Portion of Her father^s Estate"

"In Confirmation of Each & Every of y[e] articles in this our agreement wee y[e] afores[d] widdow & Children of y[e] Deceas[d] have hereunto Sett our Hands & Seals" Signed by: Rebecca Weston, Nathan Weston, Zachariah Weston (by a mark), John Weston, Edmund Weston, Benjamin Weston, Thomas Darling, Rebecca Darling (by a mark).

The witnesses were George Samson, Jr. and John Perkins.

The agreement was acknowledged by all the signers, 6 November, 1727, before Isaac Winslow, Judge of Probate, and approved by him.

DEACON JOHN FOSTER'S WILL

BY THE EDITOR

THE marriage of John Foster and Hannah Stetson, on 16 November, 1692, will be found in our thirteenth volume; and the births of nine of their children, recorded at Plymouth, are in our second volume.

Deacon John Foster's three daughters married descendants of Mayflower Passengers, as follows:

Hannah Foster married, first, William[4] Bradford (*John[3], William[2-1]*), and they had six children, recorded at Plymouth and Kingston. Hannah (Foster) Bradford married, second, George* Partridge, and survived him. She was the second wife of George Partridge, and was not the mother of all his children.

Sarah Foster married, first, William Bartlett[5] (*Benjamin[4-3], Mary[2] Warren, Richard[1]*), and they had one daughter, Ruth, who died young. Sarah married, second, Nathan Thomas. She married, third, Jedediah Bourne†, and survived him.

Mercy Foster married Ebenezer Morton[4] (*Mary Ring[3], Deborah[2] Hopkins, Stephen[1]*), and survived him. Their ten children, recorded at Middleborough, will be found in Volumes 6-9 inclusive, 12 and 13, of this magazine.

Deacon John Foster died 24 December, 1741, and his widow died 30 April, 1747, and their gravestones are on Burial Hill, Plymouth.

We here print exhaustive abstracts of Deacon John Foster's will and all records relating to the settlement of the estate found

* Not "William" Partridge, as printed in the Foster Genealogy, Chicago, 1899.

† Not "Brown", as printed in the Foster Genealogy, Chicago, 1899.

in the Plymouth County, Mass., Registry of Probate. There are no original papers in the files.

[DEACON JOHN FOSTER'S WILL]

[8 : 466] On 9 January, 1739/40, "John Foster of Plymouth . . . . being in the Seventy fourth year of my Age and . . . . in usual health" made his will. Bequests were as follows:

To "wife Hannah Foster she Resigning her Right of Dower the Sole use and improvment of my Home State dureing her naturall life or widdow Hood (and no longer) Excepting the Blacksmiths shop & warehouse & warfe which is to be Set off begining at ye Path Ten feet westward from the Shop" also "my best bed & furniture, my negro woman and One quarter part of my Houshold Goods with Liberty & choosing her share."

To "my Youngest son Seth Foster and to my Three Daughters viz Hannah Sarah & Mercy the three Remaining parts of my household Goods & all my moveable & Personall Estate (Excepting what I Shall hereafter dispose off) To be divided equally among them."

"To my Eldest son Samuel Foster . . . . One half of the Home stall Houses & land (Excepting the Shop, warf and warehouse and ye land below the Way ten feet Westward of the Shop as above) which he shall have after my wifes death or second mariage."

To "my second son Thomas Foster . . . . One half of my meadow land at ye High Pines within the bounds of Duxborough . and allso all my wearing apparrell and allso my Pine Lott of land at Billington Sea on ye Westerly side."

To "my Third son Nathll Foster . . . . my Blacksmiths shop with the Utensils thereunto belonging and the Warehouse & wharf & ye land to be Sett off ten feet Westward of the Shop as above . allso ye other Half of the Homestall Houses & Land which he shall have after my wifes death or second Marriage . also my Field & Pasture Lying in Plymo Above Littletown with the Wood Lott at the head of it: allso my Sixty acres of Land at Gunners Exchange pond 40 acres on ye South & 20 Acres on ye north side of sd Pond allso my lott of land on ye beach with ye Blacksmiths shop that stands on it with ye Utensils, allso One half of my meadow land att High Pines within the bounds of Duxborough" also "my Negro Girl Nanne and whatsoever is due to me by Book and I Order him to pay all my debts & funerall

Charges and to provide for & Support his mother Comfortably &
Honourably as long as she Continues my widdow, or to give
her yearly a Certain sum of money for her support as my son
Samuel and he Shall Agree . I allso order him to pay to my
Grandson Eliphalet Bradford Ten pounds or let him have a good
Cow and allso take Care that s^d Eliphalet be learned the Smiths
Trade or some other and when his time is up Give him two Suits
of apparill one proper for the Lord's and the other for working
days."

"my Cedar Swamp at South meadows my sons Thomas &
Nath^ll shall have One half to Thomas . . . . and the Other half
To Nath^ll".

"my two sons Samuel & Nathaniel To be Joynt Executors"

The witnesses were, Isaac Lothrop, Jr., Thomas Wethrell and
Rebecca Wethrell.

On 26 January, 1741, the "Will of John Foster late of Plym°
. . . . Blacksmith Deceasd" was probated, the three witnesses
being present, and administration was granted "unto Samuel
Foster of Kingston & Nathaniel Foster of Plymouth . . . .
Blacksmiths Joynt Executors"

[9:28] "An Inventory of the Estate of Deacon John Foster
late of Plymouth Deceass'd" was taken by Stephen Churchell,
Haviland Torrey and William Donham, on 25 March, 1742, "In
old tenour", and it was sworn to, by the two executors, on
14 January, 1742.* "the Negroes" were valued at £180.

The real estate was: "the House and Land & Barne" £380;
"Pasture and Wood Lott Adjoyning" £225; "the Shop & warfe
& Warehouse & Land thereto belonging" £100; "the Shop upon
the Point" £50; "Meadow land at the High Pines" £150; "Sedar
swamp" £35; "a Pine Lott near West Ponds" £15; "1 Lott at
Gunners Exchange ponds" £30. The total amount of the inventory was £1546, 13s.

———

FORM FOR A BEQUEST

I GIVE and bequeath to the Society of Mayflower Descendants,
a corporation organized under the laws of the Commonwealth of
Massachusetts, the sum of . . . . dollars.

---

* This would be 25 January, 1743, in New Style dating.

KENELM BAKER'S WILL

By the Editor

KENELM BAKER of Marshfield, Mass., married Sarah[3] Bradford, daughter of Major William[2] Bradford (*Gov. William[1]*), of Plymouth, but the date of the marriage has not been found.

Kenelm and Sarah (Bradford) Baker had ten children, recorded at Marshfield,* as follows: Sarah Baker[4], born 28 October, 1688; Alice Baker[4], born 3 November, 1690; Eleanor Baker[4], born 31 March, 1692; Abigail Baker[4], born 23 December, 1693; Kenelm Baker[4], born 3 November, 1695; Bethiah Baker[4], born 12 May, 1699; Keziah Baker[4], born 15 August, 1701; Samuel Baker[4], born 5 February, 1702/3; William Baker[4] and Edward Baker[4], twins, born 18 August, 1705.

Kenelm Baker made his will 29 September, 1712, and as he did not mention his wife, she probably was not then living. All of the ten children were living, and were mentioned in the will, also John Sherman, husband of Sarah Baker[4]. The testator's uncle, Capt. Nathaniel Winslow, his brother-in-law, Major John[3] Bradford, and his kinsman, Isaac[3] Winslow (*Gov. Josiah[2]*, *Gov. Edward[1]*), were named as executors of the will.

The inventory was taken, 30 March, 1713, and the will was probated, 6 April, 1713, at Marshfield.

We here print exhaustive abstracts of the will and all records, and original documents in the files, found in the Plymouth County, Mass., Registry of Probate.

[KENELM BAKER'S WILL]

[From original will] Kenelm Baker "of Marshfield" made his will 29 September, 1712. Bequests were as follows:

To "my eldest son Kenelm all my Housen and land and meadow land . . . . in the Towneshipe of Marshfield aforesd on the north side of the south River excepting my Common Righte of lands lately devided in the Towneship of Marshfield"

To "my son Samuell all my lands lying on the south side of the south River aforesd in Marshfield"

* See Mayflower Descendant, 5 : 234, 235 and 6 : 20, 21.

To "my son William all that my Common Right of lands lately devided by the Towne of Marshfield aforesd being both that above and this below both in the uper and lower devision therof and also all my Righte in the Cedar swamp", also £50, "to be payed . . . . When he shall arrive to the age of twenty one years"

"my Will is that all my marsh and meadow lying near the Cut both that I formerly purchased of Isaac Winslow of Marshfield and what I have since purchased of those allotments lately laid out in the devisions of the Common meadows in the Towneship of Duxbury be equally devided between my three sons aforesd Kenelm Samuell and William the sd devision to be made therof When my son Kenelm shall attaine to the age of twenty one years"

To "my son Edward" £120, "to be payed . . . . When he shall attaine to the age of twenty one years"

To "my Daughter Sarah the wife of John Sherman" £30, "besides What she hath allready recived to be payed . . . . within one year after my decase"

To "my Daughter Alice" £63, "to be payed . . . . Within one year after my decease"

To "my Daughter Elanor" £60, "to be payed . . . . Within one year after my deceas"

To "my Daughter Abigale" £60, "to be payed . . . . Within one year after my deceas"

To "my Daughter Bethiah" £60, "to be payed . . . . att her marriage or when she shall attaine to the age of eighteen years which shall first be".

To "my Daughter Keziah" £60, "to be payed . . . . at her marriage or when she shall attaine to the age of eighteen years Which shall first be".

"The Residue of my estate my younger children being first brought up out of it my Just Debts and funerall Charges being payed I desire may be equally devided among all my Daughters aforesd"

"Finally I Constitute . . . . my Uncle Capt Nathaniell Winslow of Marshfield my Brother maj^r John Bradford of Plimoth and my kinsman m^r Isaac Winslow of Marshfield the executors of this my last Will".

The will was witnessed by "Ichabod Bartlet", William Carver and "Israel thomas", all of whom made oath to the will, 6 April, 1713.

The will was probated, at Marshfield, 6 April, 1713, and administration granted to "Isaac Winslow Esqr Maj^r John Bradford & Capt Nathaniel Winslow Executors therin Named." [Also recorded, 3 : 236.]

[From original document] The inventory was taken, 30 March, 1713, by "Israell thomas" and "Samuel baker". The only real estate was "a forty acre lot of land not disposed by his Will" £25; "mony in the house in silver and paper" amounted to £19, 2s.; "mony Due by severall bills and bonds" amounted to £499, 2s., 6d.

On 6 April, 1713, "Isaac Winslow Esqr Capt Nathaniel Winslow & Maj^r John Bradford", the executors, made oath to the inventory. [Also recorded,. 3 : 239.]

[3 : 279-283] On 8 March, 1713, guardians were appointed for the seven children who were under age, as follows: Abigail, who was over fourteen years old, chose as guardian Major John Bradford of Plymouth, and he was appointed, as guardian, for William, who was under fourteen; Kenelm, and Bethiah, both over fourteen, chose Isaac Winslow of Marshfield, and he was appointed guardian of Edward, who was under fourteen; Keziah, who was over fourteen, chose Captain Nathaniel Winslow of Marshfield, and he was appointed guardian of Samuel, who was under fourteen. The original "Letter of Guardianship to Capt N. Winslow for Kesire Baker", dated 8 March, 1713, is in the files.

[From unrecorded bonds] On 8 March, 1713, seven bonds, of £200 each, without sureties, were given: by Maj. John Bradford, as guardian of Abigail Baker, and as guardian of William Baker; by Isaac Winslow, as guardian of Kenelm Baker, as guardian of Bethiah Baker, and as guardian of Edward Baker; by Captain Nathaniel Winslow, as guardian of Keziah Baker, and as guardian of Samuel Baker. The seven bonds were witnessed by John Rouse and John Bourn.

[4 : 245] On 12 November, 1720, Samuel Baker, under twenty-one, but over fourteen, chose Samuel Baker, yeoman, of Marshfield, as his guardian, and he was appointed. The original letter of appointment is in the files.

[4 : 247] On 12 November, 1720, Edward Baker, under twenty-one, but over fourteen, chose William Ford, Jr., of Marshfield, as his guardian, and he was appointed. The original letter of appointment is in the files.

[From unrecorded bonds] On 12 November, 1720, two bonds, of £200 each, were given: by "William foord" of Marshfield, as guardian of Edward Baker, with Samuel Baker as surety; by Samuel Baker of Marshfield, as guardian of "Samuel Baker the son of Kenelm Baker . . . . Deceased", with "William foord" as surety. Hopestill Oliver and Josiah Winslow witnessed both bonds.

[4: 282] On 22 May, 1721, Samuel Baker, of Marshfield, was chosen guardian by "William Baker the Son of yoʳ Brothʳ Kenelm Baker late of Marshfield . . . . deceased who is a minor under" twenty-one, but over fourteen, and the choice was approved. The original letter of appointment is in the files.

[From unrecorded bond] On 22 May, 1721, Samuel Baker, of Marshfield, as guardian of William Baker, with James Sprague, of Marshfield, as surety, gave a bond of £200. The witnesses were Thomas Foster and Benjamin White.

[From unrecorded document, without date] "Majr Bradfords accompt An accompᵗ of what I have done for the children of Kenellem Baker late of marshfeild deceased". Expenses of journeys to Boston and Marshfield are mentioned. "Money payed to thomas tumes for filling 2 writs" £1; "payd mʳ Cotten for Coppies" 4s.; "for diating edward and Clothing at School one year" £14. Payments for interest on money had been received from: Ephraim Bradford, "Capᵗ Cushhen", Wrestling Brewster, Joseph Ford.

The payments amounted to £21, 9s.; receipts, £21, 14s.

This account was drawn up on the back of an uncompleted bond of guardianship for "Elkanah Fuller who is a minor under the age of fourteen years".

THE WILLS OF HON. ISAAC³ WINSLOW AND HIS WIDOW SARAH

By the Editor

Isaac³ Winslow, son of Gov. Josiah² Winslow, of Marshfield, and grandson of Gov. Edward¹ Winslow, was born about 1671 and married, at Boston, on 11 July, 1700, Sarah Wensley. He lived at Marshfield, Mass., and his six children were recorded there*, as follows: Josiah⁴ Winslow, born 27 July, 1701, died without issue, before his father; John⁴ Winslow, born 27 May, 1703, married Mary Little⁵ (*Isaac⁴⁻³, Anna² Warren, Richard¹*); Penelope⁴ Winslow, born 21 December, 1704, married James⁴ Warren (*James³, Nathaniel², Richard¹*) of Plymouth; Elizabeth⁴

* See Marshfield records printed in our sixth, seventh and eighth volumes.

Winslow, born 13 December, 1707, married Benjamin Marston, of Salem, Mass.; Anna⁴ Winslow,. born 29 January, 1709/10, died without issue, before her father; Edward⁴ Winslow, born 7 June, 1714, married Hannah⁴ (Howland) Dyer, widow of William Dyer, daughter of Thomas³ Howland (*Joseph²*, *John¹*).

"The Honᵇˡᵉ Isaac Winslow Esqʳ Deceasᵈ December yᵉ 14ᵗʰ 1738", and "Mʳˢ Sarah Winslow widow of yᵉ Honʳᵇˡ Isaac Winslow Esqʳ Deceasᵈ December yᵉ 16ᵗʰ: AD 1753" according to the Marshfield town records, and Isaac Winslow's gravestone record gives the same date of death for him, adding "Aetatis 67". These three records were printed in our ninth and tenth volumes.

Isaac³ Winslow made his will, 24 May, 1736, and it was probated, 6 April, 1739. He mentioned his wife Sarah; his living sons John and Edward; his daughter Penelope, wife of James Warren of Plymouth; and his daughter Elizabeth, wife of Benjamin Marston of Salem.

Widow Sarah Winslow made her will, 5 September, 1753, and it was probated, 4 February, 1754. She mentioned her sons John and Edward; her sister Hopestill Oliver*; her daughter Elizabeth (Winslow) Marston; her grandchildren, James Warren, Jr., Ann Warren and Sarah Warren, children of her deceased daughter Penelope (Winslow) Warren.

We here present exhaustive abstracts of these two wills, and of all other records relating to the settlements of the estates, found in the Plymouth County, Mass., Probate Records. The probate files do not contain any original papers relating to these estates.

[Hon. Isaac³ Winslow's Will]

[Plym. Co. Prob., 8: 27] "Isaac Winslow of Marshfield" made his will, 24 May, 1736. Bequests were as follows:

To "my Son John Winslow my Seal Ring"

To "my Son Edward all my other Rings & my Sword or Rapier"

To "my sᵈ Sons all my armes & wareing apparrel to be Equally Divided Between them."

"I Give my Books to be Equally Divided Between my Beloved wife Sarah Winslow & my sᵈ Sons John Winslow & Edward Winslow To Each a Third part"

*Peter Oliver and Hopestill Wensley were married, 1 March, 1711/12, at Boston.

To "my s^d Wife the use & Improvement of all My Moveable Estate within Doors & without Excepting my Quck* Stock The one half of which I Dessier may be Sold Towards the payment of Debts & Charges The Other half I Give her the Improvement of together with the Other moveable Estate before Mentioned Dureing her Natural Life with full Power to make such Dispossition Thereof to & among her Children as She may Se Cause I also Give to her . . . . The Improvement of one half of My Real Estate Except Such as I Shall Herein Dispose of or may be Disposed of by My Executors . . . . Dureing her Life"

To "my Daughter Penelope Warren wife to Mr James Warren of Plymouth That Peice or Percel of Salt meadow which he the s^d James Warren has Improved for this Several years being about Twenty Acres besides what She hath already had"

To "my Daughter Elizabeth Marston The wife of Mr Benjamin Marston of Salem besides what She Hath already Rece^d" £200, "to be paid her by my Sons John Winslow & Edward Winslow In Equal Proportion in Some Convenient Time after my Decease"

"I Do Hereby Give full Power to my Executors Hereafter Named to Sell & Dispose of So Much of My Real Estate Either of the out Lands or of the Homestead of The upland or meadow as they Shall thinck most Convenient for the Payment of my Debts & for the Bring up my youngest Son Edward In his Learning thro the Course of his Studdy at the Colledge til he has Taken his Second Degree"

To "my Sons John Winslow & Edward Winslow . . . . all my Houseing & Lands Not Herein Disposed of & what Shall Not be Dispossed of by my Executors afores^d the Improvement of The one half to their Mother as Afore Excepted whether Lying In Marshfield Pembrook Middleborough or Rutland or wheresoever Elce to be Equally Divided Between them the Land formerly Given to my Son John Winslow by Deed of Gift to be accounted as Part of his Divition & that my Son Edward to Have Proportionable to that & then to be Equally Divided In Consideration whereof I Hereby Direct my Sons John Winslow & Edward Winslow to pay to their Sister Elizabeth Marston" £200 "to be paid In Silver money Bills of this Province or Such Money as Shall be Passable in the Goverment at the time"

"I Do Hereby Appointe my afores^d wife Sarah Winslow & my Sons John Winslow & Edward Winslow Joynt Executors"

The witnesses were Joshua Soule, Pelatiah West, Samuel

* " Quick ".

Weston and Nathaniel Fish; all of whom made oath to the will of "the Honble Isaac Winslow Esqr Late of Marshfield" on 6 April, 1739.

[8:28] The will was probated, at Scituate, on 6 April, 1739, and administration granted to "m^s Sarah Winslow . John Winslow Esqr & Edward Winslow Gen^t Executors in the Same will named."

[8:29] "An Inventory of the Real & Personal Estate of The Honble Isaac Winslow Esqr" was taken 16 May, 1739, by Edward Arnold, Kenelm Winslow and Jabez Whittemore. "Servants" were valued at £250. The real estate, not described, was valued at £13510. The total amount of the inventory was £14807, 11s.

The inventory was sworn to by the three appraisers, Edward Arnold, "Kenelm Winslow Esqr" and "Mr Jabez Whittemore", 16 May, 1739.

On 27 July, 1739, the executors added to the inventory: "1 p^r Goold Buttons. 1 p^r Silver Buckels . one Dozen Silver Jacket Buttons. The following Books viz. Goddolfine. Lex. Testementary. Compleat attorney. Shepards abridgment. & the Doct^r and Student"; but no value was stated, and, on the same day, "Mad^m Sarah Winslow & John Winslow Esqr and Mr Edward Winslow Executors" made oath to the inventory.

[MADAM SARAH WINSLOW'S WILL]

[Plym. Co. Prob., 13:201] "Sarah Winslow of Marshfield . . . . Widdow" made her will, 5 September, 1753. Bequests were as follows:

To "My son John Winslow the four pictures, and my Great Black Walnut Table"

To "My son Edward Winslow my largest Silver Salt Celler"

To "My Sister Hopestill Oliver . . . . Ten pounds Old Tenour"

"My will is that my wearing Apparell my Gold Chain rings and Buttons be Equally Divided Into two parts and one Half thereof I Give . . . . to My Daughter Elizabeth Marston, and in case she Die before me I Give the same to the Children, she Shall Have at my Decease; and the other Half of My said Apparell, Chain rings and Buttons, I Give to my Grand Children, Ann Warren and Sarah Warren Daughters of Penelope Warren my Daughter Deceas'd and in case either of them said Grand Daughters Shall die Before me I Give her Share and part to the Children she shall have Liveing at My Decease, and in Default of such Children then I Give the whole to the Survivor of My said two Grand daughters".

To "My Three Grand Children, Namely James Warren Junʳ Ann Warren, and Sarah Warren the Children of My Daughter Penelope afore named" £50 "Old Tenner as an Equivalent to Divers peices of Houshold Stuff that I have given to my Daughter Elizabeth Marston aforenamed Since my Husbands Decease, and in case any of my Three Grand Children last Named shall Die before me Then I Give his or her Share and porportion so Dying to his or her Children Liveing at My Decease and for Default os* such Children then I Give the whole to the Survivor or Survivors of the said James, Ann, and Sarah"

"all My personall Estate . . . . not heren before Bequeathed and all Debts to me Due, Shall be Divided Into two Equall parts & Shairs & One Half of My said Goods. Chattles. & Debts I Give . . . . to My said Daughter Elizabeth Marston and in case she Die Before Me I Give . . . . the Same to her Children that shall be Liveing at My Death and the other Half of My said Goods Chattles and Debts I Give to My said Three Grandchildren, James Warren Junʳ Ann Warren and Sarah Warren, Equally to be Divided among them, and In case the said James, ann or Sarah Die before me Then I Give his or her portion of said half . . . . to the Children of him or her (so Dying) that Shall be alive at my Death and in Default of Children of him or her so Dying then I Give the whole to the Survivor, or Survivors"

"I . . . . appoint My said Grandson James Warren Junʳ, My Soul Executor"

The witnesses were Ephraim Cobb, Nathaniel Goodwin and James Curtiss.

On 4 February, 1754, Ephraim Cobb and James Curtiss made oath that they, with Nathaniel Goodwin, witnessed the will.

[13:203] The will "of Madᵐ Sarah Winslow late of Marshfield . . . . Widdow Deceas'd" was probated at Plymouth, 4 February, 1754, and administration was granted to "James Warren Junʳ of Plimouth . . . . Marchant Soul Executor in the Same Will named".

[13:327] An inventory, dated at Plymouth, 17 July, 1754, was taken by Perez Tillson, John Thomas and Jedediah Bourn. The total amount of the inventory was £211, 1s., 9¾d.

James Warren, Jr., executor, made oath to the inventory, 17 July, 1754.

[14:59] An account of James Warren, Jr., executor, was

* Sic. Plainly an error, by the recorder, for "of".

sworn to and allowed, 3 April, 1756. Cash payments had been received : from "Edwd Winslow Esqr due on Bond" £20, 5s., 1d.; from "John Winslow Esqr due on Bond" £46, 12s., 7d.; from "Mary Tinkham to Ballance" 6s., 8d.

Payments had been made: "Gold Rings to the Bearers" £6, 10s., 2d.; to "Mrs Howland of Pembrooke"; "To 4 Pictures £5. 6. 8, 1 Large Table 2. 13. 4 D^{ld} Coll^o Winslow" £8; "To Sundrys to Mrs Marston ℣ Apprizment" £68, 19s., 4½d.; "To Sundreys to James, Ann, Sarah, Warren ℣ Ditto" £69, 0s., 6½d.; to "Messrs Winslow & White"; to "Doct^r John Thomas"; to "Mad^m Oliver"; to John Dingley; to "Mad^m Oliver for Mrs Holyoke"; to "Rich"; to "Jed. Bourn"; to Jacob Weston; to "m^r Bourn"; "To Ja^s Ann & Sarah Warren" £6, 13s., 4d.; "To Jo^s Winslow".

THE WILL OF JOHN COBB, SR.
OF MIDDLEBOROUGH, MASS.

By the Editor

John Cobb, Jr., of Plymouth and Middleborough, Mass., married Rachel^3 Soule, daughter of John^2 Soule (*George*^{1}) of Duxbury. The marriage is recorded at Plymouth, as on 7 September, 1688, and John is there called "Junior"; but on the Middleborough records the date is given as 5 September, 1688.

John and Rachel (Soule) Cobb had five children, recorded at Middleborough. They were: John Cobb^4, married, first, Joanna Thomas, married, second, Mary Conant^6 (*Elizabeth Washburn^5, Thomas^4, Elizabeth Mitchell^3, Jane^2 Cooke, Francis^1*); Martha Cobb^4, married, first, Ephraim Tinkham^4 (*Ephraim^3, Mary^2 Brown, Peter^1*), married, second, Aaron Simmons; Patience Cobb^4, married Samuel Tinkham^4 (*Ephraim^3, Mary^2 Brown, Peter^1*); James Cobb^4, married Thankful Thomas^4 (*Lydia^3 Howland, John$^{2-1}$*); Rachel Cobb^4, married Moses^4 Standish (*Ebenezer^3, Alexander^2, Myles^1*).

John Cobb, Sr., made his will, 29 May, 1727, and added a codicil, 28 September, 1727, after the death of his wife Rachel, which occurred 18 September, 1727. John Cobb died 18 October, 1727, and some of the witnesses to his will were sworn on 16 November, 1727.

We here present exhaustive abstracts of the will and codicil and all other records relating to the settlement of the estate, found in the Plymouth County, Mass., Probate Records.

[WILL OF JOHN COBB, SR.]

[From original will] "John Cob Senr of . . . . Middleburro" made his will 29 May, 1727. Bequests were as follows:

To "wife Rachell Cob my Dewling* house where I now Dwell During the whole Term of her naturall Life togethr with all my movable Estate wthin Doores & without with all my moneys to be absolutly at her Dispose for Ever Excepting my old oxen & my mare my will is that my Execu^t maintain my s^d wife three Cows both with pastureage & fodder good & Convenient both winter & Summer and twelve bushells of Corn yearly & that she have half the profit of my orchard all which to be performed by him During the whole term of her naturall Life"

"I give all my homestead to my son John Cob Except my Dwelling house which I have Reserved to my wife . . . . Excepting my three Twenty acres Lots which I now Improve which after his Decease I give to his Two sons namly Gershom Cob & John Cob . . . . with the appurtenances there unto belonging"

To "my son James Cob the Dwelling house where he now Dwells with all my Lands there to adjoying"

To "my three Daughters namly Martha Simons Patience Tinkham & Rachell Standish my whole Share of Land in the Twelve mens purchase in middleburro aboves^d with my Lot of Land in the mad mares neck So Called & my Lot of Land in Assawamsit neck . . . . to be Equally amongst them Divided"

"my two oxen and mare above Exprest I give to my two Daughters namly martha Simons & Patience Tinkham or the vaulue of them in money to be Equally Divided betwen them"

"all the Rest of my Lands & meadows and Swamps in middleburro & plimton I give to my two sons that is to say to my son John Cob two thirds & to James Cob one third"

"my will is that my three Yoak of oxen now in the possession of John Cob and James Cob & moses Standish be & Remain to as their own proper Estate"

"my Son John Cob" was appointed sole executor.

The will was signed "JoHn CoB".

The witnesses were "John Bennet," Jonathan Fuller and "Shubeal Tomson".

* Sic.

A codicil was added, 28 September, 1727, as follows: "where-as it hath pleasᵈ almighty God to Call to his mercy the othʳ day my dear Wife . . . . of these my moveables My desire & will is that my Executʳ Do out of them pay to Each of my daughtʳˢ Martha Patience & Rachel fiveteen pounds to Each of them & . . . . that the remainder of my moveables be Equally divided between my sons & my daughtʳˢ saving that I give to my sons my own Wearing Cloathes & to my daughtʳˢ all the wearing cloathes yᵗ were Hers to be Equally divided between thèm & also I give to my son James Cobb the Cow which he now hath that was my dear Wifes"

The codicil was witnessed by "Joseph Bennett", "Shubael Tomson" and "Ebenezer Cobb Juner".

On 16 November, 1727, Jonathan Fuller and Shubael Tomson made oath to the will, and the same day Shubael Tomson made oath to the codicil.

On 2 February, 1727/8, John Bennet made oath to the will, and Ebenezer Cobb made oath to the codicil.

On 6 March, 1727/8, Joseph Bennett made oath to the codicil.

The will and codicil were probated 28 March, 1728, and administration granted to "John Cobb one of the sons of the sd deceased and sole Executor in the same Will named" [Also recorded, 5: 528.]

[From original warrant] On 16 November, 1727, "mʳ John Benet mr James Soul and mr John Soul all of Middleborough" were appointed appraisers. [Also recorded, 5: 530.]

[From original document] The inventory was taken 10 January, 1727, by "John Bennet", "James Soul" and "John Soul". The real estate was as follows: "his Homstead & all his Lands Adjoyning thereto" £600; "all his meadows in Plimton & middleburro" £120; "four Lots of Land in the 12 mens purchase 290 acrs" £180; "half a 100 acre Lot in the Six & twenty mens purchase" £37; "two Lots in the South purchase ninty acres" £12; "a Lot in assawamsit neck being about 30 acres" £24; "a Lot in mad mares neck about 30 acres" £24; "3 Lots 2 near to Titucut meadows the other at assonet" £84; "one half of 2 points of maples by the great Cedar Swamp" £8; "the Land whereon James Cob Dwells about 80 acres" £110; "a Lot & half of Cedar Swamp in the great Swamp" £30; "part of a Lot in the Sixteen Shilling purchase" £3; "part of a Lot in assonet Cedar Swamp" £2; "part of a Lot on the Easterly Side of namassakit River" £5.

John Cobb, executor, and the three appraisers made oath to the inventory, 2 February, 1727/8. [Also recorded, 5: 530.]

MIDDLEBOROUGH, MASS., VITAL RECORDS

Transcribed by Miss Ethel A. Richardson

(Continued from Vol. XXIII, p. 71)

[p. 77] Rachal Smith Daughter of Abial Smith by Lydia his wife was born march the 20 1754

Hopestill Smith Daughter of Abial Smith by Lydia his wife was born June 20th 1755

Abial Smith Son of Abial Smith by Lydia his wife was born April the 27 1757

Samuel Sproutt Son of Capt Ebenezer Sproutt by Bathsheba His Wife Was born December 9th 1763

Thomas Shaw & Peter Shaw born Twins Sons of Samuel Shaw Junr by Fear his Wife was born march 20th 1763

Elkanah Sears the Son of Zebedee Sears by Mary his Wife was born April ye 10th 1764

Expearinee Sherman Daughter of Edward Sherman by Lucy his wife was born January the 16th 1764

[*] Samson Daughter of Abner Samson by Hannah his Wife Was born may 6th 1764

Ezra Samson Son to Uriah Samson by Ann his wife was born February 12th 1749

John Samson Son of Uriah Samson by Ann his wife was born March 27th 1751

Sarah Samson Daughter of Uriah Samson by Ann his wife was born April 8 1753

Hannah Samson Daughter of Uriah Samson by Ann his wife was born April 15th 1755

Uriah Samson Son of Uriah Samson by Ann his wife was born October 9th 1759

Isaac Samson Son of Uriah Samson by Ann his wife was born January 8th 1762

Ann Samson Daughter of Uriah Samson by Ann his Wife was born November 18th 1764

Zadok Samson & Daniel Samson Sons of Nathaniel Samson by martha his wife was born Twins December 15th 1764

[p. 78] Sarah Fuller the Daughter of Jabez Fuller by Hannah, his wife was born, July ye 22^d 1746

Lucy Fuller the Daughter of Jabez Fuller by Hannah his Wife was born January 17th 1747

Peter Fuller & Lucy Fuller Son & Daughter of Jabez Fuller by Hannah his wife ware both born at one beirth, may ye 13th 1748

* The baptismal name was not entered.

Zenas Fuller the Son of Jabez Fuller by Hannah his wife was born, July ye 8 1751

Betty Fuller the Daughter of Jabez Fuller by Hannah, his wife was born, September ye 13th 1753

John Fuller the Son of Jabez Fuller by Hannah, his wife was born June ye 18th 1754

Amasa, Fuller the Son of Jabez Fuller by Hannah his wife was born, march ye 6 1755

Silas Fuller the Son of Jabez Fuller by Hannah his wife was born April ye 27th 1756

Andrew Fuller the Son of Jabez Fuller by Hannah his wife was born may ye 18 1758

Hannah Fuller Daughter of Jabez Fuller by Hannah His wife was born march 4th 1764

Lewis Finney Son of Lt Nelson Finney by Rosemond His wife was born September 16th 1765

Samuel French Son of Asa French By Anne his wife was Born october 3rd 1766

Marcy Thatcher Forster Daughter of Thomas Forster By Mary his wife . was Born August 13th 1768

[p. 79] Nathan Vaughan the Son of Thomas Vaughan by Hannah, his wife was born, November ye 1st 1753

Faith Vaughan the Daughter of Thomas Vaughan by Hannah, his wife was born January ye 6th 1756

Betty Vaughan, the Daughter of Thomas Vaughan by Hannah his wife was born Febuary ye 19th 1758

Thomas Vaughan, the Son of Thomas Vaughan by Hannah his wife was born, January ye 30th 1761

mary Vaughan Daughter of Jesse Vaughan by margret his wife was born January 15th 1764

Asenath Vaughan Daughter of Jabes Vaughan J^r by Loes His Wife was born December 9th 1765

Deborah Vaughan Daughter of Daniel Vaughan by Sarah his wife was born June 24th 1749

Daniel Vaughan Son of Peter Vaughan By Joanna his wife was born October the 12th 1766

Elisabeth Vaughan Daughter of Elisha Vaughan by Esther his wife was born December 12th 1766

Simeon Vaughan Son of Simeon Vaughan by Naomi his wife was Born may 7th 1768

Daniel Vaughan Son of Jabez Vaughan Junr by Lois his wife was Born September 18th 1768

Deborah Vaughan Daughter of Jabez Vaughan Junr by Lois his wife was born March 27th 1771

[p. 80] Eli Peirce Son of Helkiah Peirce by Hannah his wife was born august 25th 1760

Chloe Peirce Daughter of Helkiah Peirce by Hannah his Wife was born December 25th 1762

Capt Abiel Peirce Son of Ebenezer Peirce by Mercy his wife was
    born September 10th 1733

William Peirce Son of Capt abiel Peirce by Hannah his wife was
    born June 1st 1758

Nathan Peirce Son of Capt Abiel Peirce by Hannah his wife was
    born November 9th 1761

Selah Peirce Daughter of Capt Abiel Peirce by Hannah his wife
    was born December 18 1763

Daniel Perry Son to Elijah Perry by Sarah his wife was born May
    6th 1752

Sarah Perry Daughter of Elijah Perry by Sarah his wife was born
    April 6th 1754

Mary Perry Daughter of Elijah Perry by Sarah his wife was born
    March 1st 1756

James Perry Son of Elijah Perry by Sarah his wife was born May
    19th 1758

Lydia Perry Daughter of Elijah Perry by Sarah his wife was born
    July 22^d 1760

Elijah Perry Son of Elijah Perry by Sarah his wife was born April
    21st 1763

George Pratt Son of Paul Pratt by Jael his wife was born July y^e
    8th 1764

Susanna Pratt Daughter to Beniah Pratt by Phebe his wife was
    born at Plimpton October 19th 1740

James Palmer Son of James Palmer by Maribah his Wife was born
    July 26th 1760

Sarah Palmer Daughter of James Palmer by maribah his wife was
    born July 13th 1763

[p. 81] Abiel Wood Son to Ebenezer Wood by Lydia his wife was
    born July 8th 1743

Levy Wood Son of Silas Wood by Priscilla his Wife was born April
    30th 1764

Joannah Wood Daughter of Abner Wood by Deborah his wife was
    born march 17th 1765

Rebeckah Wood Daughter to En^n Nathaniel Wood by Mary his
    wife was born March 27th 1765

Lavinia Weston Daughter of Edmond Weston Junr by Mary his wife
    was born September 29th 1764

Lydiah Washburn Daughter of Amos Washburn by Prudence his
    Wife was born February 25th 1765

Elenor Warren Daughter of Joseph warren by Mercy his wife was
    born November 20th 1764

Perez Wood Son of Nathan Wood by Betty his wife was born April
    3^d 1758

Nathan Wood Son of Nathan Wood by Betty his Wife Was born
    March 11th 1760 and Decesed February 24th 1761

Eleazer Wood Son of Nathan Wood by Betty his wife was born
    February 21st 1762

Molley Wood Daughter of Nathan Wood by Betty his wife was born
February 6th 1764

Azel Washburn Son to Jonah Washburn by Huldiah his wife was
born april 26: 1764

Huldiah Wood Daughter of Ephraim Wood by mary his wife was
born August 30th 1765

Seth Washburn Son of Ruben Washburn by Betty his wife was born
august 2d 1751

Joshua wood Son of Seth wood by Lydia his wife was born June
6th 1766

(*To be continued*)

PLYMOUTH COLONY WILLS AND INVENTORIES

ABSTRACTS BY THE EDITOR

(*Continued from Vol. XIX, p. 165*)

[KENELM WINSLOW'S WILL AND INVENTORY]

[3 : 1 : 56] "Kanelme Winslow senir" made his will, 8 August,
1672. Bequests were as follows:

"what estate I have formerly settled on my eldest son
Kanelme . . . . shall remaine unaltered"

"my son Nathaniel : shall have the halfe of my farme, that
I last lived upon with all the appurtenances, as I gave him by
a former Deed of Gift"

"and the other halfe of my farme to my wife, for the tearme
of her naturall life, with all my Cattle stocke and goods within
Dores and withoute; and that after the Decease of my wife
Ellinor Winslow the said halfe of the farme shall Returne unto
my son Nathaniel : and that my wife in the mean time shall not
have any power to Dispose of the movables or stocke of Cattle,
without the Consent of Major Josias Winslow and my son
Kanelme Winslow, whom I appoint overseers"

"my son Job shall have halfe of my land att Namassakett
which is about fifty acrees more or lesse; and the other fifty
acrees or therabouts; unto Kanelme Baker my Grandchild I
Give,"

"To my Daughter Ellinor I Give five pounds, That is in the
hands of Samuell Nash* Marshall, att Plymouth, for the prsent
yeer upon an execution from John Soule"

* Samuel Nash, of Duxbury, held the office of marshal at this time.

"my wife shall att her Decease Give unto Mary Addams an equall portion of the Goods and Moveables as to the Rest of my Grand Children"

"I Doe Constitute my wife sole Exequitrix"

The will was witnessed by Daniel Weld and William Bowditch. "Mr Daniel Weld and Willam Bowditch made oath as they were witnesses to this will . . . . before mee Willam Hawthorne Assistant"

"The . . . . Will of Mr Kanelme Winslow Deceased was shewed in the Court . . . . att Plymouth . . . . the fift of June 1673 and . . . . ordered heer to be Recorded"

"An Inventory of the whole estate of Mr Kanelme Winslow Deceased the 12 of September 1672 taken by us whose names are underwritten this 25 of the 7th month* 1672 and exhibited to the Court" 5 June, 1673, "on the oath of Nathaniel : Winslow". The appraisers were John Bourne, Anthony Snow and Josiah Winslow. The real estate was not valued, but was listed, as follows:

"The one halfe of the Dwelling house and housings and Meddow lands and uplands belonging to the said farme, hee had, lived on and now Died posessed off in the Towne of Marshfeild"

"The one halfe of all the lands Graunted him by the Court, with the ancient Freemen which lyeth on the west syde of Taunton River either Devided or to be Devided heerafter"

"The one halfe of the portion of land Graunted by the Court to him and his brother Josias Winslow upon the accoumpt of theire Brother Gilbert Winslow as hee was a first Comer† ".

The total value of the personal estate was £87, 15s., 4d.

[GOVERNOR THOMAS PRENCE'S WILL]

[On pages 58 to 70, inclusive, are recorded the will and inventory of Governor Thomas Prence. A literal copy of these was printed in our third volume, pages 203-216 inclusive.]

[HUMPHREY TURNER'S WILL]

[p. 71] "The last day of february 1669 I Humphery Turner of Scittuate . . . . Tanner . . . . make this my last will". Bequests were as follows:

---

* The seventh month was September, in Old Style dating.

† This Gilbert Winslow was one of the Mayflower Passengers.

To "my eldest son John* Turner twelve pence"

"wheras I have lately Given & posessed my son Joseph Turner of" £40 "as a portion for him; Item I give . . . . him more twelve pence"

"I give . . . . unto my son Young John* Turner" £5.

To "my son Daniell Turner twelve pence"

To "my son Nathaniel : Turner" £50.

To "my Daughter Mary Parker" £10.

To "my Daughter Lydia Doughtey twelve pence"

To "my Grandchild Humphery Turner" £5.

To "my Grandchild Mary Doughtey" £10.

To "my Grand Children Jonathan Turner Joseph Turner and Ezekiell Turner, being the sonnes of my eldest sonne ten shillings apeece"

To "my son Nathaniel : Turner all my quicke stocke, both of cattle horse Flesh sheep and swine"

To "my son Thomas Turner; all my wearing Clothes; and one woole bedd with the blanketts and Coverings belonging to it; and my mind and will is that the wearing Clothes and beding be Delivered within one Month, after my Decease"

"my will is that the rest of the Legacyes be payed; the one halfe of each and every legacye within twelve monthes after my Decease, and the other halfe within two yeares after my Decease"

"I Give . . . . unto my Grand Child Abigaill Turner the Daughter of My son Nathaniel : Turner" £15, "To be payed within two yeares after my Decease"

"as for my Debts I owe, or which is owing to mee, my mind and will is they be equally received; and equally payed, by my son Younge John Turner and Nathaniel : Turner; whom I Doe Make . . . . Joynt exequitors"

"my funarall expences Debts and legacyes being payed, Item I Give all the Rest of my moveable Goods and lumber both within Dores and without . . . . unto my exequitors; To be equally Devided betwixt them"

The witnesses were Mathew Gannett (by a mark), Nathaniel Tilden and James Cudworth.

"Captaine James Cudworth Gave oath to" the will, at the court at Plymouth, 5 June, 1673.

(To be continued)

---

* Humphrey Turner had two sons named John. The first John Turner married Mary[3] Brewster (*Jonathan[2], William[1]*) and her father recorded the marriage, in the Brewster Book, as follows: "Mary Brewster marryed to John Turner of Situate the Elder the 10th November. 1645". The first John appears on the records sometimes as Elder and sometimes as Senior. The second John Turner, called the Younger, also Junior, married Ann James.

NOAH WASHBURN'S ESTATE

By the Editor

Noah Washburn[5] (*Samuel*[4], *Elizabeth Mitchell*[3], *Jane*[2] *Cooke, Francis*[1]) was born at Bridgewater, Mass., 11 July, 1682, and there married, 25 January, 1709/10, Elizabeth Shaw. They had three children, recorded at Bridgewater, as follows: Hannah Washburn[6], born 13 July, 1711; Eliezer Washburn[6], born 8 February, 1713; Noah Washburn[6], born 18 July, 1716.

Noah Washburn[5] died at Bridgewater, 17 October, 1716, and his widow, on 22 July, 1717, became the second wife of Isaac Harris[5] (*Mercy Latham*[4], *Susanna Winslow*[3], *Mary*[2] *Chilton, James*[1]) of that town.

Isaac Harris[5], by his second wife, Elizabeth (Shaw) Washburn, had one child, Isaac Harris[6], born 22 July, 1720.

We here print exhaustive abstracts of all records and original documents on file, relating to the settlement of the estate, found in the Plymouth County, Mass., Probate Records.

[Noah Washburn's Estate]

[4:70] On 20 June, 1717, "Elisabeth Washbourn relict widdow of Noah Washbourn Late of Bridgwater .... dec^d" was appointed administratrix of her husband's estate.

[From original document] On 8 May, 1717, an inventory of the personal estate "of Noah Woshburne late of Bridgwater deceased" was taken "at Bridgwater" by "Joseph Shaw and Eleazar Carver both of Bridgwater", and on 20 June, 1717, "Elizabeth Washbon Relict Widow" made oath to it. [Also recorded, 4:19]

[5:105] "July 24th 1719. The accompt of Elisabeth Harris administratri[x] on ye Estate of Noah Washbourne deceased" was presented.

[From a contemporary "Coppy" on file] "The settlement of the personall Estate of Noah Washborne late of Bridgwater .... Deceased Intestate made and done July the 24 : 1719". The widow's thirds being settled on her, the balance "is also settled on Elizabeth Harris who was the widdow of sd noah Wasborne now the wife of Isaac Harris of Bridgwater aforesd to and for the bringing up of the Children of the sd Noah Wasborn deceased" [Also recorded, 5:105]

PROCEEDINGS OF THE MASSACHUSETTS SOCIETY OF MAYFLOWER DESCENDANTS

TWENTY-SIXTH ANNUAL DINNER

The Twenty-Sixth Annual Reception and Dinner were held at the Hotel Somerset, Boston, on Monday evening, 21 November, 1921.

Mr. William B. H. Dowse, Governor of the Society, presided at the after dinner exercises, and there were addresses by: Hon J. Weston Allen,* Attorney General of the Commonwealth of Massachusetts; Hon. Thomas C. Thacher, Chairman of the Provincetown Tercentenary Commission; Mr. John Packwood Tilden, Governor General of the General Society of Mayflower Descendants; and LeBaron Russell Briggs, LL.D., President of Radcliffe College, read his Pilgrim Tercentenary Poem, "1620-1920".

Secretary George Ernest Bowman read "The Compact" as usual; but this year, for the first time in the history of the Society, he read it from an original copy, owned by himself, of the first edition of Nathaniel Morton's "New-Englands Memoriall".

This very rare book, published in Boston, in 1669, contains the earliest known list of the Signers of "The Compact", and is the sole authority for their names.

Half-tone reproductions of the two pages of this edition of the "Memoriall", containing "The Compact" and the names of the Signers, were printed on the menu cards, and each guest received also a small reproduction of Marshall Johnson's painting, "The Mayflower", long owned by the Society.

The arrangements for the reception and dinner were in charge of, Frederic A. Washburn, M.D., Mrs. Channing H. Cox, Mrs. William L. McKee, Miss Clara Endicott Sears and Mr. F. Delano Putnam, the Society's Committee on Annual Dinner.

FOREFATHERS' DAY RECEPTION

The three hundred and first anniversary of Forefathers' Day was observed on Wednesday afternoon, 21 December, 1921, by an informal reception at the Society's Rooms, in charge of the Committee on At Home Days, Mrs. John Holmes Morison, Mrs. Robert H. Gardiner, Mrs. Curtis Guild, Miss Clara Endicott Sears and Miss Caroline Ticknor.

GIFTS FOR THE LIBRARY AND CABINET

From Mr. Andrew Keogh: Four photographs of the John Robinson Tablet at Leyden, Holland.

* A member of the Society.

From Miss Susanna Willard*: An old brooch, containing a piece of Plymouth Rock, made for her mother, Susanna Hickling (Lewis) Willard, before 1869.

From Dr. Rendel Harris: "Souvenirs of the Mayflower Tercentenary", Numbers, 1, 2, 3 and 4.

From Miss Amelia D. Campbell*: Three numbers of "Americana".

From Mr. Wallace Fay Tenney, the compiler: "Genealogical Data concerning the family of Captain Edward Brown of Newbury, Massachusetts".

From Mrs. Frederic W. Bakeman*: Thirty-six back numbers of The Mayflower Descendant.

From Miss Helen L. Church*: Four copies of Genealogical Magazines.

From Mr. Samuel Usher: Twenty-four back numbers of The Mayflower Descendant.

From Mr. Edwin C. Gilman*: Six bound volumes of The Mayflower Descendant.

From Miss Alice M. Hawes, the author*: "Plymouth Mayflowers 1621-1921".

From the University of Illinois: "The Pilgrim Tercentenary Celebration at the University of Illinois, 1920".

From Mr. George Ernest Bowman*: Thirty copies of Genealogical Magazines.

Mrs. Leonard C. Bliss, a life member, died 4 October, 1921, at Edgartown, Mass. She was a descendant of John Howland, and was elected a member 23 September, 1907, her membership number being 998.

Mr. Harry M. Howard died 21 October, 1921, at Brookline, Mass. He was a descendant of Francis Cooke, and was elected a member 23 June, 1897, his membership number being 228.

Mr. Charles A. Dunham died 25 October, 1921, at New Brunswick, N. J. He was a descendant of Edward Fuller, and was elected a member 30 April, 1900, his membership number being 582.

Mr. William D. Wright died 16 November, 1921, at Knoxville, Tenn. He was a descendant of John Howland, and was elected a member 13 January, 1919, his membership number being 1569.

Mr. Wallace L. Kimball died 7 December, 1921, at Haverhill, Mass. He was a descendant of Richard Warren, and was elected a member 27 August, 1914, his membership number being 1310.

Mrs. Edwin D. Hauthaway died 28 December, 1921, at Brookline, Mass. She was a descendant of James Chilton, and was elected a member 15 January, 1906, her membership number being 924.

---

*Member of the Massachusetts Society of Mayflower Descendants.

MEMBERS ELECTED

10 October, 1921.

No. 2346. Miss Lucretia Stevens Heckscher, Strafford, Pa., ninth from Richard Warren.

No. 2347. Edward Oliver Wells, Rockwood, Tenn., ninth from Richard Warren.

No. 2348. Mrs. Robert McLure Fairleigh, Hopkinsville, Ky., tenth from Richard Warren.

14 November, 1921.

No. 2349. Austin Lothrop Baker, Medfield, Mass., eighth from John Howland.

No. 2350. Loring Quincy White, Cohasset, Mass., ninth from William Brewster.

No. 2351. Alfred Davenport, Malden, Mass., tenth from John Alden.

No. 2352. Mrs. Marshall Franklin Blanchard, Cambridge, Mass., ninth from Richard Warren.

No. 2353. Mrs. Franklin Amos Pond, Greenfield, Mass., tenth from Richard Warren.

21 November, 1921.

No. 2354. Archibald MacLeish, Cambridge, Mass., ninth from William[1] Brewster, eighth from Love[2] Brewster.

No. 2355. Freeman Cudworth Rogers, Pueblo, Colo., eighth from William[1] White, seventh from Peregrine[2] White.

No. 2356. Mrs. Freeman Cudworth Rogers, Pueblo, Colo., eighth from William[1] White, seventh from Peregrine[2] White.

No. 2357. Lewis Edward Keith*, Lynn, Mass., ninth from Stephen[1] Hopkins, eighth from Gyles[2] Hopkins.

No. 2358. Mrs. Onias Paige, Taunton, Mass., eighth from Thomas Rogers.

No. 2359. Mrs. Fred Fremont Rogers, Washington, D. C., tenth from John Alden.

No. 2360. Mrs. Arthur Hinton Gardner, Nantucket, Mass., ninth from John Howland.

16 December, 1921.

No. 2361. Mrs. Frank Hugo Sterling, Normal, Ill., tenth from William Brewster.

No. 2362. Mrs. John Kemp Bartlett, Jr., Baltimore, Md., ninth from William Brewster.

No. 2363. Mrs. George Washington Dixon, Cory, Col., ninth from William Brewster.

No. 2364. Mrs. Robert Dennis Hall, Brookline, Mass., tenth from Francis[1] Cooke, ninth from John[2] Cooke.

* Life Member.

No. 2365. Mrs. Charles Holcombe Reade, South Hero, Vt., ninth from Degory Priest.

No. 2366. Mrs. Ralph Gerhardt Johnson, Chicago, Ill., twelfth from Edward[1] Fuller, eleventh from Samuel[2] Fuller.

No. 2367. Edward Southworth Hawes, Boston, Mass., eighth from John Alden.

No. 2368. Mrs. George Boardman Wheeler, West Somerville, Mass., eighth from William Bradford.

No. 2369. Mrs. George Albert Miles, West Somerville, Mass., eighth from William Bradford.

No. 2370. Hall Edward Shepherd, Bronxville, N. Y., tenth from Stephen[1] Hopkins, ninth from Constance[2] Hopkins.

No. 2371. Mrs. Thomas Lincoln Handy, Bay City, Mich., tenth from Stephen[1] Hopkins, ninth from Gyles[2] Hopkins.

No. 2372. Mrs. John Duncan Menish, Port Huron, Mich., ninth from John Alden.

31 December, 1921.

No. 2373. George Frederick Kendall, Cambridge, Mass., ninth from William Brewster.

No. 2374. James Henry Kendall, Holden, Mass., ninth from William Brewster.

No. 2375. Roy Waldo Miner, Yonkers, N. Y., ninth from John Alden.

No. 2376. Charles Seaver Scott, Waverley, Mass., ninth from William Brewster.

No. 2377. Mrs. William Henry Doble, Quincy, Mass., eighth from Thomas Rogers.

SUPPLEMENTAL LINES ACCEPTED

[The By-Laws require an additional fee of two dollars ($2.00) for each supplemental line filed.]

November, 1921.

No. 1608. Walter G. Parsons, ninth from Richard Warren.

No. 2158. Mrs. Nevin C. Lescher; ninth from John Alden; ninth from Thomas Rogers.

No. 2272. John C. Pearson, eighth from Samuel Fuller.

No. 2281. Mrs. Algie C. Hodges, tenth from Isaac[1] Allerton, ninth from Mary[2] Allerton.

No. 2295. Mrs. Thomas D. Barroll, tenth from William Brewster.

December, 1921.

No. 2023. Mrs. Robert Johnston, tenth from James[1] Chilton, ninth from Mary[2] Chilton.

Attest: GEORGE ERNEST BOWMAN,
Secretary.

THE
MAYFLOWER DESCENDANT

| Vol. XXIV | APRIL, 1922 | No. 2 |

NATHANIEL MORTON'S "NEW-ENGLANDS MEMORIALL"

By George Ernest Bowman

Nathaniel Morton's "New-Englands Memoriall", published in 1669, when its author had been Secretary of Plymouth Colony for more than twenty years, contains a brief history of the Old Colony; but it is of especial interest to all descendants of the Mayflower Passengers, because it contains the oldest known list of the Signers of The Compact, and is our sole authority for their names, the original document having been lost for many years.

The accompanying illustration, a reprint of one of the plates in "The Mayflower Compact and Its Signers", published by the present writer, on 21 November, 1920, reproduces the fifteenth page of the first edition of the "Memoriall". This page contains the Compact and twenty-one names of the Signers, the remaining twenty names being printed at the top of the sixteenth page.

Seven editions of the "New-Englands Memoriall" have been published, and the Massachusetts Society of Mayflower Descendants has long owned copies of the fourth, sixth and seventh; but, on account of the rarity of the first edition, the possibility of securing a complete set seemed very remote, and no special effort was made to secure the other three editions.

In November, 1921, however, we had an opportunity to purchase an imperfect copy of the first (1669) edition, and, as the leaf containing the Compact and the names of the Signers was complete, it seemed best to secure this copy, rather than to wait, possibly many years, for a perfect one.

The Society has no funds available for such purchases, and a prompt decision was necessary, therefore I bought the book myself, and owned it for four months, until the Society could raise the amount of the purchase price, by gifts from members.

The eventual addition to our library of this rare first edition of the "Memoriall" having been assured, I determined if possible to secure for the Society copies of the second, third and fifth editions; and at the twenty-sixth annual meeting, held in Boston on 28 March, 1922, the four copies needed to make up a complete set of the seven different editions were presented to the Society, and these seven books were then exhibited.

At this meeting the copy of the first edition was formally presented by the present writer, in behalf of the forty-eight members who had contributed to the fund for its purchase. [The list of the contributors will be found at the end of this article.]

A letter was then read from Mrs. Theodore C. Keller, of Evanston, Ill., a member of the Society, presenting a copy of the second edition.

The present writer then personally presented a copy of the third edition.

The Society's copy of the fourth edition was then shown. This had been presented, in 1897, by Mr. Henry Southworth Shaw, of Milton, Mass., a member of the Society.

Mrs. Charles H. Bond of Boston, a member of the Society, then personally presented a copy of the fifth edition.

The Society's copy of the sixth edition was then shown. This had been presented in 1899, by the late Mrs. Henry E. Raymond, a member of the Society.

The Society's copy of the seventh edition, which was obtained by exchange in 1904, was then shown, completing the set.

Mrs. Theodore C. Keller also very kindly loaned for this exhibit another copy of the second edition, with the name of a different bookseller on the title-page.

Brief accounts of the seven different editions are here given, with notes on the variations in the two impressions of the second edition.

[First Edition—Cambridge, Mass., 1669]

The first edition of the "Memoriall" was printed in 1669, at Cambridge, Mass., by Samuel Green and Marmaduke Johnson, for John Usher of Boston.

In the following literal copy of the title-page no attempt has been made to indicate the arrangement of the lines, or the numerous styles and sizes of type used.

"New-Englands Memoriall: or, A brief Relation of the most Memorable and Remarkable Passages of the Providence of God, manifested to the Planters of New-England in America; With special Reference to the first Colony thereof, Called New-Plimouth.

"As also a Nomination of divers of the most Eminent Instruments deceased, both of Church and Common-wealth, improved in the first beginning and after-progress of sundry of the respective Jurisdictions in·those Parts; in reference unto sundry Exemplary Passages of their Lives, and the time of their Death.

"Published for the Use and Benefit of present and future Generations, By Nathaniel Morton, Secretary to the Court for the Jurisdiction of New-Plimouth.

"Deut. 32.10. He found him in a desert Land, in the waste howling wilderness he led him about; he instructed him, he kept him as the Apple of his Eye.

"Jerem. 2. 2, 3. I remember thee, the kindness of thy youth, the love of thine Espousals, when thou wentest after me in the wilderness, in a Land that was not sown, &c.

"Deut. 8. 2, 16. And thou shalt remember all the way which the Lord thy God led thee this Forty Years in the wilderness, &c.

"Cambridge: Printed by S. G. and M. J. for John Usher of Boston . 1669."

A copy of this first edition was purchased for the Society's library with funds contributed by the forty-eight persons here named, all being members of the Massachusetts Society of Mayflower Descendants, except in two cases noted.

Francis R. Allen, Mrs. J. Paul Baker, Mrs. John C. Bannister, Mrs. Herschell Bartlett, Mrs. Morris B. Belknap, Mrs. Charles H. Bond, George Ernest Bowman, Miss Harriet H. Brayton, Frederick Brooks, Joshua L. Brooks, Mrs. William F. Brooks, Miss Mabel E. Cheney, Mrs. Matthias W. Conrow, William F. Cushman, Mrs. Fred R. E. Dean, Mrs. Fred C. Eaton, Miss Lucy H. Eaton, Miss Nellie L. Edwards, Edric Eldridge, Miss Edith Eliot, Luther O. Emerson, Mrs. Robert M. Fairleigh, Mrs. Wendell B. Folsom, Frederick Foster, Mrs. Richard W. Francis, Mrs. Arthur H. Gardner, Mrs. William B. Gibson, Mrs. Theodore C. Keller, Dr. Philip Leach, Miss Edith Lombard, James A. Noyes, Mrs. Jess O. Park, Edward L. Parker, Royal Parkinson, Merritt G. Perkins (member of New Jersey Society), Virgil C. Pond, D.M.D., Miss Ella H. Read, C. Perry Rockwell, Warren C. Rowley, Mrs. Flora E. Shepard, Charles W. Sherman, Mrs. William E. Sherwood, Miss Cordelia E. Stone, Charles I. Thayer, John

Packwood Tilden (member of New York Society), Mrs. Lillian A. Ward, Loring Q. White, and A Member.

[SECOND EDITION—BOSTON, MASS., 1721]

The second edition of the "Memoriall" was printed at Boston, Mass., in 1721, by John Allen.

The entire title-page of the first edition, through the quotation from Jeremiah, was reprinted for this edition, but a smaller page necessitated a change in the styles of type and in the arrangement of the lines; and there are a few changes in spelling and punctuation.

At the bottom of the title-page of the copy presented to the Society by Mrs. Theodore C. Keller is printed: "*Boston*, Reprinted for *Daniel Henchman*, at the Corner Shop, over-against the Brick-Meeting-House . 1721."

At the bottom of the title-page of another copy, owned by Mrs. Keller, but loaned to this Society, is printed: "*Boston*, Reprinted for *Nicholas Boone*, at the sign of the BIBLE in *Cornhill* . 1721."

On the first page of the last leaf of each of these two copies is printed:

"Advertisement . Pharmacopœia Londinensis; Or, The *London* Dispensatory further Adorned by the Studies and Collections of the Fellows now living of the said College . . . . By Nich. Culpeper, Gent. Student in Physick and Astrology

"*Boston*, Printed by *John Allen*, for *Nicholas Boone*, at the Sign of the Bible in *Cornhill*; and *Daniel Henchman* over-against the Brick Meeting-House . 1720."

This advertisement leaf supplies the explanation of the two different title-pages for the second edition of the "Memoriall". The copies printed to be sold by Nicholas Boone "at the sign of the Bible" bore his name on the title-page; and Daniel Henchman's name was put on the title-page of the copies to be sold at his "Corner Shop".

The two impressions of the second edition are the same, with the exception of the change of name on the title-page.

It is interesting to note that after Mrs. Keller had decided to present to this Society the copy with Daniel Henchman's name on the title-page, which she had bought from a dealer in Boston, she tried to secure another copy for herself, and in a short time had the unusual good fortune to secure, from a dealer in Chicago, one of the copies printed for Nicholas Boone.

[THIRD EDITION—NEWPORT, R. I., 1772]

The third edition of the "Memoriall" was printed at Newport, R. I., in 1772, by Solomon Southwick.

The title-page is the same as in the second edition, through the quotation from Jeremiah, with a few slight changes in spelling and punctuation, and a different arrangement of the lines, caused by another change in the size of the page.

At the bottom of the title-page we find: "BOSTON: printed. NEWPORT: Reprinted, and sold by S. Southwick . M,DCC,LXXII."

Following the last page of the text are printed eight pages of "Names of the Subscribers for" this edition, including five hundred and sixty different names. The total number of copies subscribed for in advance was eight hundred and sixty-eight (868), distributed as follows: "Elijah Tilton, for himself and a number of others at Martha's Vineyard 37"; Nathaniel Russell, 36; Clarke Brown, Azariah Lathrop, Francis Rotch, Daniel Skinner, 12 each; Cornelius Simmons, 9; Thirty-one took 6 each; One took 5; One took 4; Four took 3 each; Fifteen took 2 each; and Five hundred and one took one copy each.

The residences of the subscribers were not given, but the names would seem to indicate that the great majority of them were from Rhode Island and southeastern Massachusetts.

The Society's copy of this edition was given by the present writer.

[FOURTH EDITION—PLYMOUTH, MASS., 1826]

The fourth edition of the "Memoriall" was printed at Plymouth, Mass., in 1826, by Allen Danforth. The title-page is the same as in the preceding edition, through the quotation from Jeremiah, with a few slight changes. At the bottom of the title-page we read: "Plymouth, Mass. Reprinted by Allen Danforth . 1826."

The Society's copy of this edition was presented, in 1897, by a member, Mr. Henry Southworth Shaw.

[FIFTH EDITION—BOSTON, MASS., 1826]

The fifth edition of the "Memoriall", with voluminous notes, and an appendix, by Judge John Davis, was "Printed by Crocker and Brewster, No. 47, Washington Street, late No. 50, Cornhill . 1826", in Boston. It was copyrighted, 13 December, 1826, by the Pilgrim Society of Plymouth.

This edition has an entirely new title-page, but reprints also the title-page of the first edition.

The Society's copy of this edition was presented by a member, Mrs. Charles H. Bond.

[SIXTH EDITION—BOSTON, MASS., 1855]

The sixth edition of the "Memoriall" was published at Boston, Mass., in 1855, by the Congregational Board of Publication, but the printing was done at Cambridge, Mass., by "Allen and Farnham, Printers."

This edition has an entirely new title-page, which reads as follows:

"New England's Memorial. By Nathaniel Morton, Secretary to the Court for the Jurisdiction of New-Plimouth. Sixth Edition. Also Governor Bradford's History of Plymouth Colony; Portions of Prince's Chronology; Governor Bradford's Dialogue; Gov. Winslow's Visit to Massasoit; with Numerous Marginal Notes and an Appendix, containing numerous articles relating to the Labors, Principles, and Character of the Puritans and Pilgrims. Itur in antiquam sylvam. Boston: Congregational Board of Publication . 16 Tremont Temple . 1855."

The Society's copy of the sixth edition was presented by a member, the late Mrs. Henry E. Raymond.

[SEVENTH EDITION—BOSTON, 1903]

The seventh edition of the "Memoriall" is a facsimile reproduction of the first edition, to which is prefixed an introduction by Hon. Arthur Lord of Plymouth.

The title-page reads: "New-Englands Memoriall By Nathaniel Morton With an Introduction by Arthur Lord Boston The Club of Odd Volumes 1903".

Only one hundred and fifty copies were printed, at the University Press, John Wilson and Son, Cambridge, Mass.

The Society's copy was obtained in 1904, in exchange for duplicates.

FORM FOR A BEQUEST

I GIVE and bequeath to the Society of Mayflower Descendants, a corporation organized under the laws of the Commonwealth of Massachusetts, the sum of..............................dollars.

MIDDLEBOROUGH, MASS., VITAL RECORDS

(Continued from page 41)

[p. 82] March yᵉ 28 1760 married Joshua Caswell & Zilpah Ransom both of middleborough

May yᵉ 29ᵗʰ 1760 Married John Eddy Junʳ & Hannah Pomroy both of middleborough

October yᵉ 2ᵈ 1760 Married Philip Dean of Taunton and Abigail Shaw of Middleborough

November yᵉ 19ᵗʰ 1761 Married Archippus Cole & Drusilla Howland both of Middleborough.

February yᵉ 11ᵗʰ 1762 Married Job Richmond & Jenny Washburn both of middleborough, And Isaac Richmond of Taunton & Mehetable Richmond of middleborough

June yᵉ 3ᵈ 1762 Married Isaac Thomas & Phebe Thomas 3ᵈ both of Middleborough

August yᵉ 5ᵗʰ 1762 Married Samuel Barrows & Sarah Thomas 3ʳᵈ both of Middleborough

December yᵉ 27 : 1762 Married Jesse Curtis of middleborough and Esther Herrington of Raynham

April yᵉ 21ˢᵗ 1763 Married Isaac Shaw & Betty Beals both of Middleborough

A Trew Coppy Attest Solomon Reed Clerk

November yᵉ 1ˢᵗ 1763 Married Elijah Eaton & Sarah Shaw both of Middleborough A Trew Coppy attest Solomon Reed

December yᵉ 8ᵗʰ 1763 Married Zebedee Pratt of middleborough & Dordana Keith of Bridgwater   Solomon Reed

Middleborough November yᵉ 10ᵗʰ 1763 Then Isaac Samson and Mercy Caswell both of Middleborough were Joyned in marriage by me Ebenezer Hinds Baptist minester

[p. 83] Middleborough November yᵉ 21ˢᵗ 1763 Then Nathaniel Mayo & Dorithy Smith both of Middleborough were Joynᵈ In marriage by me Ebenʳ Hinds Baptist minester

Middleborough December yᵉ 1ˢᵗ 1764 Then David Peirce of Rochester & Martha Canedy Ware Joynᵈ In Marriage by me Ebenʳ Hinds Baptist minester

Plimouth Ss: march 19 : 1764 This Certifys that Nathaniel Cobb Jʳ of Plimpton and Penelepey Standish of Bridgwater were this Day joynᵈ in marriage by me Joseph Tinkham Justic Peace

This Certifies that Hugh Canedy of middleborough and Bathsheba Baker of Rochester were joynᵈ in marriage on april 11ᵗʰ 1764 by Ebenezer Jones Baptist minster

Plimouth Ss. may 10 : 1764 This Certifys that Abner wood of middleborough & Deborah Bearce of Hallifax were joynᵈ in marriage by me Joseph Tinkham Justic Peace

may 3ᵈ 1764 Married Jonathan Woods Junʳ and Kezia Keith both of
   Bridgwater   Solomon Reed

Plimouth Ss: may 24 : 1764 this Certifies that John Rickard and
   Ruth Pratt both of middleborough were Joynᵈ in marriage by me
   Joseph Tinkham Justice Peace

Middleborough march yᵉ 24ᵗʰ 1763 Then I married Job Thrasher &
   Lydia Smith both of middleborough

April 26ᵗʰ 1763 I Married Edmond Richmond of Taunton Abigial
   Wood of middleborough

July 28ᵗʰ 1763 I married Archelus Leonard & Lydia Caswell, both of
   middleborough

August 10ᵗʰ 1763 I married John House of Dartmouth & Elenor
   Barden of middleborough

November 24ᵗʰ 1763 I married George Fish of Dighton, & Thankfull
   Raynolds of Middleborough

December 1ˢᵗ 1763 I married David Shermond of middleborough &
   Lydia Stap[*] of Taunton

Middleboro Janʸ 5ᵗʰ 1764 I married George Leonard of Taunton &
   Charity Nelson of Middleborough

may 14 1764 I married Ephraim Hackett & Elisabeth Paddock both
   of middleborough Pr Caleb Turner

the foregoing marriages Sent to Plimouth august 6 176[*worn*]

[p. 84] middleborough march 26 : 1764 Then Robart Simon Inden
   man and Sarah Thomas Inden woman both of middleborough
   were Joynᵈ in marriage by me Ebenʳ Hinds Baptist minister

middleborough may the 27 1764 Then Caleb Tinkham and Deborah
   Babbit both of middleborough were married by me Ebenezer
   Hinds Baptist minister

middleborough June the 14 : 1764 Then Isaac Barker of middleborough and Abigail Robbins of Rochester were joynᵈ in marriage by me Ebenʳ Hinds Baptist mini

middleborough July the 26 : 1764 Then Thomas Simmons & Rebekah Peirce both of middleborough were joynᵈ in marriage by
   me Ebenʳ Hinds Baptist minister

Plimouth Ss: July 24 : 1764 this Day Samuel Bennett & ann Bennett both of middleborough were joynᵈ in marriage by me Joseph
   Tinkham Just Peace

Plimouth Ss: august 23 : 1764 this Day Caleb Williamson Junʳ &
   mercy Jackson both of middleborough were joynᵈ in marriage
   by me Joseph Tinkham J. Peace

Plimouth Ss: august 30ᵗʰ 1764 this Day mʳ Calven Delano of Dartmouth & miss mary alden of middleborough were joynᵈ in marriage by Joseph Tinkham Justice Peace

Plimouth Ss: September 13 : 1764 This Day William Peirce of
   Taunton & Joanna Dagget of middleborough Were joinᵈ In
   marriage by me Joseph Tinkham Justic Peace

* Worn off. The name probably was " Staples ".

October 1764 N : B all the above & foregoing marriages and carried
to the County Record attest Joseph Tinkham T : C

Plimouth Ss October 11th 1764 this Day John Randol & Jemima
Washburn both Residents in middleborough were join^d in marriage by me Joseph Tinkham Justic Peace

Plimouth Ss November 1st 1764 this D Mr Batchaler Bennet & miss
Mary Samson both of middleborough were joined in marriage:
as also David Thomas and Deborah Howland both of middleborough were joined in marriage by me Joseph Tinkham Justic Peace

Plimouth Ss January 3^d 1765 This Day Zebulon Vaughan & Mercy
Pratt both of middleborough were joyn^d in marriage by me
Joseph Tinkham Justic Peace

Plimouth Ss January 15th 1765 This Day m^r Seth Billington & m^rs
Betty washburn both of middleborough were joined in marriage
by me Joseph Tinkham Justic Peace

[p. 85] middleborough October the 18 : 1764 then William Smith the
3^d & Keziah Hinds both of middleborough were Joyn^d in marriage by me Eben^r Hinds Baptist minster

middleborough October 19th 1764 then Benjamin Spooner Junr &
mary Peirce both of middleborough were Joyn^d in marriage by
me Eben^r Hinds Baptist minister

Middleborough December the 18th 1764 then Nathaniel Smith the
4th & Anne Dillingham both of middleborough were Joyn^d in
marriage by me Eben^r Hinds Baptist minis[ter]

middleborough December the 20th 1764 then Elijah Thomas &
martha Pratt Both of middleborough were Joyn^d in marriage
by me Eben^r Hinds Baptist minister

april 8 : 1756 woodw^d Tucker of Bridgwater & mercy Tinkham of
middleborough were married by Silvanus Conant

april 15 1756 Jacob Tomson of Hallifax and waitstill miller of middleborough were married by Silvanus Conant

april 22 : 1756 John Elmes & Lydia Rider both of middlebor^r were
married by Silvanus Conant

July 7 : 1756 Jonah washburn and Huldia Sears both of middleborough were married by Silvanus Conant

July 27 : 1756 manasseh wood and Sarah Pomeroy both of middleborough were married by Silvanus Conant

august 5 : 1756 Nathaniel Billington & Eleanor warren both of middleborough were married by Silvanus Conant

Novr 17 : 1756 Lemuel Ransom of Freetown and mary Rickard of
middleborough were married by Silvanus Conant

Novr 18 : 1756 Silas Stertevant of Plimpton and Elisabeth Samson
of middleborough were married by Silvanus Conant

Novr 25 1756 Hushia Thomas & Lucy Vaughan both of middleborough were married by Silvanus Conant

Decem^r 1 : 1756 Ebenezer Fuller of Plimouth and Lois Rider of
middleborough were married by Silvanus Conant

Decem^r 13 : 1756 Ensign Charles Ellis of middleboro & Bathsheba Fuller of Hallifax ware married by Silvanus Conant

Dece^r 16 : 1756 Samuel Shaw & fear Thomas both of middleborough ware married by Silvanus Conant

Decr 30 1756 Seth Billington and Deborah Smith both of middleborough were married by Silvanus Conant

Jan^r 13 : 1757 Simmon* Freeman of Rochester & paticence wood of middleborough were married as also Isaac Bennet and Zilpah Peterson both of middleborough were married by Silvanus Conant

Jan^r 26 : 1757 Thomas Darling Junr & Ruth Howland both of middleborough were married by Silvanus Conant

march 1 1757 John Smith Junr & Betty Tucker both of middleborough were married by Silvanus Conant

April 14 : 1757 John weston Junr and Elisabeth Leonard both of middleborough were married by Silvanus Conant

[p. 86] Abigail Miller Daughter of David Miller Junr by Sarah his wife was born December 17th 1761

Fredrick Miller Son of David Miller Junr by Sarah his wife was born December 20th 1764

Hannah Miller Daughter to John Miller 3rd by Zilpah his Wife was born March 25th 1765

Mary Marshall Daughter of Josiah Marshall by Sarah his wife was born February 19th 1758

Olive Miller Daughter of Thomas Miller by Mary his wife was Born october the 24th 1766.

Mary Miller Daughter of Thomas Miller by Mary his his wife was Born March 2nd 1768

Susanna Miller Daughter of Abraham Miller by Susanna his wife was born on Saterday April 1st 1769.

Lydia Miller, daughter of John Miller 3^d by Zilpha his wife was born, June 2^d 1766

Abishai Miller, son of John Miller 3^d by Zilpha his wife was born November 17th 1767

Zilpha Miller daughter of John Miller 3^d by Zilpha his wife was born Novr 3^d 1769

John Miller son of John Miller 3^d by Zilpha his wife was born July 24th 1771.

Priscilla Miller daughter of John Miller 3^d by Zilpha his wife was born April 16th 1773.

Susanna Miller, daughter of John Miller 3^d by Zilpha his wife was born . Decr 10th 1776

Minerva Miller daughter of John Miller 3^d by Zilpha his wife was born February 28th 1779

(*To be continued*)

* On 1 November, 1756, the intention of marriage of " Simeon Freeman of Rochester & Patience wood of middleborough " was recorded, in original Volume 2, Part 1, page 91.

ABSTRACTS OF BARNSTABLE COUNTY, MASS. PROBATE RECORDS

BY THE EDITOR

(Continued from Vol. XXIII, p. 69)

[EDWARD PERRY'S WILL]

[2 : 1] On "December : 29 : 1694 Edward Perry of Sandwich" made his will. Bequests were as follows:

"my Body to be Desently Buiered at Spring hill Buring place among my friends there"

To "Wife Mary yᵉ use and proffit of all my housing and Land for her Comforte during yᵉ term of her Natural Life and after her decease . . . . my Eldest Son Samuel Shall have my now dwelling house and all my out housing and yᵉ Land thereunto belonging . bounded Southerly up on yᵉ highway or Country Road and westerly on the way that Leads to a place knowne by yᵉ Name of yᵉ great Sprinng from Sᵈ Road bounded Easterly by John Wing and notherly by Scoton River Including all yᵉ meadow as well as upland with in Sd boundaries and on Lott of about nine Acres . . . . which is with in fence Lying on yᵉ South Side of yᵉ Sd high way or Country Road and bounded with yᵉ fenċe that is now about it this Land and meadow with all yᵉ housing there on I give as afore Sd to my Son Samuel"

To "my Son Edward . . . . all yᵉ Remaining part of yᵉ tennement on which I dwell both upland and marsh lying on yᵉ westerly Side of yᵉ lands above given to Samuel And is bounded Southerly by yᵉ highway or Country Road and Northerly by Scoton River and westerly by yᵉ land in yᵉ occupation of Joseph Hallet and Easterly by yᵉ afore Sd way which Leads from yᵉ Country Road to yᵉ great Spring afore Said which Sd way is to be yᵉ division between yᵉ lands of my two Sons afore Sd and is to lye comon for yᵉ use of both and yᵉ Crick that Runs from. Sd great Spring into Scoton River is to be yᵉ division of their marsh and . . . . Edward Shall have as belonging to Sd tenement all my land on yᵉ South Side of yᵉ Sd high way Except yᵉ lott given to Samuel"

To "my youngest Son Benjamin all my Lands both upland and meadow on Scoton Neck"

"it is to be understood that all my Lands given to my three

Sons Shall be for yᵉ use of my Sd wife during yᵉ term of her Natural Life as above Sd"

"my two Daughters Peace and Rest Shall have" £20 "apiece in money which Shall be paid to them by my Son Samuel as a Legace out of yᵉ Land given to him within one year after my wifes decease"

"my Daughter Deborh Shall have twenty pounds in money paid to her by my Son Edward as a Legacy out of yᵉ Lands given to him within one year after my wifes decease : and my Daughters Peace and Rest Shall have each of them ten pounds in money"

"my Son Benjamin Shall pay in Legaces out of yᵉ Land given to him thirty pounds in money within one year after he Comes to twenty one years of age and to Injoy yᵉ Land given him, ten to my Daughter Dorchas and ten to my Daughter Sarah and five to my Daughter Peace and five to my Daughter Rest"

"my Daughter mary Shall have five pounds besides what She hath all Redy had to be paid to her by her mother my executrix here after Named in such time and manner as She She Shall See meet : and Six pounds to my Grand Daughter hannah Easton"

To "my Sd wife all my moveable Estate . . . . for her Comfort and Support in her age, and what She Shall not have need to Expend : to be disposed of as She Shall See Caues, She having paid yᵉ Bequest given to my daughter Mary"

"wife Mary to be . . . . Executrix"

"I . . . . appoint Stephen Skeffe and John otis to be yᵉ over Seers of this my last will"

The witnesses were Ebenezer Wing, John Hoxcy and John Otis.

The will was probated, at Sandwich, 9 April, 1695, on the testimony of "mʳ John Otis" and Ebenezer Wing, and administration granted to Mary Perry the executrix.

"we Peace Perry & Rest Perry Beeing both of competent age do Testifie and Say that when our honoured Father Edward Perry Lay upon his Death Bead (while he was of a disposing minde and memory) did desire and appointe his Son in Law John Winge to Accept of and performe yᵉ Service that he him self was desired and Impowered to do by vertue of yᵉ Last Will of William Newland Late of Sandwich Deceased in Relation to yᵉ disposing of yᵉ Land there in mentioned for or toward yᵉ Support of John Newland

"The above Sd Peace Perry and Rest Perry did . . . . Appeare April yᵉ 28ᵗʰ day : 1696 and being quakers I put it to them : If they could testifie that ye above written was ye truth as they weare in ye presence of God and they Said it was the truth

"Before Barnabas Lothrop Justice of ye peace" Recorded 5 May, 1696.

[p. 3] The inventory was taken, 9 March, 1694/5, by Edmund Freeman, Sr., and Thomas Boureman. The real estate was : "his housing and Lands" £500. "Sheep lett out by him to Judah Butler & three Stocks of Bees at home" were valued at £10.

Mary Perry, the executrix, testified to the truth of the inventory, 9 April, 1695.

[On fly-leaf, facing page 1] "November the 25th 1709 then Wee Christopher Gifford and Deborah his wife both of Dartmouth . . . . Received of our Brother Edward Perry Son of our Father Edward Perry Late of Sandwich . . . . Deceased" £20 "in money being in full of a Legacy Given to us or one of us by our sd Father in his Last Will" The receipt was acknowledged by both, the day of its date, before Barnabas Lothrop, Judge of Probate, and was recorded 10 December, 1709.

[WILLIAM NEWLAND'S WILL]

[p. 4] "William Newland of ye Towne of Sandwich" made his will 26 August, 1690. Bequests were as follows:

"First my minde and will is that . . . . my Body be decently buried by ye advice and assistance of my Deare friends ye people of God called quakers in their Buring place in Sandwich"

To "wife Rose Newland ye use of all my whole Estate of housing and lands except & Rezerving those my lands . . . . on Spring hill in Sandwich ye said Lands beeing accounted about thirty acres and also Rezerving that parcel of meadow which lyieth in ye pine Islands ye which afore Sd Rezerved lands and meadow is for a use here after Named and ye afore Sd use of all my Sd Estate of housing and lands besids ye above mentioned Rezerved is for ye Supplye and Support of my aforesd wife during her Natural life & all my movable Estate do I give to her to dispose of Excepting all my wearing cloathes and ten Shillings out of ye s^d moveables with ten Shillings I give unto my Son in law William Edwards and also Rezerving out of ye Sd moveables one bed and Bolster and Such Bed Clothes with it as Shall be sufficient to make it a comfortable lodging ye which Bed & Beding I give to my Daughter Mercy Edwards"

"all that my above mentioned Excepted and Rezerved Lands

and meadow togeather with my wearing cloathes do I give unto my Brother John Newland for his supplie and support and y^e, ordering and disposing of ye afore Sd lands and cloaths so given . . . . I committ to my over seers of this my will here after Named to whom I do give full power to dispose of ye Sd lands both upland and meadow either by Sale or otherwaies as they shall see cause & if in ye sale of sd lands my sd wife shall desire to have it then Shee paying for it to ye satisfaction of my sd over seers shall have it before any other : And If any part of this my Gift unto my sd Brother Shall be Remaining after his decease what so ever it may be I do Comitt ye ordering and disposing of it to my overseers of this my will by them to be Improved for ye use and Service of ye truth which they with me and I with them we do profess"

"After my abovesd wifes decease upon these following conditions I do give unto my Daughter Mercy Edwards ye use of all that my estate of housing and lands which is given to my wife during her life so ye use of it do I give unto my Sd Daughter if she do and shall forsake that unclean spirit which hath led her into an unclean conversation to ye great grieff of my heart and shall not concearne her self with any man after ye manner of man and wife besids her husband William Edwards during his life : but if my Sd Daughter doth goe on in such an uncleane practice which is to ye Dishounour of God and of his truth and to ye Greef of ye honest hearted and shall concern herselfe with any man besids her sd husband tending to ye bringing fourth of children : then this shall make void this my gift unto her this same Namely that what my before mentioned and here after Named overseers shall Judg meet for her to have of it so it shall be : to whom I do hereby give full power to order it as they shall see cause and after her decease my abovesd housing and lands which is so given ye use of it as is above mentioned I do give it to my Grand Daughter Elizabeth Edwards"

"I do make my Deare wife . . . . executricks . . . . and appoint my loving and beloved friends my Brother in law William Allin and Edward Perry to be ye overseers of this my will to whome I do give power that if they or either of them shall be disabeled for ye performanc of this place and concern : whether by death or otherwise that they chuse and put another or others in their stead"

The witnesses were Robert Harper, Zechariah Jenkins and Daniel Butler, the last signing by a mark. The will was probated, 6 May, 1695, on the testimony of the three witnesses.

[p. 5] "This Will of William Nulands was proved but approved only so far as concerned yᵉ Real Estate there in contained yᵉ executrix being ded before yᵉ Testater, So that leatters of Administration were granted to Administer on yᵉ personal Estate
Barnabas Lothrop Judg : of Probats"

[WILL OF THOMAS GAGE, SR.]

On 30 June, 1695, "Thomas Gage Seʳ of Harwich do will to my Son Benjamin Gage all my whole Estate be it in what So ever and where So ever it is only to my wife I do give one Shilling : and to my Son Thomas 5 Shillings and to all my other children to each a Shilling".

The will was signed by a mark. The witnesses were John Chase and Isaac Chase, both of whom testified 23 July, 1695.

The inventory was taken 19 July, 1695, by John Chase and Manoah Ellis, at the request of Benjamin Gage. The only real estate was : "the house Land and meadow" £8. Benjamin Gage made oath to the inventory, 23 July, 1695.

On 5 August, 1695, "Letters of Administration was Committed unto Benjamin Gage of Harwich . . . . Son of Thomas Gage . . . . And at yᵉ same time by the above Said Judg Barnabas Lothrop yᵉ Settlement of yᵉ estate of the above Sd Thomas Gage . . . . Intestate is as followeth : that his widow have and Injoy to her Self and at her dispose all yᵉ Goods or Estate that Shee Carried away from her husband Sᵈ Gage in his life time She Relinquesing and giving up her Right to all yᵉ Rest of her late husbands estate parsonal and Real : And when Debts and funaral charges are paid If any thing be left then according to yᵉ minde of yᵉ deceased : Benjamin Gage Son of Thomas Gage deceased to have all yᵉ Remainder of his Sd father Gage his Estate both personal and Real he paying to his Brother Thomas Gage fiye Shillings and to each of yᵉ Rest of his Fathers Children one Shilling apiece"

[SARAH TAYLOR'S ESTATE]

[p. 6] "An Invintory of yᵉ estate of Sarah Taylor of Barnestabl Deceased yᵉ : 31 : day of July 1695 : Taken this 16 day of August 1695", by James Gorham and Henry Cob. There was no real estate. The total was £32, 6s., 6d. Samuel Cob owed the estate 10s., and it owed Joseph Bearse £2, 2s., 6d.

"Deacon Job Crocker and Samuel Cob made oath to" the inventory, 13 September, 1695.

On 23 September, 1695, "Deacon Job Crocker and Samuel Cob Brothers in Law of Sarah Taylor Late of Barnstable deceased Intestate" were appointed administrators.

"The Estate of Sarah Taylor late of Barnestable deceased Intestat : was on yᵉ thirteenth day of September 1695 Setled as followeth viz that when her Debts and funeral Charges are Satisfied and paid that then yᵉ Rest of yᵉ Estate of Sd deceased to be Equally devided between all yᵉ Brothers and Sisters of Sd deceased (that is to Say) To John Taylor Joseph Taylor Mary Marchant* Martha Bearse Elizabeth Cob Hannah Crocker and Ann Daves to every one an equal part of said estate"

(To be continued)

CHATHAM, MASS., VITAL RECORDS

TRANSCRIBED BY THE EDITOR

(Continued from Vol. XVII, p. 99)

[p. 150] october 12ᵗʰ 1765 Then Thomas Nickerson 3ʳᵈ of Chatham Entred his Intentions of marriage with Ruth Hinkley jʳ of Harwich ·In order for Publishment thereof to be made there of by James Covel Town Clerk

October 26ᵗʰ 1765 Then James Eldredge jr of Chatham Entred his Intentions of marriage with Experience Sears of said Chatham In order for publishment there of to be made by James Covel Town Clerk

october 30ᵗʰ 1765 Then Crisp Rogers jr of Harwich Entred his Intentions of marriage with Deborah Riadon of Chatham In order for publishment thereof to be made by James Covel Town Clerk

November 16ᵗʰ 1765 Then John Clerk of Chatham had his Intention of marriage with Elisabeth Brown of Eastham In order for publishment thereof to be made In Chatham by James Covel Town Clerk

November 29ᵗʰ 1765 Then was the Intentions of marriage betwixt Calvin Haman of Dartmouth and Patience Young of Chatham Entred by Prence Young In order for publishment Thereof to be made In Chatham by me James Covel Town Clerk

December 6ᵗʰ 1765 Then Israel Nickerson jr of Yarmouth Entred his Intentions of marriage with Bathsheba Smith Jʳ of Chatham In order for publishment thereof to be made In Chatham by James Covel Town Clerk

*"Taylo" was first written, but was crossed out and the entry finished as printed.

December 14th 1765 Then Nathan Phillips of Harwich Entred his Intentions of marriage with Bathshabe Godfrey jr of Chatham in order for publishment thereof to be made In Chatham by James Covel Town Clerk

December 21 : 1765 Then Heman Young of Eastham had his Intentions of marriage with Phebe Godfrey jr of Chatham Entred by obed Smith In order for publishment thereof to be made In Chatham by James Covel Town Clerk

December 27th 1765 Then Daniel Howes of Yarmouth Entred his Intentions of Marriage with Sarah Collings of Chatham In order for Publishment thereof to be made In Chatham by James Covel Town Clerk

December 28 : 1765 Then Joseph Smalley of Harwich Entred his intentions of marriage with marcy Godfrey jr of Chatham In order for publishment thereof to be made by James Covel Town Clerk

February 15th 1766 Then Timothy Nickerson of Chatham Entred hi[s] Intentions of marriage with Elisabeth otherwise Called Betty Farri[s] of Yarmouth In order for Publishment thereof to be ma[de In] Chatham by me James Covel Town [Clerk]

[p. 151] February 20th 1766 Then Joseph Hunter of Nantuckit Entred his Intentions of marriage with Annah Hawes of Chatham In order for publishment thereof to be made In Chatham by me James Covel Town Clerk

February 22nd 1766 Then Richard Howes of Chatham Entred his Intentions of marriage with Tabethy Collings of sd Chatham In order for publishment thereof to be made In Chatham by James Covel Town Clerk

March 7th 1766 Then Joseph Chase jr of Yarmouth Entred his Intentions of marriage with Phebe Bassett of Chatham In order for publishment Thereof to be made In Chatham by James Covel Town Clerk

March 8th 1766 Then Nathaniel Myrick of Harwich Entred his Intentions of marriage with Hannah Slator of Chatham In order for publishment thereof to be made In Chatham by James Covel Town Clerk

March 15th 1766 Then George Godfrey jr of Chatham Entred his Intentions of Marriage with Rebecca House of said Chaham In order for Publishment thereof to be made In Chatham by James Covel Town Clerk

April 12th 1766 Then James Nickerson a Resident of Chatham Entred his InTentions of marriage with Rebecca Harding of Chatham In order for Publishment There of to be made In Chatham by James Covel Town Clerk

April 12th 1766 Then Jeremiah Nickerson a Resident In Chatham Entred his Intentions of marriage with Ruth Hinkley of

Chatham In order for publishment there of to be made In Chatham by me James Covel Town Clerk

June 21 : 1766 Then Elija Smith Entred his Intentions of marriage with Mary Collings (being both of Chatham) In order for publishment thereof to be made In Chatham by James Covel Town Clerk.

August 2nd 1766 Then James Rider of Chatham Entred his Intentions of marriage with Tabitha Eldredge of sd Chatham in order for publishment thereof to be made in Chatham by James Covel Town Clerk

September 4th 1766 Then Joseph Harding of Chatham Entred His Intentions of marriage with Zeruiah Collings [of] Chatham In order for publishment Thereof to be [made] In Chatham by James Covel Town Clerk

[p. 152] September 19th 1766 Then Elijah Smalley of Harwich Entred His Intentions of marriage with Barbary Godfrey of Chatham In order for publishment thereof to be made In Chatham by James Covel Town Clerk

September 27 : 1766 Then Reuben Rider of Chatham Entred his Intentions of marriage with Mehatable Hopkins of Harwich In order for publishment there of to be made In Chatham by James Covel Town Clerk

October 18th 1766 Then the Intentions of marriage betwixt Micah phillips Juner of Harwich and Dorcas Nucom of Chatham was Entred (by Thomas Basset) In order for publishment thereof to be made In Chatham by James Covel Town Clerk

October 18th 1766 Then Thomas Kenwrick jr of Harwich Entred his Intentions of marriage with Phebe Smith of Chatham In order for publishment therof to be made In Chatham by James Covel Town Clerk

November 29th 1766 Then Joseph Doane Juner of Chatham Entred His Intentions of marriage with Abigail Gould of Harwich In order for Publishment There of to be made In Chatham by James Covel Town Clerk

December 13th 1766 Then Obediah Smith Entred his Intentions of marriage with Susanna Taylor of Sd Chatham In order for Publishment there of to be made In Chatham by James Covel Town Clerk

December 20th 1766 Then Reuben Cahoon of Harwich Entred his Intentions of marriage with Hannah Eldredge of Chatham In order for publishment thereof to be made In Chatham by James Covel Town Clerk

March 7th 1767 Then william Long jr of Harwich Entred his Intentions of marriage with Elisabeth Harding of Chatham In order for publishment thereof to be made In Chatham by James Covel Town Clerk

March 14th 1767 Then Eliezer Simmons a Resident In Chatham Entred his Intentions of marriage with Prissilla mayo of Chatham In order for publishment thereof to be made in Chatham by James Covel Town Clerk

March 21st 1767 Then David Collings Juner of Chatham Entred his Intentions of marriage with Deborah Sears jr of yarmouth In order for publishment thereof to be made In Chatham by James Covel Town Clerk

April 1st 1767 Then William Baker of yarmouth Entred His Intentions of marriage with Prissilla Smith of Chatham In order for publishment There of to be made In Chatham by James Covel Town Clerk

June 6th 1767 Then Phillip Jackson of Chatham Entred his Intentions of mariage with Barbary Basset of sd Chatham in order for publishment thereof to be made In Chatham by James Covel Town Clerk

[p. 153] April 4th 1767 Then John Sears Juner of Chatham Entred his Intentions of marriage with Silvester Sisson of Tivertown In order for publishment Thereof to be made In Chatham by James Covel Town Clerk

July 21st 1767 Then Jeremiah Eldredge Junr of Chatham Entred his Intentions of marriage with Elisabeth Nickerson ye 3rd of Sd Chatham In order for publishment thereof to be made In Chatham by James Covel Town Clerk

August 22nd 1767 Then mr Thomas Howes of Chatham Entred his Intentions of marriage with mrs Hope Doane of sd Chatham In order for publishment There of to be made In Chatham by James Covel Town Clerk

September 22nd 1767 Then Elisha Eldredge Junr and Mary Rider Both of Chatham had their Intentions of Marriage Each to the other Entred In Chatham In order for publishment There of to be made In Chatham by James Covel Town Clerk

October 10th 1767 Then Isaiah young of Chatham Entred his Intentions of marriage with Debby Atwood of sd Chatham In order for Publishment there of to be made In Chatham by James Covel Town Clerk

October 13th 1767 Then mr John Ward Gilman of Exetor In New Hampshire Entred his Intentions of Marriage with mrs Hannah Emery of Chatham In order for Publishment thereof to be made In Chatham by James Covel Town Clerk

october 31 : 1767 Then James Knowles of Chatham Entred his Intentions of marriage with Sarah mayo of Eastham In order for publishment there of to be made In Chatham by James Covel Town Clerk

November 10th 1767 Then Elisha Dunbar of Hingham Entred his Intentions of marriage with Fear Eldredge junr of Chatham In order for publishment there of to be made In Chatham by James Covel Town Clerk [p. 154] November 12th 1767 Then Israel Nickerson Junr of yarmouth Entred His Intentions of marriage with Betty Doane of Chatham in order for publishment thereof to be made In Chatham by James Covel Town Clerk

November 28th 1767 Then was the Intentions of marriage Betwixt Samuel Basset and penine Basset Both of Chatham Entred In order for publishment there of to be made In Chatham by James Covel Town Clerk

December 4th 1767 Then Nathaniel Burges of Harwich Entred His Intentions of marriage with mercy Crowel of Chatham In order for publishment Thereof To be made In Chatham by James Covel Town Clerk

January 2nd 1768 Then John Harding of Chatham Entred his Intentions of marriage with Deborah Nickerson junr of sd Chatham In order for Publishment there of to be made In Chatham by James Covel Town Clerk

January 16th 1768 Then Joseph Smith of Sherbourn on Nantuckit Entred his Intentions of marriage with Thankful Nickerson Junr of Chatham In order for publishment There of to be made In Chatham by James Covel Town Clerk

January 30th 1768 Then Richard Basset of Chatham Entred his Intentions of marriage with Phebe Phillips of Harwich In order for Publishment there of to be made In Chatham by James Covel Town Clerk

February 6th 1768 Then Stephen Phillips of Harwich Entred his Intentions of marriage with Desire Rider Junr of Chatham In order for publishment thereof to be made In Chatham by James Covel Town Clerk

February 20th 1768 Then Seth Taylor of Chatham Entred his Intentions of marriage with Rebecca mayo of said Chatham In order for Publishment there of to be made In Chatham by James Covel Town Clerk

February 22nd 1768 Then Thomas Doane a Resident In Chatham Entred his Intentions of marriage with Elisabeth Lewes of Eastham In order for Publishment there of to be made In Chatham by James Covel Town Clerk

March 16th 1768 Then Thomas Hamilton 3rd of Chatham Entred his Intentions of marriage with Elisabeth Weston of Harwich In order for publishment Thereof to be made In Chatham by James Covel Town Clerk

(*To be continued*)

UNRECORDED BARNSTABLE COUNTY DEEDS

ABSTRACTS BY THE EDITOR

(*Continued from Vol. XXII, p. 169*)

THE abstracts presented in this issue have been made from original deeds recently presented to the Massachusetts Society of Mayflower Descendants by Miss Eleanor T. Lewis, a member of the Society.

These three deeds were duly recorded, but were not re-recorded after the fire, in 1827, which destroyed most of the records in the Barnstable County, Mass., Registry of Deeds.

[CROCKER ESTATE TO ANNABLE AND GORHAM]

On 15 July, 1720, "James Paine of the Town and County of Barnstable . . . . administrator to the estate of Thomas Crocker Late of Barnstable deceased", for £3, 9s., 6d., "to me in hand paid by Samuel annable and John Goreham both of Barnstable aforesd . . . . have in my Capacitie aforesd by vertue of licence or authority given me by His Majes^ts Justices of the Superiour Court of Judicature held for the County of Barnstable . . . . Convayed and Confirmed . . . . unto the Sd Sam^ll Anable and John Gorham the several pieces or parcels of Land Following which are a part of the estate which was sd Thos Crocker's: viz: To sd John Gorham four shares and three quarters in the 26 Lot of the Last division of the Late Comon Land in sd Barnstable which Lot Containes 28 shares in the whole and unto the Sd Sam^ll annable Seventy and seven shares and a halfe in the 59th Lot in the third division of Sd Comon Land at Sandy Nack the whole Lot Containing 100 shares all which pieces or percels of Land are more particularly known both as to scituation butts and bounderies by the Records kept of Sd divisions special Reference thereunto being had".

The deed was signed "James Paine". The witnesses were "Danl Parker" and "Mary Paine". It was acknowledged, 15 July, 1720, before "Danl Parker", Justice of the Peace, and was recorded, 6 March, 1720/1, in Barnstable County Deeds, 10: 361, by John Thacher, Register. It has not been re-recorded, since the fire.

It is endorsed on the back "Mr Paine To Annable and John Goreham".

[SAMUEL ANNABLE TO HIS SON THOMAS]

On 5 May, 1727, "Samuel Annable of Barnstable . . . . yeoman For and in Consideration of yᵉ Love good will and parental affection which I have and bear unto my Loving son Thomas Annable of sd Barnstable, Do herby Give . . . . unto him my sd son . . . . that percell of upland Scituate in Barnstable aforsd To yᵉ Southward of my Dwelling house Containing Six acres more or Less bounded Easterly by yᵉ Cart way that Leads up into yᵉ woods between my sd House and yᵉ House of Giddean Hadway Southwardly by Mʳ John Lathrops wood Lot Westerly and Notherly by the Lands of Mʳ James Pain . . . . Reserving to my Selfe Liberty to Cut wood of from sd Land During my natural Life".

The deed was signed "Samuel Annable". The witnesses were "Silvanus Bourn" and "mehetabel dimouck". It was acknowledged, 5 May, 1727, before John Bacon, Justice of the Peace, and was recorded, 18 June, 1728, in Barnstable County Deeds, 14: 168, by John Thacher, Register. It has not been re-recorded, since the fire.

It is endorsed on the back "Mr Samˡ Annable to Thomas Annable".

[GREEN AND LOTHROP TO WIDOW SALLY LEWIS]

On 28 September, 1807, "Isaiah L Green and Robert Lothrop both of Barnstable . . . . Gentlemen", for $50.00, sold to "Sally Lewis of said Barnstable widow of Joseph Green Lewis late of said Barnstable . . . . all the right title & interest which we have in & to several tracts & parcels of Real estate conveyed to us by a Deed from the said Joseph Green Lewis & Sally Lewis bearing date the 10ᵗʰ day of July AD 1805 . which Deed is recorded in the 61ˢᵗ Book of records for the County of Barnstable folio 149 . Excepting . what we conveyed to William Lewis by a Deed dated Janʸ 1807".

The deed was witnessed by "Homes Allen" and Ezra Crowell. It was acknowledged, by both grantors, 28 September, 1807, before "Homes Allen", Justice of the Peace, and was recorded, 7 January, 1808, in Barnstable County Deeds, 65: 80, by Eben Bacon, Register. It has not been re-recorded, since the fire.

PLYMOUTH COLONY WILLS AND INVENTORIES

ABSTRACTS BY THE EDITOR

(*Continued from page 43*)

[WILL OF DOLAR DAVIS]

[3 : 1 : 72] "Dolar Davis of Barnstable" made his will, 13 September, 1672. Bequests were as follows:

"I haveing alreddy Given my son Symon and Samuell theire full portions and Deeds for theire lands which I have settled on them; I Doe heerby bequeath to my . . . . wife Joanna five pounds, which I have Due to me by bill to be payed att Mr Brattles in Boston and four pounds p^r annum to be payed by my exequitor To her During the tearme of four yeares after my Decease in English Comodities or otherwise as my wife and my said exequitor shall agree incase my said wife live soe longe"

To "my eldest son John my house and barne and orchyard with severall p^{r}sells of land lying in Concord in the Collonie of the Massachusetts; heerafter mensioned: viz: all my land about the said house, bounded by the highway Downe by the brooke; and by the land Given to my son Symon; and butting on the North River Containing by estimation twenty acrees (more or lesse) as alsoe a p^{r}sell of upland and meddow Containing six acrees more or lesse neare my son Symons house bounded by the highway on one syde and by the twenty acrees on the other syde, as alsoe thirteen acrees of upland (more or lesse) adjoyning to my seaven acrees of meddow on one syde, which said seaven acrees of Meddow are alsoe heerby bequeathed to him which said upland and meddow is bounded with James bloods land on the one syde, my son Symons four acrees (more or lesse) on the other syde, and the rest bounded by the twenty acrees; as alsoe thirty two acrees of upland; and swampish meddow Compased about with Richard Temples land on three sydes, and bounded with Thomas Batemans land on the other syde; as also five acrees of upland Fenced in, bounded by John Heales feild on the one syde; my son Symons land on another syde; and the highway on a third syde; and buting on the North River which said five acrees my will is; are heerby bound over; and Ingaged for the payment of the four pounds p^r annum for the said four yeares incase my exequitor refuse to pay the said four pounds for the tearme aforsaid, then my said wife shall have power to sell the said five acrees onely I Doe heerby reserve the use of my said five acrees to my Son Samuell for the next Cropp in the yeare" 1673, "my will alsoe is that incase my said five acrees be nott sufficient to answare the said four pounds for four yeares to my said wife, That then a peece of Pasture land is heerby aded therto on that accoumpt, and engaged to her to Dispose of for her satisfaction, which said pasture land, is p^rte of the twenty acrees about the house; bounded by the North River on one syde; a little brook on another syde and Samuell Hunts on a third syde; and the feild lotts head on the other syde"

"my son Symon shall have another Cropp after this yeare from that peece of my land that lyes neare his house for which he is to pay mee my executor or assignes twenty shillings"

To "my son John, a bill of foure pounds Due to me from Roger Chandler; of Concord to satisfy for the Charges of my Coming from Barnstable to Concord; and to provide his son Joseph (who Came to attend mee) a serge suite" also "all my Carpenter tooles and my serge suite and Cloake"

To "my son in law Lewis my Cloth suite and Coate and hatts, and to my Daughter mary his wife a Cow which is att p^rsent in my Son Samuell his keeping; as alsoe fifty shillinges the halfe of a bill of five pounds Due to me from my son Samuell as alsoe all my beding pewter and brasse and other houshold stuffe now in my Dwelling place att Barnstable"

To "my Daughter Ruth Hall besides what shee hath received from mee, a Cow which her husband hath att p^rsent in his keeping, as alsoe fifty shillings, the other halfe of the aforesaid bill Due from my son Samuell; provided that her husband or herselfe pay five shillings for mee to Willam Buttericke"

To "the poor of the Towne; wher it shall please God that I Die whether at Concord or att Barnstable the sume of ten shillings to be payed to the Deacons of the Church there"

"I Doe . . . . appoint my said son John, the sole executor . . . . and my . . . . frinds Willam Butterick Richard Hassell and Thomas Browne the overseers heerof"

The will to this point was witnessed by Thomas Browne.

"I Doe further Declare that I Doe Give unto my son John Davis twenty acrees of wood land; which is by the twenty scoare acrees, which belongeth unto twenty men, or Did belong unto them in the Towne of Concord . . . . which land is not mensioned in my will abovewritten"

"alsoe I Doe give my red mare unto my wife Joanna which is not; before Disposed of"

"Signed and sealed in the pʳsence of Nathaniel: Bacon Junⁱʳ Samuell Bacon"

"This will . . . . was acknowlidged by Dolar Davis . . . . according as it is witnessed in both places and Sealed before mee Nathaniel; Bacon Assistant The 13ᵗʰ of September 1672"

The will was proved, at Plymouth, 2 July, 1673, "and John Davis the Reputed son of the said Dolar Davis is alowed . . . . to be the sole executor"

"A Testimony relateing unto the above written will was shewed in the Court" 2 July, 1673, and "ordered to be heer Recorded"

"Willam Crocker aged about 65 yeares being Deposed Testifyeth, that Dolar Davis Desireing him to Goe with him in order to an agreement between him and Joannah his late wife, as to the settleing of matters respecting theire estate before theire marriage, the sume of the Conclusion or agreement between them was, That Notwithstanding theire Marriage and Improvment of theire stock together for the support and Comfort of theire family yett that should not give Right unto or Intitle either of them into the estate of each other; which hee or sheé had before theire Marriage but each of them Might Disposé of such his or her estate as hee or shee should see Cause, to his or her owne Relations and not either of them Dispose of the others estate but To remaine his or her owne; and further Testifyeth that hee hath heard the said Dolar Davis since his Marriage often times off his owne accord say and owne that hee Could not nor [p. 75*] nor would not Dispose of any thinge that was hers before theire marriage, but it remained to her owne free Dispose, or words to the like effect that theire estate should be kept Distinct and that hee would not have her wronged; in any pʳte of that estate that was hers before they were married" . Sworn in June, 1673, before Thomas Hinckley, Assistant.

"Mʳ John Chipman off Barnstable made oath to this abovewritten Testimony before the Court held att Plymouth" 2 July, 1673.

(*To be continued*)

* Page 74 was omitted in numbering.

DEACON BENJAMIN⁸ ALDEN'S ESTATE
WIDOW HANNAH ALDEN'S DEATH
ELIZABETH⁴ ALDEN'S ESTATE

BY GEORGE ERNEST BOWMAN

BENJAMIN³ ALDEN (*David²*, *John¹*) of Duxbury, Mass., married, about 1709, Hannah⁴ Brewster (*Wrestling³*, *Love²*, *William¹*) of Duxbury, and they had eight children, as follows: Mary⁴ Alden, born 1 January, 1709/10, married Dr. John Wadsworth⁵ (*Mercy Wiswall⁴*, *Priscilla Pabodie³*, *Elisabeth² Alden*, *John¹*); Sarah⁴ Alden, born 5 April, 1712, died, unmarried, before her father; Elizabeth⁴ Alden, born 12 September, 1714, died, unmarried, 9 July, 1771; David⁴ Alden, born 14 February, 1717; Ichabod⁴ Alden, born 5 October, 1719, died, unmarried, before his father; Bezaleel⁴ Alden, born 15 May, 1722; Wrestling⁴ Alden, born 11 October, 1724; Abiathar⁴ Alden, born 29 July, 1731.

The record of the marriage of Benjamin³ Alden and Hannah⁴ Brewster has not been found, but the proof that they were married was printed in our twentieth volume, pages 112-115; and a literal copy of the original record of the births of their children was printed on page 185 of our tenth volume.

The deaths of Benjamin³ Alden and his widow Hannah, and of their unmarried daughter, Elizabeth⁴ Alden, were recorded together, on the seventh page of the oldest original book containing vital records of the town of Duxbury, and exact copies of these three entries were printed, in October, 1906,* in my literal transcript of the Duxbury, Mass., Vital Records, begun in our eighth volume. For convenient reference these three records are here reprinted.

"Deacon Benjamin Alden Deceased And was Drownded April
  yᵉ 14ᵗʰ Anno Dommni 1741
The Widow Hannah Alden his wife Deçeased January yᵉ 8ᵗʰ 1763
Elisabeth Alden Deceased July yᵉ 9ᵗʰ Anno Dommni 1771"

Two of these three deaths were also recorded, on pages 249 and 252, in the oldest volume of the records of the First Church

* Mayflower Descendant, 8:233.

in Duxbury, and literal copies of these two church records are here given.

[1 : 249] "Jany ye 8th 1763 . died Hannah Alden aged 74 ₁⁴₂
    Years"
[1 : 252] "July 9 . 1771 . died Elisabeth Alden aged 56 Years
    and 10 months. Apoplexy"

The foregoing records are the only known contemporary records of the deaths of Deacon Benjamin³ Alden, his widow Hannah, and their daughter Elizabeth⁴ Alden.

There was no other Deacon Benjamin Alden in Duxbury; and there was no other Benjamin Alden with a wife Hannah in Duxbury. Unfortunately, however, serious errors printed in the History of Duxbury, the Alden Memorial, and the "Vital Records of Duxbury Massachusetts" published by the New England Historic Genealogical Society, have made it appear that there were in Duxbury two almost contemporary Deacon Benjamin Aldens, each with a wife Hannah.

Justin Winsor, on page 216 of his History of Duxbury, published in 1849, stated that Benjamin³ Alden, son of David² Alden (*John¹*), married "Hannah, who died Jan. 8, 1763, aet. 74½ years", and correctly assigned to this couple the eight children named in the first paragraph of the present article. But, on the next page of his book, Winsor stated that "Dea. Benjamin" Alden (calling him son of Jonathan² Alden) married Hannah ———, and died 14 April, 1741; and that the widow Hannah died 8 January, 1763. Winsor thus made two couples out of one.

Jonathan² Alden (*John¹*) left no son Benjamin, as shown by my articles printed in our sixth and fourteenth volumes, and it is evident that Winsor had not consulted the probate and land records. Apparently, also, he failed to notice that he had listed two Benjamin Aldens, of the same generation, each with a wife Hannah, and that he had both of these Hannahs dying the same day.

If Winsor had consulted the probate and land records he would have found that the Deacon Benjamin and Hannah Alden who died in 1741 and 1763 were the parents of the children he had named on his page 216.

Dr. Ebenezer Alden, on pages 10 and 11 of his Alden Memorial, published in 1867, copied, without further investigation, Winsor's statements that there were two Benjamin Aldens, each with a wife Hannah; but he called attention to the statement that two wives of the same name had died the same day.

Winsor's error in making two Benjamin Aldens out of one, and two Hannah Aldens out of one, was given wider publicity by its repetition in the Alden Memorial, and has caused a great deal of confusion.

This confusion has been greatly increased by a very serious error in the "Vital Records of Duxbury Massachusetts", published, in 1911, by the New England Historic Genealogical Society. In that book we find printed, among the deaths of persons named Alden, the following statements,* purporting to be abstracts of entries on the records of the town of Duxbury.

"Benjamin, Dea. [h. Hannah], drounded, Apr. 14, 1741."
"Hannah, w. Dea. Benjamin, Jan. 8, 1743.
    Hannah, wid. Dea Benjamin, Jan. 8, 1763 [dup. a. 74 y. 4 m.].
    [a. 74 y. 4 m., C. R. 1.]"

The only logical deduction from these three statements would be that there were two almost contemporaneous Deacon Benjamin Aldens in Duxbury, each with a wife Hannah. But nowhere in the records of the town of Duxbury, in the church records of that town, or among the gravestone records in the cemeteries of that town, is there a record that any Hannah Alden, either as wife or widow of any Deacon Benjamin Alden, died on 8 January, 1743, and the printed statement that such a death is on record at Duxbury is merely the result of a careless error made by the New England Historic Genealogical Society's copyist, as will be shown in the following notes.

In 1851, Ichabod Alden made for the town of Duxbury, in two large record books, what purported to be a copy of all the births, marriages and deaths recorded in the earlier record books of the town. But this copy contains many very careless errors in names, in dates, and in ages from death records; and some original records were overlooked entirely, by the copyist, although he copied the records which immediately preceded and followed them.

Fortunately, however, Alden usually noted in the margin of his copy the volume and page of the original record from which he took each entry. It is, therefore, a simple matter to check up a large part of his copy and show that most of its conflicting dates are merely errors resulting solely from his very careless work in copying.

* "h" means husband of. "w" means wife of. "dup." means a duplicate record. "C. R. 1" means Records of the First Church of Duxbury.

On the first page of the second volume of this Alden copy, under the heading Deaths, we find:

"Alden Benjamin Deac. Died drowned 14 April 1741
Alden Hannah his wife deceased 8 January 1763
Alden Elisabeth Died 9 July 1771"

And in the margin we find that these entries were taken from page seven of the first book of original records. Comparison of these copies with the original records (printed earlier in the present article) will show that in this case the Alden copy correctly states the facts.

But in the transcript* of this Alden copy, made for the New England Historic Genealogical Society, for use in printing its "Vital Records of Duxbury" in 1911, we find that the second of these three Alden entries was incorrectly copied, and reads as follows, "Alden Hannah his wife deceas'd 8 January 1743". The work of the Genealogical Society's transcriber evidently was not properly checked up, and as a result that Society accepted this error as if it were an actual death record, and, as already shown, printed it, among the deaths, in the following form: "Hannah, w. Dea. Benjamin, Jan. 8, 1743", thus making it appear that there were two Deacon Benjamin Aldens, instead of only one, and that there were two Hannahs, instead of only one.

In brief, there was only one Deacon Benjamin Alden in Duxbury, Hannah Brewster was his only wife, and she survived him nearly twenty-two years, dying 8 January, 1763, and not in the year 1743. Moreover, there is nothing on the town records, the church records, or the cemetery records, or on the probate records of Plymouth County, which indicates that there was any Hannah Alden, either maiden, wife or widow, who died in the year 1743.

Deacon Benjamin³ Alden died intestate, on 14 April, 1741, and the eldest son David and the widow Hannah were appointed administrators, and if any one desires further proof that the widow did not die in 1743, it will be found in the fact that on 1 May, 1759, her dower in Deacon Benjamin Alden's real estate was set off to her, by order of the probate court.

Exhaustive abstracts are here given of all records and original documents on file, in the Plymouth County, Mass., Registry of Probate, relating to the settlement of the estates of Deacon Benjamin³ Alden and his daughter Elizabeth⁴ Alden.

* Now deposited at the State House, Boston.

[DEACON BENJAMIN³ ALDEN'S ESTATE]

[From original letter] On 21 May, 1741, "David Alden yeoman & Hannah Alden widdo of Duxbor°" were appointed administrators on the estate of "Benjᵃ Alden Late of Duxbor° aforesᵈ yeoman . . . . Dyed Intestate". [Also recorded, 8: 371.]

[From unrecorded bond] On 21 May, 1741, David Alden, yeoman, and Hannah Alden, widow, as administrators, with Edward Arnold, Esq., and Benjamin Loring, saddler, as sureties, all of Duxbury, gave a bond for £3000. Hannah Alden signed by a mark. The witnesses were Gershom Bradford and Daniel Lewis, Jr.

[8: 375] On 21 May, 1741, Edward Arnold, Esq., Ransom Jackson and Isaac Partridge, yeomen, all of Duxbury, were appointed to appraise the estate of "Dea. Benjamin Allden".

The inventory was taken by the three appraisers, at Duxbury, 9 June, 1741. The real estate was "the Homestead" £1100; "the Salt meadow" £600; "Cedar Swamp" £100; "the fourth part of a Sawmill" £5. The inventory was sworn to by David Alden, administrator, on 10 June, 1741.

[8: 410] The account of David Alden and Hannah Alden, administrators, was sworn to and allowed 12 August, 1741, "45£ being first Set of to yᵉ Widdow as necessarys". Payments had been made to Jacob Dingley, Benjamin Pryor, Benjamin Peterson, Dr. Otis, Shereck Keen, Isaac Little, Joseph Bartlett, Ephraim Norcutt, William Carver, Israel Hatch, Nicholas Sever, Esq., Lucy Little, John Brewster, Francis Adams, Joshua Brewster, Philip Chandler, "mʳ Isaac Lothrop Junʳ", Samuel Bartlett, Esq., John Murdock, Esq., Dr. Lebaron, Robert Brown, Esq., Amos Ford, Isaac Keen, John Thomas, "mʳˢ Waterman", David Samson, Jedediah Bourne, Edward Arnold, Esq., Josiah Bishop, Lazarus Samson, Duxbury Trustees, Samuel Ford, Joseph Delano, Joshua Delano, James Thomas, Keziah Holmes, Thomas Croade, Esq., Jeremiah Crooker, David Alden, Mary Wadsworth, Elizabeth Alden.

[From original letter] On 12 August, 1741, "bezaleel Alden of Duxbor° . . . . Son of Benjᵃ allden Late of sᵈ Duxburo Decᵈ" chose Ransom Jackson, of Duxbury, yeoman, as guardian, and the choice was allowed. The witnesses were Abiel Fuller and David Alden. [Also recorded, 8: 482.]

[8: 417] On 12 August, 1741, "Wrestling Allden of Duxbor° . . . . son of Benjamin Allden of sᵈ Duxbor° Decᵈ Have named . . . . my uncle Wrestling Brewster of Kingston . . . . yeoman to be my Gaurdian" and the appointment was made. The witnesses were "Jnº" Wadsworth, Jr. and Abiel Fuller.

[From unrecorded bond] On 12 August, 1741, "Wrastling Brewster" as guardian of Wrestling Alden, with John Brewster as surety, both yeomen of Kingston, gave a bond for £600. The witnesses were David Alden and "bezaleel Alden".

[8: 431] The division of the estate was made 5 October, 1741, as follows:

"Whereas it has been Represented to me that the Real Estate of Benj^a Allden late of Duxborough . . . . Gen^t Deceas^d Intestate cant admit of Division without prejudice to . . . . the whole and the s^d estate haveing been apprized at 1800£ . . . . & David allden ye Eldest son of ye s^d Deceasd accepting of ye same and to pay his Brothers and Sisters there Ratable parts of the Apprized Value thereof . . . . I Do . . . . Assign all ye Housing & land of the s^d Deceas'd Unto his s^d Eldest son David Allden . . . . (Saveing to his mother her Right of Dower therein) He haveing allready paid out of ye same unto his Brothers & Sisters there proportion thereof the Debts & Charges being first Deducted Namely to Bezaliel Allden" £169, 16s., 6d.; "to Wrestling Allden" £169, 16., 6; "To Abiathar Allden" £169. 16. 6; "To Elizabeth Allden" £169. 16. 6; "to Mary Wadsworth £107. 9. 3 which with £62. 7. 3 which was advanced to her by s^d Intestate in his Life time Towards her portion makes £169. 16. 6"; "he haveing allso Given bond with Sureties to Each of his s^d Brothers and Sisters for payment of" £85, 14s., 3d. "at ye Decease of there mother m^{rs} Hannah Allden, all which makes up there full shares of the whole Estate Real & personall . . . . and Each partie to whom a share is alloted shall Give bond . . . . That in Case debts hereafter be made to appear, they will Refund . . . . to the s^d David allden theire Ratable parts and of his Charges."

[11: 110] On 22 March, 1748, "Abiather Alden a minor a Son of Benjamin Alden Late of Duxborough . . . . Deceased" chose "My Brother Wrestling Alden of s^d Duxborough yeoman To be my Guardian" The witnesses were Briggs Alden and Edward Winslow.

[From unrecorded bond] On 22 March, 1748, "Wrastling alden" yeoman, of Duxbury, as guardian of Abiathar Alden, with Samuel Alden, gentleman, of Duxbury, as surety, gave a bond for £500. The witnesses were Briggs Alden and Edward Winslow.

[15: 156] The account of "Joshua Brewster who was Bondsman to Ransom Jackson Guardian to Bezaliel Aldin" was allowed, 27 April, 1759. Payments had been made to Miles Stan-

dish and David Alden. "The Sum of" £27, 4s., 2 farthings,
"is now Due to the s^d Bezaliel Alden from ye s^d Ransom Jackson
& Joshua Brewster which they are hereby order^d to Pay to Discharge the same"

[19: 77] On 3 April, 1759, "Messrs Samuel Alden, George
Partridge, Israel Sylvester, & Nathaniel Simmons all of Duxborough & Nathaniel Loring of Pembroke . . . . Yeomen" were
appointed to "sett off to Hannah Allden widow & relict of
Benjamin Allden late of s^d Duxborough Yeoman dec^d her Dower
or thirds in the real estate"

The dower was set off, to "Hannah Allden widow & consort
to Dea^n Benj^a Allden", on 1 May, 1759, as follows: "It beginneth at the northeast Corner of m^r Isaac Partridge,s Land thence
north half a point easterly 54. rods to a stake & Stones for a
Corner thence west 4 degrees south 45 rods to a stake a corner
thence south nine degrees west nine rods to a stake & stones
thence north 86 . degrees west six rods to a stake & stones thence
north 26 . degrees west eleven rods to a large red oak tree at
[p. 78] At the foot of the Hill next south river thence north
sixteen & half degrees west to a Stake & large stone on the north
side of the cart way thence the same course to the abovesaid
River thence up Stream by s^d river to the aboves^d Isaac Partridge,s land thence by s^d Partridge,s land to the first mentioned
corner all within the abovesaid Boundaries . & further of the
woodland laying on the westerly side of s^d River. We do assign &
sett off another piece & it is bounded as follows, viz, it beginneth
at a Stake at the said River which is Doctor Le-Baron,s northeast corner bounds & from thence north 78 . degrees west about
99. . rods to a stake standing in the swamp in the range of Sam^ll
Sprague Jun^rs Land thence north ten degrees east 51 . rods to
two maples growing out of one root & from thence north
74 . degrees east 89 . rods to the abovesaid river thence up
Stream by said river to the stake first mentioned all within the
aboves^d Boundaries. And furthermore do assign & sett off a
piece of Salt meadow call^d Bumps neck laying adjacent to a river
called the Mill River & Duck hill river & is bounded as follows
viz. It begins at a Stake at the river last mentioned thence
ranging south fifteen degrees west ten rods & 18 . links to a
Stake stand on the easterly end of an Island called high Island
thence south 68½ . degrees west six rods to the river called the
Mill river & by said river to the stake firstmentioned all within
the s^d Boundaries . . . . together with the westerly lower room
in the dwelling house & one third part of the Cellar & also to
improve the oven."

Samuel Alden, George Partridge, Israel Sylvester, Nathaniel Simmons and Nathaniel Loring made oath to the division, at Duxbury, 3 May, 1759, and it was allowed, [—*]June, 1759.

[ELIZABETH⁴ ALDEN'S ESTATE]

[Plym. Co. Prob., 21: 128] On 16 May, 1772, "Abiathar Alden of Biddeford in the county of York" was appointed "administrator on the estate of Elizabeth Alden late of Duxborough . . . . spinster deced".

[From unrecorded bond] On 16 May, 1772, "Abiaʳ Alden" of Biddeford, as administrator, with Ebenezer Chandler and Calvin Partridge, yeomen, of Duxbury, as sureties, gave a bond for £80. The witnesses were "Briggs Alden Justice of 'Peace" and Judah Delano.

[21: 128] An inventory of the estate, taken by Isaac Partridge, Ebenezer Chandler and Calvin Partridge, showed "a bond as colateral security agᵗ David Alden old tenʳ 85 . 14 . 3", £11, 8s., 7d.; "a note agᵗ David Alden" £16; "a bond agᵗ David Alden, John Robinson & Samˡ Cates dated Decʳ 8 . 1758." £64. There was no real estate. The total amount of the inventory was £133, 2s., 10d.

The three appraisers made oath to the inventory, 19 May, 1772, at Plymouth, and the administrator made oath to it, 20 May, 1772, at Plymouth.

CAPT. EZRA WESTON AND AHIRA WADSWORTH WERE MARRIED AT BRISTOL, R. I. NOT AT DUXBURY, MASS.

BY GEORGE ERNEST BOWMAN

In the original volume of Duxbury, Mass., records labelled "General Records 1781–1825", there are no intentions of marriage, no births, no deaths, and only two marriages. Literal copies of these two marriages, both recorded on the forty-second page of the volume, are here printed:

*The day of the month was not entered.

"I hereby certify that Capt. Ezra Weston of Duxboro in the State of Massachusetts and Mrs. Priscilla Virgin Daughter of Richard Cooper of Plymouth in s^d State were lawfully Joined together in marriage on the fourth day of July A. D. 1817 . by me the subscriber—Daniel Bradford Ch. Justice C. C. Pleas County of Bristol State of R. Island &c."

"Bristol State of Rhodeisland
"This is to certify that Mr. Ahira Wadsworth was lawfully married to Miss Olive Wadsworth by the law of God and laws of man the 20th of May 1822 by Thomas Diman Just. Peace."

These two records show that Capt. Ezra Weston and the widow Priscilla (Cooper) Virgin were married by the Chief Justice of the Bristol County, Rhode Island, Court of Common Pleas, and that Ahira Wadsworth and Olive Wadsworth were married by a Bristol, Rhode Island, justice of the peace.

Both of these records were included in the copy of its earlier records made for the town of Duxbury, in 1851, by Ichabod Alden, and in the margin of his copy he added a reference to the original volume and page. Alden's copy does not follow the wording of the original record; but it includes all the information in both marriages, except the "Capt." before Ezra Weston's name, and the statement that Weston was "of Duxboro".

In 1911, the New England Historic Genealogical Society, of Boston, Mass., published "Vital Records of Duxbury Massachusetts to the Year 1850", and the transcript of the Duxbury records, made for use in preparing that book, is now at the State House in Boston. The Genealogical Society's transcriber, when copying the original* record of these two marriages, incorrectly wrote "Thomas Deman" instead of "Thomas Diman"; and when copying the Ichabod Alden (1851) copy made two more errors, "Ch Justice, C. C. Pleas" being copied as "the Justice C. C. Pleas", and "Diman" being copied as "Damon".

Notwithstanding the positive evidence, contained in the original record, and also duplicated in the Ichabod Alden copy, that these two marriages took place in R. I., they were printed in the New England Historic Genealogical Society's "Vital Records of Duxbury", under the heading "Duxbury Marriages", in the following form:

* In "General Records 1781–1825", as previously stated.

"Wadsworth, Ahira and Olive Wadsworth, May 20, 1822."
"Weston, Ezra, Capt. [dup. omits Capt.], and Mrs. Priscilla
Virgin, d. Richard Cooper of Plymouth, July 4, 1817."

The two records, as thus printed, fail to mention either the
county or the town of Bristol, R. I., and persons consulting this
book are, therefore, entirely misled, as they suppose that these
two marriages took place in Duxbury, with the possibility that
the Weston marriage might have been at Plymouth.

As a Rhode Island official could not legally perform a marriage ceremony in Massachusetts, the printing of these two marriage records without stating the fact that the marriages actually
took place in Rhode Island was a very serious error.

It is interesting to note here that the Weston-Virgin marriage was also put on record at Bristol, R. I.; but it could not
have been recorded there if the ceremony had not been performed
there, as neither of the contracting parties was a resident of that
town.

RICHARD AND HESTER WRIGHT'S CHILDREN

By the Editor

RICHARD WRIGHT of Plymouth married, about 1644, Hester[2]
Cooke, daughter of Francis[1] Cooke, the Mayflower Passenger,
and they had six children, Adam, John, Esther, Isaac, Samuel,
Mary; but the birth records of only two of these children, Esther
and Isaac, have been found.

Adam Wright[3], born about 1645, married, first, Sarah[3] Soule
(*John*[2], *George*[1]); married, second, Mehitable Barrows. He had
six children by the first wife and four by the second wife.

John Wright[3], died before his father, without issue, and
apparently unmarried.

Esther Wright[3], born at Plymouth, in 1649, married Ephraim
Tinkham[3] (*Rebecca*[2] *Brown*, *Peter*[1]), and had six children.

Isaac Wright[3], born at Plymouth, 26 August, 1652, died in
1675 or 1676, without issue, and apparently unmarried.

Samuel Wright[3], died before his father, without issue, and
apparently unmarried.

Mary Wright[3], married ———— Price.

John Wright[3], in his will, dated 7 December, 1675, and probated 7 July, 1676, mentioned his father Richard Wright, his

brothers Adam Wright[3], Isaac Wright[3] and Samuel Wright[3], and his sisters Esther and Mary Wright.

A receipt by Esther Wright[3] and Mary Wright[3], for a legacy from their brother John, shows that they were both unmarried on its date, 9 June, 1676. This receipt is of especial importance as no record of the date of marriage of Ephraim Tinkham and Esther Wright[3] has been found. Their daughter Martha (Tinkham[4]) Soule was born about 1678, according to the age on her gravestone* at Middleborough, Mass., and was born before any of the other known children of Ephraim and Esther Tinkham.

As the estate of Isaac Wright[3] was settled 7 July, 1676, he died before that date, but after 7 December, 1675, when he was mentioned in his brother John's will.

Samuel Wright[3], mentioned in John's will, evidently died before his father's will was made, but no settlement of his estate has been found.

Richard Wright, the father, died at Plymouth, 9 June, 1691. In his will, made the day before he died, and printed in full in our fourth volume, he mentioned only his son Adam, his daughter Esther, and his widowed daughter Mary Price.

Hester[2] (Cooke) Wright, the mother, died after 8 June, 1666, when she signed an agreement of heirs† of her father, Francis[1] Cooke, and probably before 7 December, 1675, the date of her son John's will.

We here print exhaustive abstracts of all records relating to the estates of John Wright[3] and Isaac Wright[3], found on the Plymouth Colony Records.

[WILL OF JOHN WRIGHT[3]]

[Plym. Col. Wills, 3 : 1 : 177] The will of John Wright, dated 7 December, 1675, was "exhibited to the Court held att Plymouth" 7 July, 1676, "on the oathes of Mr Willam Crow and Lydia Tildin", the witnesses.

"I John Wright being now to goe forth to warr Doe make these p^rsents to be my last will".

"I Give all my land . . . . in the Towne of Plymouth unto my two brothers Isacke Wright and Samuell Wright to be equally Devided between them"

"I Give unto my Deare father Richard Wright all my wages that is Due to mee from the Collonie of New Plymouth"

* Mayflower Descendant, 14 : 132.

† Mayflower Descendant, 3 : 103, 104.

"I Give unto my brother Adam Wright my five swine"

"I Give unto my two sisters Ester and Mary Wright my Cow mare and horse"

"my Debts and legacyes being first payed I Give unto my three aforsaid brothers and two sisters to be equally Devided amonst them all my other estate"

"I Doe . . . . ordaine my Loveing brother* executor of this my last will"

The will was witnessed by William Crow and Lydia Tilden (by a mark).

"Received of Adam Wright Adminnestrator to the Estate of John Wright one Cowe and one Mare and horse that was Given to us by Will; by the aforsaid John Wright our Brother". This receipt was dated 9 June, 1676, and signed by Esther Wright (by a mark) and Mary Wright (by a mark). It was witnessed by Jacob Cooke and William Crow.

"I Richard Wright Doe acknowlidge to have Received of my son Adam Wright soe much of the estate of my son John Wright Deceased as will pay all my son Johns Debt; and therfore Doe . . . . engage . . . . to pay the said Johns Debt; and Doe alsoe acquitt the said Adam of the Legacye Given mee by my son John". The receipt was dated 9 June, 1676, and was signed by a mark. The witnesses were Jacob Cooke and William Crow. It was acknowledged in court, 4 July, 1676.

The inventory was taken 8 June, 1676, by Edward Gray and William Crow.

Debts were due the estate from: "the Collonie or Towne of Plymouth" for wages; from Adam Wright; George Russell; "the Collonie of Plymouth for" £3 "in silver that the testator payed to the Doctor and other expences to Cleare himselfe when hee Came from Road Iland";

The estate owed: Edward Gray; William Crow; Ester Wright, 14s.; Elizabeth Cooke; Samuel Fuller; Adam Wright.

"Wee are Informed that the Testator Died posessed of fifty acrees of upland and about four acrees of meddow By a Deed from his father att Winnatucksett in the Towne of Plymouth"

The inventory was exhibited at the court held at Plymouth, 7 July, 1676, "on the oath of Adam Wright".

[Plym. Col. Court Orders, 5:139] At a court held at Plymouth, 7 June, 1676, "In Reference unto the estate of John Wright Deceased the Court have ordered that his Land att Winnatucksett be settled unto and upon Adam. Wright his brother".

* The name of the brother was not recorded.

"Libertie of Adminnestration is Graunted unto Adam Wright to Adminnester on the èstate of John Wright Deceased".

On the same ·day Adam Wright, as administrator, gave a bond of £40. This is entered at the bottom of page 139 of the original record. There were no sureties.

[ESTATE OF ISAAC WRIGHT³]

[Plym. Col. Court Orders, 5: 139]

"The Court have settled the sume of four pound, which was the peculiare estate of Isacke Wright Deceased on Richard Wright his father".

EASTHAM AND ORLEANS, MASS., VITAL RECORDS

TRANSCRIBED BY THE EDITOR

(Continued from Vol. XX, p. 158)

[p. 145] John mark and Rebkah Lent indians both of Eastham were married october yᵉ 26ᵗʰ: 1744 by mʳ Isaiah Leuis minister

October yᵉ 31ˢᵗ 1744 Eldad Nickerson Chatham and Mary Cahoon of Eastham were married by Mʳ Isaiah Lues minster

november yᵉ 8ᵗʰ 1744 Ezekiel Harding and mary young both of Eastham were married by Mʳ Isaiah Leuis minester

february yᵉ 18ᵗʰ 1744/5 Isace peirce of Eastham and Esther Couell Harwich were married by mr Isaiah Leuis minester

february yᵉ 28ᵗʰ 1744/5 Thomas mayo of Harwich and Hannah Atkins of Eastham were married by mʳ Isaiah Luis minester

Simeon Nucomb and Jemimah Treat both of Eastham were married march yᵉ 1ᵗʰ 1744/5 by mʳ Isaiah Lewis minester

Richard Ary and thankfull Atwod both of Eastham were married may 30ᵗʰ 1745 by mʳ Isaiah Lewis minester

Simon Newcomb yᵉ 3ᵈ and marcy Brown Both of Eastham were married September yᵉ 5ᵗʰ 1745 by mʳ Isaiah Lewis minester

Anthony Baker of yarmouth and Thankfull young of Eastham were married november yᵉ 13ᵗʰ 1745 by mʳ Isaiah Lewes

Cornelias Jenney of Dartmouth and Eleaner young of Eastham were married December yᵉ 3ᵈ 1745 by mʳ Isaiah Lewis minest[er]

the above list of marriages has ben Sent in to the county clerk

December yᵉ 10ᵗʰ 1746 then Capt Zoheth Smith and mrs Ruth Mayo both of Eastham ware married by Joseph Doane Justis peace

October yᵉ 31ᵗʰ 1745 then Nathaniel Bacon and apphia cole both of Eastham were married by mʳ Joseph Crocker Clerk

November ye 30th 1745 then Beniamin Smith and Ruth Snow both of Eastham were married by m^r Joseph Crocker Clerk

January ye 2^d 1745 then alexander martin and thankfull Rich were married by m^r Joseph Crocker Clerk

february the 20th 1745 then Samuel Ary of Truro and Ruth Snow of Eastham were maried by m^r Joseph Crocker Clerk

[p. 146] Isiaiah higgens and ann* mayo boath of Eastham ware marryed by Mr Isaiah Lewis minester in aprel 17: 1748 Entred pr Thomas Knowles Town Clark

Joanah Higgens Daughter of Isaah And Joanna higgins was Borne the 24 Day of march 1749

Apphiah Higgens Daughter of Isaiah and Joannah Higgens was Born in Eastham September the 15 . 1751

aron Higgens Son of Isaiah and Joanna higgens was Born In Eastham march the 25 1754

Isaiah higgens Son of Isaiah and Joannah Higgens was Born march the 11 : 1757

Cornelus hamblin and Jane young boath of Eastham ware marred by Mr Isaiah Lewes minester in June 23 : 1748 Entred pr Thomas Knowles Town Clark

Look for the Rest of Isaiah Higgins Childrens in page 140

philip higgens and mary wiley boath of Eastham ware marryed by Mr Isaiah Lues minestar in July 27 : 1748 Entred pr Thomas Knowles Town Clark

Jonathan harding of Truro and Abigil treat of Eastham ware married by Mr Isaiah Lewes minestar in octobar 13 : 1748 Entred by me Thomas Knowles Town Clark

richard Atwood and mary Atwood boath of Eastham ware marryed by Mr Isaiah Lues minestar in octobar 27 : 1748 Entred pr Thomas Knowles Town clark

Elisha bickfoord and Lucia holbrook boath of Eastham ware married by Mr Isaiah Lewes minester in november 10 : 1748 Entred pr Thomas Knowles Town Clark

[p. 147] Joshua Cook of provenc town and Content Coombs of Eastham ware marryed by Mr Isaiah Lewes minestar in novembar 17 : 1748 Entred pr Thomas Knowles town clark

Barnabas harding and ruth Atwood boath of Eastham ware marreyd by Mr Isaiah Lewes minestar in febuary 23 : 1748/9 Entred pr Thomas Knowles Town Clark

Jonathan young Jur and rebaca harding boath of Eastham ware marreyed by Mr Isaiah Lewes minestar in April 12 : 1749 Entred pr Thomas Knowles Town Clark

Cristopher Atwood and susanah smith boath of Eastham ware marreyed by Mr Isaiah Lues minestar in Aprel 27 : 1749 Entred pr Thomas Knowles Town clark

* "Joanna" was first written, but the first two letters and the last were crossed out, in the same ink.

David Brown and Expearenc higgens boath of Eastham ware marred by Mr Isaiah Lewes minestar in may 11 : 1749 Entred pr
Thomas Knowles Town Clark

[p. 148] James Atwood Jr and asenath higgens boath of Eastham
ware marreyed by Mr Isaiah Lewes minestar in may 11 : 1749
Entred pr Thomas Knowles Town Clark

Barnabas Atwood the sun of James and asenath Atwood was Born
in Eastham febuary 19 : 1750

John homer of yarmuth and Abigail osban of nantucket ware married
in Eastham by Joseph Done Justes peas in septembr 28 : 1749
Entred pr Thomas Knowles Town Clark

Edman Done and the widdo Elisabath pain boath of Eastham ware
marrid in Eastham by Joseph Done Esqr in novembr : y^e : 10 :
1749 Entred pr Thomas Knowles Town Clark

Jonathan Sparrow Jur and Elisabath heard boath of Eastham ware
marrid in Eastham by Joseph Done Esqr in novembar y^e : 9 :
1749 Entred pr Thomas Knowles Town Clark

Joshua Sparrow the sun of Jonathan and Elisabath sparrow was
Born in Eastham July : 12 : 1750

Elisabath sparrow the Dafter of Jonathan and Elisabath sparro[w]
was Born in Eastham January 19 : 1752

Jabez sparrow the sun of Jonathan and Elisabath sparrow was Born
in Eastham may 26 : 1754

stephen sparrow the sun of Jonathan and Elisabath sparrow was
Born in Eastham march 3 : 1756 : Carried Below

Enock Done the sun of Enock Done Disseast and hanah Done was
Born the furst of novembar 1738

bethier Done the Dafter of Enock Done Disseast and hanah Done
was Born the 28 Day of Desembar 1740

Isack Son of Jonathan and Elisabath Sparrow was Born in Eastham
march 27 : 1762

[p. 149] Enock higgens and Sarah Dmes* boath of Eastham ware
marrid in Eastham by solomon Lumbart Esqr in febuary in the
evning betwen the fourth and fifth day 1749 Entred pr Thomas
Knowles Town Clark

Rhoda higgens the Dafter of Enock and sarah higgens was born in
Eastham may the : 5 : 1751

nathaniel higgens the sun of Enock and sarah higgens was Born
in Eastham may : 18 : 1753

Thomas higgens the sun of Eanock and sarah higgens was Born in
Eastham Aprel 24 : 1755

look in page 116 for the rest of the Children

Jonathan Cole and suzanah horten both of Eastham ware marred
by m^r benimin webb minester in Eastham in Aprel : 2 : 1741
Recorded pr Thomas Knowles Town Clark

---

* Sic. The "Intention", on page 197 of the original, reads "Deanes".

David Cole sun of Jonathan Cole and suzanah Cole was born in Eastham July : y^e : 2 : 1741

Elisabath Cole Dafter of Jonathan and suzanah Cole was born in Eastham may : y^e : 11 : 1744

Jonathan Cole ju the sun of Jonathan and suzanah Cole was born in Eastham January : 2 : 1746/7

Hannah Cole Daughter of Jonethen Cole Borne in Eastham may the 6th 1750

Susanah Cole Daughter of Jonothen Cole Born In Eastham fabuary the 14th 1753

Abigal Cole Daughter of Jonathan Cole was Born in Eastham aprel the 24th 1756

Asa Cole Son of Jonathan Cole was Borne in Eastham febuary the 19th 1759

Carred to paige 162

marcy freeman Dafter of gidan freeman and hanah freeman was Born at Eastham in January 22 : 1748/9*

Mehetable walker the Dafter of samuel and Rebaca walker was Born in Eastham march 18 : 1754

Sarah walker the Dafter of Samuel and Rebaca walker was Born in Eastham september 11 : 1756

John walker Son of Samuell and Rebecca walker was Born in Eastham December 23 Day 1759

Rebacca walker wife of Samuell walker Dyed January 26 Day 1764

[p. 150] samuel walker the sun of samuel walker and Rebaca walker was born novembar : y^e : 22 : 1743 and Disseast may : 1 : 1744

marcy walker the Dafter of samuel and Rebaca walker was Born octobar 22 : 1744

susannah walker Dafter of samuel and Rebaca walker was Born Aprel : ye 4 : 1747

Liddia walker Dafter of samuel and Rebaca walker was Born August y^e : 28 : 1749

Rebaca walker Dafter of samuel and Rebaca walker was born in Easth[am] septembar : y^e : 15 : 1751

look in paig 149 for the rest

John Cole Jr and martha young boath of Eastham ware marrid in Eastham by Joseph Done Esqr in march : y^e : 1 : 1749 Entred pr Thomas Knowles Town Clark

theoapulas Coale sun of John Coale Jr and marther Cole was borne in Eastham Aprel the 9 : 1751

Elkeny Cole the sun of John and martha Cole was Born in Eastham Aprel 19 : 1753

John Cole the sun of John and martha Cole was Born in Eastham febuary 28 : 1755

Look in the new Book in page 42 for the Rest of the Children

* Apparently an attempt was made to cross this entry out.

Thomas Knowles Son of henry and mary Knowles was Born in
    Eastham November 1771
Nathaniel Knowles Son of Henery Knowles and Mary Knowles was
    born in Eastham april 26 Day 1765
Thomas Knowles son of henry and mary Knowles was Born in
    Eastham on the 9 Day of march 1763
mary Knowles Daughter of henry & mary Knowles was Born in
    Eastham april 9 : 1761
August : 30 : 1749 then henry Knowles and mary Knowles boath
    of Eastham ware married in Eastham by m^r Joseph Croker min-
    estar Entred pr Thomas Knowles Town clark
frances Knowles Dafter of henry and mary Knowles was Born in
    Eastham January : 8th : 1749/5*
cared to pag 167
phebee Knowles the Dafter of henry and mary Knowles was Born
    in Eastham octobar 26 : 1751
Henry Knowles the sun of henry and mary Knowles was Born in
    Eastham febuary : 26 1753 and Died ·march : 7 : 1753
Henry Knowles the sun of henry and mary Knowles was Born in
    Eastham septembr : 3 : 1754
nathaniel Knowles the sun of henry and mary Knowles was Born
    in Eastham march 12 : 1757 and Died fabuary the 21 1759
azubah Knowles Daughter of Henry and mary Knowles was Born
    in Eastham april 1767
Look above
August 17 : 1749 then Elkanah Doane and Jeruase Cole boath of
    Eastham ware marrid in Eastham by Mr Isaiah Lues minester
    of Eastham Entred pr Thomas Knowles Town Clark
[p. 151] Jonathan webber of yarmath and hannah snow of Eastham
    ware marrid in Eastham August 31 : 1749 by Mr Isaiah Lues
    minestar Entred pr Thomas Knowles Town Clark
Joseph word and mary Treat boath of Eastham ware marrid by
    Isaiah Lues clark in Eastham octobar : 16 : 1749 Entred pr
    Thomas Knowles Town Clrk
nathaniel Cole and phebe higgens boath of Eastham ware marrid in
    Eastham by Isaiah Lues minestar in november : y^e : 16 : 1749
Ebnezar Atwood iur and Rachal harding boath of Eastham ware
    marrid in Eastham by Isaiah lues minestar in novembar : y^e : 30 :
    1749
Daniel Atwood Son of Ebenezer and Rachal atwood was born in
    Eastham october 18 : 1750 and Died may 29 : 1751
hephzibah atwood Daughter of Ebenezer and Rachal atwood was
    born in Eastham march 30 : 1752 Died octr 27 : 1752
Eldad atwood Son of Ebenezer and Rachal atwood was born in
    Eastham December 15 : 1755

    * Sic.

Ebenezer Atwood Son of Ebenezer and Rachal was born in Eastham april 23 1753

Nathan atwood Son of the above named was Born in Eastham January : 8 : 1758

Ruth atwood Daughter of Ebenezer and Rachal was born in Eastham· January 22 : 1760 :

Benjamin atwood Son of Ebenezer atwood was born in Eastham february 13 : 1762

[p. 152] Joseph Atkehs of trurow and Jemima mayo of Eastham ware marrid in Eastham by Isaiah lues minestar in Desembar yᵉ : 14 : 1749

Joshua Rich and hanah Bacor boath of Eastham ware marrid in Eastham by Isaiah Lues minestar in January : yᵉ : 18 : 1749/50

Mʳˢ Rebaca mayo wife to Mʳ Theopeulus mayo Died Desembar : yᵉ : 22 : 1748

nathaniel freeman sun of Joseph freeman and pheba freeman was Born at Eastham novembar : yᵉ : 18 : 1749

Joshua hopkens Jr and Rebaca sparrow boath of Eastham ware marrid by Joseph Crocker Clark in may : yᵉ : 14 : 1747

freeman higgens and marther Cole boath of Eastham ware marrid in Eastham by Joseph Crocker Clark in novembar : 13 : 1747

(To be continued)

PROCEEDINGS OF THE MASSACHUSETTS SOCIETY OF MAYFLOWER DESCENDANTS

WASHINGTON'S BIRTHDAY, 1922

His Excellency, Channing H. Cox, Governor of the Commonwealth of Massachusetts, extended to the members of the Society an invitation to the Governor's Reception, at the State House, Boston, on Washington's Birthday, 22 February, 1922. Mrs. Cox, who is a member of this Society, received with the Governor.

TWENTY-SIXTH ANNUAL MEETING

The Twenty-Sixth Annual Meeting was held at the Twentieth Century Club, Boston, on Tuesday afternoon, 28 March, 1922, with Mr. William B. H. Dowse, Governor of the Society, in the chair.

An important feature of this meeting was the formal presentation to the Society of copies of the first, second, third and fifth editions of the "New-Englands Memoriall", first published in 1669. An account of the presentation, with a list of the different editions printed, and the names of the donors, will be found in the article, Nathaniel Morton's "New-Englands Memoriall", printed in this issue.

The Society's complete set of the seven different editions was exhibited at this meeting.

Officers for the ensuing year were unanimously elected, as follows:

Governor,	Charles A. Coolidge
Deputy Governor,	Frederick Foster
Secretary,	George Ernest Bowman
Treasurer,	J. Colby Bassett
Historian,	Miss Ethel Bradford Davis
Captain,	Frederic A. Washburn, M.D.
Elder,	Rev. Paul Revere Frothingham, D.D.
Surgeon,	Edwin A. Daniels, M.D.
Assistants,	Frederick Brooks
	Mrs. Channing H. Cox
	Edric Eldridge
	Mrs. Randolph Frothingham
	Samuel Hammond
	Mrs. John Holmes Morison
	Mrs. Bayard Thayer

At the close of the business meeting, Mr. Charles A. Coolidge, the newly elected Governor of the Society, gave a very interesting illustrated talk on "Early Gravestones in Boston and Vicinity".

FROM THE SECRETARY'S TWENTY-SIXTH ANNUAL REPORT

Since the last annual meeting, two hundred new members have been elected, and five former members have been re-instated. There have been twenty-four deaths and ten resignations, and thirty-one have been dropped for non-payment of annual dues. The net gain in membership, therefore, has been one hundred and forty, and our present membership is 1,532.

Two Minor Life Members have been elected during the year, and three such members have reached the age of eighteen years, and have, therefore, automatically become regular Life Members. Attention is called to the fact that Minor Life Members do not have the right to vote, but in all other respects have the same rights and privileges as other members.

During the past year, 518 books and pamphlets, 70 old documents, 12 photographic reproductions of old documents, and a number of miscellaneous articles, have been presented to the Society.

Just before our last annual meeting we had completed our quota of the amount required for the Cole's Hill Memorial at Plymouth, and this Society's check for $6,419.34 was later forwarded to the General Society. This amount was $1,139.22 more than the quota of any other Society.

The fund to pay the expense of the Massachusetts Society's Memorials to the Mayflower Dead at Provincetown and Boston now amounts to $1,381.00, and it is hoped that this will be enough to complete the work.

As previously announced, the design for our memorial at Provincetown has received the approval of the various commissions, and this memorial probably will be completed and dedicated during the coming summer.

The most important gift for many years has been the collection of seven books printed by Elder William Brewster at Leyden, Holland, in 1617 and 1618, presented by myself. The Society's collection of Brewster Imprints now includes ten specimens, and only three larger collections are known to me.

In the April, 1921, issue of "The Mayflower Descendant" was printed an article on the known Brewster Imprints, with a preliminary announcement of an illustrated book about them which I have in preparation.

During the past year, twenty-five life membership fees and two minor life membership fees have been added to our Building Fund, which now amounts to $9,319.64.

The fire last month, in a building back of the Society's rooms, emphasizes the importance of a fireproof building of our own, to protect our priceless relics, and our quarter of a century's collection of manuscript data for "The Mayflower Genealogies".

Much of this manuscript data could never be replaced if destroyed by fire, and it would cost many thousands of dollars to duplicate the rest of it.

Our large safe protects our most valuable relics, but they are only a small part of the Society's property, and members are urged to help increase our Building Fund, by cash gifts, or by making themselves life members.

Any United States bonds, to the amount of $100.00, will be accepted in payment of either a Life Membership fee or a Minor Life Membership fee.

GIFTS FOR THE LIBRARY AND CABINET

From The Provost and the Fellows of Trinity College, Dublin, Ireland: "Dublin University and the New World".

From Mrs. George T. Street*: Four back numbers of "The Mayflower Descendant".

From Mr. Theodore S. Lazell*: Five copies of the Genealogical Advertiser.

From Mr. Henry Whitmore*: Publications of the Colonial Society of Massachusetts, Vol. 22, Plymouth Church Records, Part I.

From Miss Irma A. Rich: "The Wheeler Family in America".

From Miss Eleanor T. Lewis*: Six Deeds of Land in Barnstable County, Mass., dated 1720 to 1831, three of them unrecorded; Nineteen back numbers of "The Mayflower Descendant"; Twenty-one back numbers of "Pilgrim Notes and Queries".

*Member of the Massachusetts Society of Mayflower Descendants.

From Mrs. Archibald McGregor*: The Family Bible of her great grandfather, Samuel Gushee, born 1788.

From Mrs. Theodore. C. Keller*: A copy of the Second Edition of Nathaniel Morton's "New-Englands Memoriall"†.

From Mr. George Ernest Bowman*: A copy of the Third Edition of Nathaniel Morton's "New-Englands Memoriall"†.

From Mrs. Charles H. Bond*: A copy of the Fifth Edition of Nathaniel Morton's "New-Englands Memoriall"†.

J. Louis Gammons, M.D., died 11 January, 1922, at Yonkers, N. Y. He was a descendant of Thomas Rogers, and was elected a member, 28 October, 1914, his membership number being 1316.

Mr. James C. Briggs died 5 February, 1922, at New Bedford, Mass. He was a descendant of Francis Cooke, and was elected a member, 10 January, 1921, his membership number being 2118.

Mr. Henry D. Coolidge died 7 February, 1922, at Cambridge, Mass. He was a descendant of William White, and was elected a member, 11 February, 1918, his membership number being 1532.

Mrs. Cyrus Walker, a life member, died 20 February, 1922, at San Mateo, Cal. She was a descendant of Richard Warren, and was elected a member 19 December, 1904, her membership number being 874.

Miss Catherine D. Pontius died 5 March, 1922, at Kansas City, Mo. She was a descendant of William Bradford and William Brewster, and was elected a member, 27 September, 1916, her membership number being 1431.

Mr. Erving Winslow died 10 March, 1922, at New Haven, Conn. He was a descendant of James Chilton, and was elected a member, 24 May, 1916, his membership number being 1415.

Mr. Fred C. Hinds died 12 March, 1922, at Newton, Mass. He was a descendant of Francis Eaton and Samuel Fuller, and was elected a member, 21 November, 1899, his membership number being 530.

Mr. William F. Warden died 22 March, 1922, at New York, N. Y. He was a descendant of Stephen Hopkins, and was elected a member, 26 March, 1920, his membership number being 1881.

Miss Lucy C. Sweet, a life member, died 23 March, 1922, at Attleborough, Mass. She was a descendant of Stephen Hopkins, and was elected a member, 9 October, 1916, her membership number being 1438.

---

* Member of the Massachusetts Society of Mayflower Descendants.

† See page 50.

MEMBERS ELECTED

9 January, 1922.

No. 2378. Mrs. Philip Hamilton Warren, Worcester, Mass., eleventh from Richard Warren.

No. 2379. Mrs. Frank King Nash, Brookline, Mass., eighth from Degory Priest.

No. 2380. Mrs. Henry Grover Perkins, Brookline, Mass., eighth from George Soule.

No. 2381. James Hunter Hall, Ossining, N. Y., tenth from John Alden.

No. 2382. Mrs. Franklin Swift Akin, Fall River, Mass., eighth from Myles Standish.

No. 2383. Mrs. Frederick Charles Eaton, Warren, Pa., eighth from John Howland.

No. 2384. Miss Eunice Thomas, Pasadena, Calif., eighth from John Howland.

13 February, 1922.

No. 2385. Sherman Skinner Rogers, Cambridge, Mass., ninth from Thomas[1] Rogers, eighth from Joseph[2] Rogers.

No. 2386. Mrs. Clarence Reuben Sloan, Marietta, Ohio, ninth from William Bradford.

No. 2387. Claud Frederick Lester, Philippi, W. Va., tenth from William Brewster.

No. 2388. Miss Katherine Adella Hill, Hammonton, N. J., tenth from James[1] Chilton, ninth from Mary[2] Chilton.

No. 2389. Mrs. John Porter Clark, Spencerport, N. Y., ninth from Degory Priest.

No. 2390. Mrs. Joel Edward Lawrence, Boston, Mass., ninth from Richard Warren.

No. 2391. Mrs. Henry Hawley Lynch, Brookline, Mass., ninth from Francis Cooke.

No. 2392. Mrs. William Baker Gibson, Huntington, N. Y., seventh from John Howland.

No. 2393. Mrs. James Shanks Evans, Manchester, N. H., eighth from Samuel Fuller.

No. 2394. Miss Edith Louise Baldwin, Chestnut Hill, Mass., tenth from William Bradford.

No. 2395. Mrs. John Newton Riley, Marietta, Ohio, ninth from Myles Standish.

No. 2396. Mrs. Harry Barnes Gear, Chicago, Ill., tenth from Myles Standish.

No. 2397. Miss Margaret Dibble Gear, Chicago, Ill., eleventh from Myles Standish.

13 March, 1922.

No. 2398. Ferris Robert Vaughan, Brattleboro, Vt., eighth from John Howland.

No. 2399. Mrs. Samuel Burns, Omaha, Nebr., tenth from William Brewster.

No. 2400. Ward Goodrich Case, Des Moines, Ia., ninth from John Alden.

No. 2401. Miss Catherine Elizabeth Chipman, Newton Highlands, Mass., ninth from John Howland.

No. 2402. Marcellus Zaccheus Thompson, East Craftsbury, Vt., eighth from Francis Cooke.

No. 2403. Mrs. Richard Waldo Francis, Springfield, Mass., eleventh from William Brewster.

No. 2404. Mrs. John Conkey Bannister, Boston, Mass., ninth from Francis Cooke.

No. 2405. Mrs. Maitland Leroy Osborne, Everett, Mass., tenth from John Howland.

28 March, 1922.

No. 2406. Arthur Winslow, Boston, Mass., eighth from James[1] Chilton, seventh from Mary[2] Chilton.

No. 2407. Mrs. Robert Winthrop Putnam, Red Wing, Minn., ninth from William Bradford.

No. 2408. Miss Henrietta Sonntag, Cleveland, Ohio, tenth from Richard Warren.

No. 2409. Mrs. William Francis Fuller, Worcester, Mass., eighth from Francis Eaton.

SUPPLEMENTAL LINES ACCEPTED

[The By-Laws require an additional fee of two dollars ($2.00) for each supplemental line filed with the Society.]

January, 1922.

No. 1054. Frederick Foster; tenth from John Howland.

No. 2258. Mrs. Harvey I. Cashman; ninth from John Alden; tenth from Thomas Rogers.

March, 1922.

No. 662. Mrs. J. Ravenel Smith; ninth from Thomas[1] Rogers, eighth from Joseph[2] Rogers.

No. 2070. Henry Whitmore; ninth from Francis Cooke; ninth from Stephen Hopkins; ninth from Richard Warren.

No. 2274. Mrs. Gertrude Capen Whitney; eighth from Francis Cooke.

Attest: GEORGE ERNEST BOWMAN,
Secretary.

THE
MAYFLOWER DESCENDANT

| Vol. XXIV | JULY, 1922 | No. 3 |

WILLIAM BREWSTER'S AUTOGRAPH SIGNATURE ON A LEASE OF SCROOBY MANOR HOUSE

By George Ernest Bowman

ONLY a few autograph signatures of Elder William Brewster are known, and it is especially pleasing to me, as one of his descendants, to be allowed to reproduce, in the accompanying illustration, a signature which is of unusual interest because it was written by Brewster when witnessing a lease of part of the Manor House at Scrooby, England.

We are indebted to the Rev. Roderick Terry, D.D., of Newport, R. I., the owner of the original parchment lease, for the privilege of exhibiting this valuable document at the Forefathers' Day reception of the Massachusetts Society of Mayflower Descendants, held at the Society's Rooms, on 21 December, 1921, and also for the privilege of reproducing the signature.

By this indenture, dated 22 February, 1604, Old Style (4 March, 1605, in New Style dating), Vincent Waterhouse, Esq., of Braythwell, County of York, England, leased a part of Scrooby Manor House to Richard Jackson, of Scrooby, County of Nottingham, England, for a term of ten years, to begin on 9 October, 1608, and the lease was witnessed by John Clyman, William Brewster, Edward Pewtinger and Anthony Cade.

Duplicate copies of the lease were, according to custom, written on a single sheet of parchment, one copy being signed by the lessor, the other by the lessee, and it is probable that the same four witnesses signed each copy. The two leases were then cut apart, along an irregular line, the irregularities supplying evidence that they were originally written on a single parchment.

The copy signed by Richard Jackson was delivered to Vincent Waterhouse, the lessor, and this is the copy now owned by Rev. Dr. Terry. The duplicate, signed by Waterhouse, was given to Jackson, the lessee.

This lease from Waterhouse to Jackson, as already noted, was dated 22 February, 1604, Old Style (4 March, 1605, New Style), but was to run from 9 October, 1608, to 9 October, 1618.

As the document recites that Waterhouse held the property by a lease from Sir Samuel Sandys*, of Ombersley in the County of Worcester, dated 20 July, 1604, but running from 20 October, 1608, to 20 October, 1618, it is evident that Waterhouse held a still earlier lease from Sandys, expiring 20 October, 1608; otherwise Waterhouse could not have given Jackson a valid lease to run from 9 October, 1608.

We here present a literal transcript of the duplicate lease signed by Richard Jackson.

[VINCENT WATERHOUSE TO RICHARD JACKSON]

This Indenture made the two and twenty daye of Februarie in the second yeare of the Raign of our Soveraign Lord Kinge James by the grace of God Kinge of England, France, and Ireland, and of Scotland the Eight and thirty, Betwene Vincent Waterhous of Braythwell in the County of Yorke Esquier of th'one partie : And Richard Jackson of Scrooby in the County of Nottingham of th'other party, Witnesseth That wheras Sr Samuel Sandys of Ombersley in the County of Wigorn† Knight, by his Indenture of Leasse bearinge date the twentie daye of July last before the date hereof Hath demysed graunted & to farme letten unto the said Vincent Waterhous That his pcell of the manor house of Scroby, together wth all and singuler landes, medowes, pastures, leasures, comons and other Comodities what-soev^r unto the said manor house of Scrooby belonginge, or in any wise apperteyninge wth th'appurtenances To have and to hold all and every the premisses wth th'appurtenancs unto the said Vincent Waterhous & his Assignes from the twenteth day of October wch shalbe in the yeare of our Lord one thousand sixe hundreth & eight, unto the end & tearme of Ten yeares from thence next & imediatly followinge fully to be complete, and

* Scrooby Manor was the property of the see of York, and was leased by Archbishop Sandys, in 1582, to his eldest son, Sir Samuel Sandys.

† County of Worcester.

ended Yeldinge and payinge therefore yearely unto the said Sʳ Samuel Sandis, his Executoʳˢ, or Assignes : And unto the Lord Archbyshop of yorke, and his Successors certayn yearely rents reserved . wᵗʰ divers other Covenants therin conteyned, as by the said Indenture, more at large yt doth appeare . This Indenture now witnesseth That the said Vincent Waterhous for divers good causes & consideracons him thereunto espetially movinge Hath demysed, graunted, & to farme letten, and by these pnts doth demyse, grant and to farme lett unto the said Richard Jackson, That pcell of the said manor house of Scrooby standinge at the East syde of the great Court there wᵗʰ all the Chambers, barne, stables, & other Edifices builded upon the East, & south sides of the said great Court, together wᵗʰ the Orchard & Courtes about the manor : And also all that pte of Scroby Parke lying next to Scrooby as yt is now devided . And one Closse of medow lyinge upon the East syde of the said Parke Comonly called the Parke Closse : And one pcell of medow ground lyinge in Dunnard ynges comonly called the Steward ynge : And one Closse of medow, or pasture adjoyninge unto the said pcell of the manor house comonly called yᵉ pond yard (All wᶜʰ pʳmisses now are in the tenure & occupacon of the said Richard Jackson & his Assignes) To Have and to hold the said pcell of the manor house, Chambers, barnes, stables, and other edifices, Orchardes, & Courtes, And the said parte of Scroby Parke, Parke close, Steward ynge, & pond yarde wᵗʰ all & singuler their appurtenancs unto the said Richard Jackson his Executors, Administrators, & Assignes, From the nynth daye of October wᶜʰ shalbe in the yeare of our Lord one thousand sixe hundreth and eight unto the full end & terme of Tenne yeares from thence next & imediatly followinge fully to be complete and ended . yeldinge and payinge therfore yearely duringe the said tearme of tenne yeares unto the said Vincent Waterhous his Executors, or Assignes the yearely rent of twenty poundes of lawfull English money At the Feasts of the Anuntition of the blessed Virgin Mary ; and Sᵗ Michael the Archangell by even & equall porcons . And if yt happen the said yearely rent of twenty poundes to be behynde or unpayed in parte, or in all by the space of tenne dayes after eyther of the said Feasts wherin yt ought to be payed, That then yt shalbe lawfull to & for the said Vincent Waterhous his Executors and Assignes into all & every of the premisses to reenter . & the same to reposses and have againe, as in his or their formʳ estatt, anythinge in this Indenture to the contrary notwᵗʰstandinge : And the said Vincent Waterhous doth further Covenant and graunt to and wth the said Richard Jackson and his assignes by these presents That yt shalbe lawfull to & for the said Richard and his Assignes to take and have all such [*] boote, fyre boote, and other boote of wood whatsoever in such maner & for such purpose accordingly as yt is allowed & granted unto the said Vincent Waterhous and his Assignes by the aforenamed demise from the said Sr Samuel Sandys. And the said Richard doth by these p^rsents Covenant & graunt to and wth the said Vincent Waterhous to performe, discharge, & kepe all and ev^ry such Covenants (Concirninge the premyses demysed unto the said Richard) as on the parte and behalfe of the said Vincent Waterhous are to be pformed, discharged & kept, contayned in the aforesaid Indenture of Leasse made from the said Sr Samuell Sandis to the said Vincent Waterhous. And yt is also further Covenanted and agreed betwext the said pties That the said Richard and his Assignes shall have and receive yearely duringe the aforesaid terme of yeares the moyetye or halfe parte of the mast of the whole foresaid Parke of Scrooby. And also that the said Richard and his Assignes shall at ev^ry Christide duringe the said terme geve unto the said Vincent Waterhous his Executrs, & Assignes two Cople of fowle : And also that the said Vincent Waterhous shall have two bayes of the Longe south barne next towardes the East end for his own pp use if he so stand need therof. It is also further Covenanted and agreed. That the said Richard Jackson or his Assignes shall kepe one Hound for the said Vincent Waterhous every yeare duringe the aforesaid terme from Easter till Michaeltyde : And further that the said Richard Jackson shall geve every yeare duringe the aforesaid terme unto the said Vincent Waterhous one daye plowinge in Plumtre Park when the said Vincent Waterhous shall call for. Provided allwayes, and yt is conditioned, That if the said Vincent Waterhous, or his Assignes at any tyme hearafter be disposed to renew his, or their estate of, or in the premisses, and that notice thereof be geven in writinge unto the said Richard or his Assignes, under the hand of the said Vincent Waterhous, or his Assignes at the now dwellinge house of the said Richard in Scrooby aforesaid. That then this present Indenture of demyse to surcease and to be of · no effect. So that the said Vincent Waterhous his Executors and Assignes make unto the said Richard Jackson his Executors & Assignes sufficient security for the peaceable and quiet enjoyinge of the premisses, for and duringe such terme of yeares

* One word illegible here.

as shalbe then unexpyred . In witnes whereof the partyes either
to other have interchangeably setto their handes And seales the
daye & yeare first above written : Anno Dni 1604

.Ric: Jacksonn
(seal)

[On the back]

Sealed signed And Deliv^red interchangeably by the first wthin
named parties

in the p^rsence of John Clyman   Edw: Pewtinger
Willm Brewster   Anthonye Cade

CHATHAM, MASS., VITAL RECORDS

(Continued from page 68)

[p. 155] March 26th 1768 Then Joseph Paine j^r of Chatham Entred
his Intentions of Marriage with Betty. Hedge of Yarmôuth In
order for Publishment there of to be made In Chatham by
James Covel Town Clerk

April 2nd 1768 Then Thomas Lewis j^r of Barnstable had his Inten-
tions of marriage with Dorcas Nickerson 3rd of Chatham Entred
In order for Publishment thereof to be made In Chatham by
James Covel Town Clerk

June 18th 1768 Then David Smalley Junr of Harwich Entred his
Intentions of Marriage with Elisabeth Atkins of Chatham In
order for Publishment There of to be made In Chatham by
James Covel Town Clerk

September 10th 1768 Then Jacob Davis of Harwich (by mr Joshua
Atkins) Entred his Intention of marriage with Mary Howes of
Chatham In order for publishment thereof to be made In
Chatham by James Covel Town Clerk

October 21st 1768 Then Elisha Smith a Resident In Chatham Entred
his Intentions of marriage with Susanna Wing of Harwich In
order for Publishment there of to be made In Chatham by
James Covel Town Clerk

October 29th 1768 Then Henry Atkins of Chatham Entred his Intentions of Marriage with Deborah Lothrop of Barnstable in
order for publishment there of to be made In Chatham by James
Covel Town Clerk

November 18th 1768 : Then Zecheriah Sears of yarmouth Entred
his Intentions óf Marriage with Mary Howes of Chatham In
order for Publishment thereof to be made In Chatham by James
Covel Town Clerk

March 11th 1769 Then Richard Godfrey j^r of Chatham Entred his
Intention of Marriage with Mary Nucumb of Harwich In order

for publishment there of to be made In Chatham by James Covel Town Clerk

April ye 15th 1769 Then John Nickerson a Resident in Chatham Entred his intentions of marriage with Thankful Long of Harwich in order for publishment there of to be maid in Chatham by Nathan Basset Town Clark

April ye 28th 1769 then Joshua Ellis of harwich Entred his intentions of marrage with aBigail Tayler of Chatham in order for Publishment theirof to be made in Chatham By Nathan Basset Town Clark

[p. 156] June ye 10th 1769 then Solomon Godfrey of Chatham Entred his Intentions of marrage with mercy Crowell of Chatham in order for publishment in sd Chatham pr Nathan Basset Town Clark

July ye 18th 1769 then Joseph Rider of Chatham Entred his Intentions of marrage with Elisabeth Eldredge of Chatham in order for Publishment in said Chatham by Nathan Basset Town Clark

July ye 19th 1769 then Enus Nickerson of Chatham Entred his Intentions of marrage with Elisabeth Ellis of Harwich in order for Publishment in Chatham by Nathan Basset Town Clark

September ye 2^d 1769 then Nathanel Godfrey of Chatham Entred his Intentions of marrage with Sarah Eldredge of Chatham in order for Publishment in Chatham by me Nathan Basset Town Clark

September ye 23^d 1769 then John Colman Jur of Scituate Entred his Intentions of marrage with Dilla Hamilton of Chatham in order for Publishment in Chatham by Nathan Basset Town Clark

October ye 21st 1769 then John Rider of Chatham Entred his Intentions of marrage with Lydia Phillips of Harwich in order for Publishment in Chatham by Nathan Basset Town Clark

November ye 25th 1769 then James Nickerson of Yarmouth Entred his Intentions of marrage with Keziah Godfrey of Chatham in order for Publishment in Chatham Pr Nathan Basset Town Clark

December ye 23^d 1769 then Josh'ua Eldredge Jur of Chatham Entred his Intentions of marrage with Jane Rider of Chatham in order for publishment in Chatham by Nathan Basset Town Clark

January ye 20th 1770 Then Samuel Covel of Chatham Entred his Intentions marrage with Jarusha Hall of Harwich in order for Publishment in Chatham by Nathan Basset Town Clark

January ye 20th 1770 Then Hezekah Doane of Chatham Entred his Intentions of marrage with Mary arey of Chatham in order for Publishment in Chatham by Nathan Basset Town Clar

March ye 3^d 1770 then Samuel Hamelton of Chatham Entred his Intentions of marrage with Margret King a Resident in Chatham in order for Publishment in Chatham by Nathan Basset Town Clark

March ye 24th 1770 then Silvenus Harding Jur of Chatham Entred his Intentions of marrage with Presillah young of Chatham in order for Publishment in Chatham by Nathan Basset Town Clark

[p. 157] April ye 23^d 1770 then mosses mayo Jur of Harwich Entred his Intentions of marrage with Elisabeth Smith of Chatham in order for publishment in Chatham by Nathan Basset Town Clerk

September ye 1st 1770 then moses pain of Truro Entred his intentions of marrage with Lidia Hinkley of Chatham in order for Publishment in Chatham by Nathan Basset Town Clerk

November ye 10th 1770 then William Brown of Truro Entred his Intentions of marraig with Temprence Hinkley of Chatham in order for Publishment in Chatham by Nathan Basset Town Clerk

November ye 24th 1770 then Elnathan Eldredge of Chatham Entred his intentions of marriag with Dorratha Freeman of Harwich in order for Publishment in Chatham by Nathan Basset Town Clerk

December ye 29th 1770 then Prence Young Jur of Harwich Entred his Intentions of marriage with Jarusha Godfrey of Chatham in order for Publishment there of to be made in Chatham By Nathan Basset Town Clerk

January ye 12 1771 then Nathenel Nickerson of Chatham Entred his Intentions of marriag with Hannah Burges of Harwich in order for Publishment in Chatham By Nathan Basset Town Clerk

March ye 9th 1771 then Thomas Howes of Chatham Entred his intentions of marriag with Prisilla Baker of Chatham in order for Publishment in Chatham By me Nathan Basset Town Clerk

March ye 23^d 1771 then William Cheever a Resident in Chatham Entred his Intentions of marriage with Zeruiah Rider of Chatham in order for publishment to be made there of in Chatham by me Nathan Basset Town Clerk

March ye 30th 1771 then James Eldredge ye 3^d of Chatham Entred his Intentions of marriage with Hannah Collins of Chath in order for Publishment to be made in Chatham by me Nathan Basset Town Clerk

March ye 30th 1771 then Samuel Doane of Chatham Entred his Intentions of marriage with Mary Eldredge of Chatham in order for Publishment there of to be made in Chatham by me Nathan Basset Town Clerk

April ye 27th 1771 then Joshua Howse of Chatham Entred his Intentions of marriag with Martha Godfrey of Chatham in order for Publishment to be made there of in Chatham By me Nathan Basset Town Clerk

(*To be continued*)

MICAH⁴ SOULE OF DUXBURY, MASS.
HIS WIFE AND CHILDREN
AND HIS WILL

BY GEORGE ERNEST BOWMAN

MICAH⁴ SOULE *(Josiah³, John², George¹)* of Duxbury, Mass.,
was born in that town, on 12 April, 1711, and was there married,
on 31 May, 1740, by Rev. Samuel Veazie, to Mercy Southworth⁵ *(Constant⁴, Mary Pabodie³, Elizabeth² Alden, John¹)*, by
whom he had eight children. The names of these children are
not on the town records, but seven of them are found in the
baptismal records of the First Church of Duxbury, and the name
of the eighth is obtained from the father's will, and from records
of deeds.

On page seven of the oldest book of the church records, in a
list of "Persons Baptized upon their Parents Faith", we find
baptisms of six of "Micah Souls Children" as follows: "Aphela
Sole" baptized 19 April, 1741; "Josiah Sole" baptized 21 March,
1743; "Constant Southworth Sole" baptized 13 May, 1745;
"Rebecka Soule Baptized by the Revʳ Mr Gay of Hingham" 11
August, 1751; "Asaa Soul baptised by the Revᵈ mr gay" in
"May 1753"*; "Ester Soul Baptised by the Revrd Mr Mac-
carter" 29 September, 1754. And among the baptisms on page
133 of the same book we find: "Micah Souls Children Lydia
Soul octobʳ 16ᵗʰ 1757"; but Lydia was the only child there
recorded.

The will of Priscilla Southworth⁵, sister of Constant South-
worth⁴ *(Mary Pabodie³, Elizabeth² Alden, John¹)*, printed in our
nineteenth volume, mentions her niece "Marcy Soul wife Micah
Soul", and a deed from Micah⁴ Soule and others, printed in the
present article, supplies additional evidence of the parentage of
Mercy (Southworth) Soule, whose birth record has not been
found.†

---

* This date was incorrectly printed as "May 1, 1753", in the New England
Historic Genealogical Society's "Vital Records of Duxbury", Boston, 1911.

† Mercy could not have been born in 1707, as stated on pages 38 and 44 of the
Southworth Genealogy (Boston, 1905), as her parents were not married until 10
February, 1714/15. [This marriage record was printed in our eleventh volume.]
The name of Mercy's first child was incorrectly printed as "Apphia" in the same
genealogy.

On page 255 of the first book of church records, we find, under deaths in 1778:

"October 14th Rebeccah Soul died—aged 27 years 11 months" .

The third entry below reads:

"October 19th Lydia Soul died—aged 20 Years" .

Again the third entry below reads:

"Novr 4th Micah Soul died—aged 67 years 8 months" .

Apparently the deaths of two of his daughters, on October 14th and 19th, led Micah Soule to make his will on 20 October, 1778, the day following Lydia's death. In the will he mentions his wife Mercy; his sons Josiah⁵ Soule, Constant⁵ Soule (his middle name was not given in the will), Jonathan⁵ Soule and Asa⁵ Soule; his unmarried daughter Esther⁵ Soule; and his daughter "Nephele Simons yᵉ wife of Consider Simmons" .

As already shown, Micah⁴ Soule's first child was baptized as "Aphela", on 19 April, 1741. The next reference to her I have found is the record of her marriage, on page. 256 of the first book of the church records, where, in a list of marriages "by Charles Turner Pastor", we read, "Febʸ yᵉ 25th 1763 . Consider Simmons and Nephele Soul." On page 261, in a list of "Persons who renewed their covenant only", we read, "June 28th 1766 . Consider Simmons Nephelee Simmons". And on page 270, in a list of "Persons who renewed their Covenant & came up to all the Ordinances", we find, "Nephele Simmons August 11 1776" .

The marriage of Consider Simmons was reported to the town clerk as usual, and in the town book now labelled "General Records 1710-1786 Miscellaneous 1816-1826", on page 266, we find, "Consider Simmons and Nephela Soul were married February yᵉ 25th 1763" .

In 1851, Ichabod Alden of Duxbury made for the town a copy of the old records of births, marriages and deaths, and copied this marriage from the church records, giving a reference to the volume and page of the original record, but spelling the bride's name "Nephela Soule" .

In the New England Historic Genealogical Society's "Vital Records of Duxbury", published in Boston, in 1911, this marriage is printed in the following forms:

Simmons, Consider and Nepheta Soul [dup. Nephela Soule], Feb. 25, 1763. [Nephele Soul, C. R. 1.]*

Soul, Nepheta [dup. Nephela Soule] and Consider Simmons, Feb. 25, 1763. [Nephele Soul, C. R. 1.]*

* " C. R. 1. " means First Church Records.

After a long search for "Nepheta" Soul on the original church
and town records of Duxbury, and on the probate and land
records of Plymouth County, I went to the State House, in
Boston, where the transcript made for use in compiling the
N. E. H. G. Society's book is now deposited, and found that in
this transcript the marriage, as found in the original book "General Records 1710-1786" etc., had been incorrectly copied as a
marriage of "Consider Simmons and Nepheta Soul", and this
error, as already shown, was printed in a way which leads readers
to believe that it was the original entry and, therefore, the
most authoritative record.

In the Plymouth County, Mass., Registry of Deeds, are
recorded eight transfers of land in which Consider Simmons of
Duxbury, with his wife "Nephele" or "Nephela" or "Nephala"
or "Naphela" releasing dower rights, sells land to various persons. The earliest deed was dated 5 June, 1784. The last deed
was dated 2 May, 1823, and was acknowledged, 9 August, 1823,
by Consider Simmons only.

The evidence is conclusive that the wife of Consider Simmons was not named "Nepheta" and she was nowhere so
recorded. The printing of that name was solely the result of a
serious error in the transcript made for the N. E. H. G. Society.

As shown by the deeds mentioned, Nephele (Soule) Simmons was living on 2 May, 1823; but I have not found any later
reference to her by that name. Bearing in mind, however, that
Micah⁴ Soule's first child was baptized as "Aphela", although
she was later called "Nephele" (as in her marriage record, in
her father's will, and in the deeds referred to), it is possible that
at the time of her death she was called "Aphelia", and that it
is her death record which was entered on page 45 of the second
book of the First Church records. On that page, under deaths
in 1827, we find:

"Dec. 1. Mrs. Aphelia Simmons" .

Unfortunately, the foregoing record does not give the age
of the deceased, which would have been helpful in our attempts
to identify her. The fact, however, that this death was entered
on the church records indicates (but does not definitely prove)
that "Aphelia" was connected with the church, and I have found
no record of any other person in Duxbury who could have been
called "Mrs. Aphelia Simmons" except the "Aphela" Soule who
later became "Nephele" (Soule) Simmons.

As already stated, the evidence secured does not positively
identify "Mrs. Aphelia Simmons", but it is here printed in order
to facilitate further investigations.

Ichabod Alden, in his 1851 copy, entered this death (with marginal reference showing that he took it from the original church records, 2:45) in the following form:
"Aphelia Simmons Wife of Died 1 December 1827."

As Alden's marginal reference proves that this is merely his method of copying the church record which I have already quoted, it is evident that he assumed that "Mrs. Aphelia Simmons" was either a married woman or a widow, but not knowing her husband's name could not enter it.

For convenient reference I here print together the only known contemporary record of her death, from the church records; the Alden (1851) copy from the original church records; and the record as it was incorrectly printed, in 1911, by the New England Historic Genealogical Society, from literal transcripts of the two preceding entries.

"Dec. 1. Mrs. Aphelia Simmons" . [Ch. Rcds. 2:45, under Deaths in 1827]

"Aphelia Simmons Wife of Died 1 December 1827." [Alden, 1851, copy]

Simmons, ———, w. Aphelia, Dec. 1, 1827. [N. E. H. G. Soc. book, under Deaths]

For the information of those who do not have access to the N. E. H. G. Society's book, it should be stated that, in accordance with their method of printing deaths, the entry quoted from their book means that a woman whose surname was Simmons, but whose baptismal name was not recorded, died on 1 December, 1827, and that she had been the wife of "Aphelia" Simmons, thus making it appear that there was a man, then living in Duxbury, who bore the—for a man—extraordinary baptismal name "Aphelia".

In this connection it is interesting to note that the same book, under Births, prints the baptism of Micah Soule's daughter "Aphela", but adds, in its proper alphabetical place, "Ophelia (see Aphela)" .

We here print an exhaustive abstract of a deed from Micah⁴ and Mercy (Southworth) Soule, and Mercy's sister Mary Southworth, to William Southworth, brother of Mercy and Mary.

We also print exhaustive abstracts of the will of Micah⁴ Soule and of all probate records relating to the settlement of his estate, found in the Plymouth County, Mass., Registry of Probate.

The abstracts of the probate records were made at the expense of Mrs. Anthony D. Hall, a descendant of Micah⁴ Soule, and a member of the Massachusetts Society of Mayflower Descendants.

[SOULE AND SOUTHWORTH TO SOUTHWORTH]

[Plym. Co. Deeds, 41:10] "We Miah* Soule Yeoman &
Mercy Soul his Wife & Mary Southworth Spinster all of Duxborough . . . . Which s^d Mercy & Mary were Daughters to Constant Southworth late of s^d Duxborough Deceased", for £436,
"in Bills of the Old Tenour, That is, Two Hundred & Eighteen
Pounds to Each of them well and truly paid by William Southworth of s^d Duxborough Husbandman . . . . Quit Claim unto
him ye s^d William Southworth all our Right . . . . to all & every
part of the Real or Personal Estate of the s^d Constant Southworth Deceased . . . . In Witness & Confirmation whereof We
ye s^d Micah, Mercy, & Mary have hereunto Set our Hands &
Seals this" 26 December, 1748.

The deed was signed by "Micah Soule", "Mercy Soule"
and "Mary Southworth", and witnessed by Rebecca Southworth,
Nathaniel Brewster and Samuel Alden.

"January the 16 . 1748⁹: The Within written Micah Soul
Mercy Soul and Mary Southworth acknowledged" the deed,
before Edward Arnold, Justice of the Peace, and it was recorded,
2 October, 1750.

[MICAH⁴ SOULE'S WILL]

[From original will] Micah Soule, yeoman, of Duxbury,
made his will on 20 October, 1778. Bequests were as follows:

To "wife marcy Soul ye Improvement of one hafe of my
homsted farme & ye one haf of me Salt medow So long as She
Shall Remain my widow also ye Improvement of one haf of my
in Dore movibels after my Debts legases & funeral Charges are
paid out of my monys or Notes of hand which I Call indor :
movibels"

To "my Son Josiah Soul all my homsted farm . one haf at
my deces ye other haf at my wifes deces or Second marrig I
allso Give my Son Josiah Soul one haf of my Salt medow I
allso Give to him one bed & ye beding thereto Belonging & I do
allso Give to him my son Josiah ye one haf of my out dore
movibels"

"ye other haf of my out Dore movibels I Give to my Son
Constant Soul I allso Give to my Son Constant Soul all that
peic of a wood lot that layeth by Capn Benjamin wadsworths
which was Given me in my fathers last will"

---

*This is plainly an error in recording. It should read " Micah ".—Editor.

"I also Give to my three Sons Constant Jonathan & asa Soul yᵉ one haf of my Salt medow at my wifes Deces to be Divided Equily Betwen them"

"I Give to my Dafter Ester Soul one bed & beding thereto belonging I also Give to my Dafter Ester Soul that haf of my Indore movibels at my wifes Deces which She my wife has to Improve her life time"

"I also Give to my two Sons Constant & Jonathan two beds at my wifes Deces with yᵉ beding thereto Belonging"

"I also Give to my Dafter Nephele Simons yᵉ wife of Consider Simmons ten pounds"

"I also Give to my two Sons Jonathan & asa Soul ten pounds apece"

"I give to my Son Josiah Soul all yᵉ Rest of my Indore movibels which is not hear in yet Disposed of his paing all my Debts legeces and funeral Charges out of my mony & Notes of hand if there be anoufe to pay them if not a Noufe to pay them my will is he Shall pay what is wanting out of his one Estate"

"Lastly my will is that my Son Josiah Soul be the Soul Executer of this my last will"

"I Give to my wife yᵉ Improvement of tow Cows her lif time"

The will was signed "Micah Soule". The witnesses were Enoch Freeman, Joseph Brewster, Jr., and Judah Delano. [The will was also recorded, 25 : 124.]

[From original letter] On 7 December, 1778, the will was probated, on the testimony of Enoch Freeman and Judah Delano, two of the witnesses, and administration granted to Josiah Soule the executor named therein. [Also recorded, 25 : 125.]

[From original warrant] On 7 December, 1778, Judah Delano, Calvin Partridge and Enoch Freeman, all yeomen, of Duxbury, were appointed to take an inventory of the estate. [Also recorded, 28 : 377.]

[From original inventory] On 22 December, 1778, the three appraisers took the inventory, at Duxbury. The total value of the property was £2481. The real estate was : "the Homestead farm with the Buildings" £1288; "half a Wood lot" £150; "salt Medow" £125.

On 29 January, 1779, the three appraisers made oath to the inventory; and Josiah Soule, the executor, made oath to it, on 28 February, 1780. [Also recorded, 28 : 378.]

HARWICH, MASS., VITAL RECORDS

TRANSCRIBED BY THE EDITOR

(Continued from Vol. XXIII, p. 122)

[p. 10] William Freeman Son to William Freeman ju^r deceasd and hannah Freeman was born in march 22th 1740/41

Sarah Freeman Daughter to Daniel Freeman and marcy Freeman his wife was born in november the 14 day 1740

Eliz^a Clark Daughter of Nath^{ll} & Lidia his wife born Dcmb^r 7th 1743

Winaford Clark Daughter of Nath^{ll} Clark & Lidia his Wife born June 2^d 1747

Lidia Clark Daughter of Nathl Clark & Lidia his Wife born May 24th 1749

Soloman Clark Sone of Nath^{ll} Clark & Lidia his Wife bon July 8 1751

Isaiah Hopkins Sone to Joseph Hopkins Junr & Mary Hopkins his Wife was born ye 29th Day of February 1741

Edward Hopkin Sone of Joseph Hopkin Ju^r & Mary his Wife borne Sept 25th 1744

Luse Maker Daughte of Soloman Maker & Sarah his wife born April 8th 1754

Solomon Maker of Soloman & Sarah his wife born Aug^s 31^t 1751

Mary Stone Daughter to Nathl Stone Ju^r & Mary his Wife born June 7th Ano Domi 1742

Selvanu Stone Sone to Nathl & Mary Stone Ju^r his Wife borne July 17th 1743

Hannah Stone Daughte to Nathl & Mary Stone Ju^r his wife borne Augst 4th A Dom 1744

Selvanus Stone Sone of Nathl Stone Ju & Mary Stone his Wife born April 4th A D 1746

Abigail Stone Daughter to Nathl Stone Ju^r & Mary his Wife born Dcemb^r 29th 1747

William Stone Sone of Nathl Stone & Mary his Wife born Jany 31st: 1750

Lucy Stone Daughte of Nathl Stone Ju & Mary his Wif born Feby 22 1752

Eunice Stone Daughte of Nathl & Mary born Feby 9th 1754

Nathan Stone Sone of Nathl Ston & Mary hi Wif born May 13th 1756

Mercy born March 6 1758

Sarah born March 4th 1760

Olive Daughte of Nathl & Mary born Oct 23^d 1762

[p. 20] Sarah Snow the Wife of m^r Edward Snow died August 23 day 1739

Capt Nathl Mirick Died ye 13th Day of November 1743

Jeremiah Hopkins Sone to David Hopkins Died July 19th 1744

Bethiah Crosbe Daughter of Thomas Crosbe Jr Died June 12th 1752

Sarah Freeman Daughter of Thomas Freeman Died Feby 23^d 1753

Obed Freeman Sone of Thomas Died Janu^y 16th 1754

Nathl Snow Died March 1749

Samuel Sears Sone of Samuel Died Novr 5th 1754

Abigail Sears Daughter of Samuel Died Feby 17th 1756

Eleazer Crosbe Died Novr 8th 1759

Abigail Sears of Saml Died Feby 17th 1756

Elizabeth Sears of Samu^{ll} Died June 1st 1758

Joseph Snow Died April 30th 1761

Hannah Snow Wife of John died Feby 16th 1764

Mary Sears Daughter of Samuel died July 8 1761

Thomas Freeman Died ye 19th Day of July 1766

Darkis Chase born Daughte of Silvanu Chase & Charity hi Wif born Nov 13 1757

Mahitable born May 2^d 1759

Selvanu Born 17th Sept 1751

Seth Crowel Son of Seth & Mary his wife born May 31st 1756

Mary Crowel Daughte of Seth & Mary Crowel his Wif bon Sept 11th 1760

Mehitable Robins Daughte of Nath^{ll} & Lydia Robins born March 27 1767

Nath^{ll} Robins Son of Nathl & Lydia born 31st May 1769

[p. 21] December the 4 day 1741 then Oakes philips and mary Small ware married by Joseph Doan Justice peace

october the 8 day 1741 then William gray and Jude Nickerson ware married by Judah Thacher Justice peac

March 25th 1742 then Samuel Pain of Eastham and Mary Gould of Harwich ware Married in Harwich by Joseph Doane Justice Peace

May 28th 1741 Joseph Mayo Junr and Sarah Cobb Married in Harwich by ye Revd Nathl Stone

June 18th 1741 Elijah Hersey and Achsah Stone married in Harwich by ye Revd Nath^{ll} Stone

Lemuel Berry & Lidea Clark Married in Harwich [*] 20th 1741 p ye Revd Nathl Stone

Octob^r 8th 1741 Thomas Mirick & Hanah Hopkins were Married in Harwich p ye Revd Nathl Stone

Octr 13th 1741 Samuel Hambleton & Marcy Ellis were Married in Harwich p ye Revd Nathl Stone

Novemb^r 12th Nathl Mirick Junr & Thankfull Lincoln married in Harwich P Revd Nathl Stone

Benjamin Nickoson and Sarah Covil ware Married in Harw[ich] Octr 13th 1741 P^r ye Revd Nathl Stone

---

*The month is illegible, and "January" has been interlined in a modern hand. There was not, however, sufficient space, in the original entry, for "January."

Novembr 12th 1741 Abner Bangs and Sarah Hopkins ware Married in Harwich Pr ye Revd Nathl Stone

Decembr 15th 1741 Ebanezer Hallet & Elizabeth Bangs ware Married in Harwich ℣ ye Revd Nathl Stone

January 21st 1741 Peter Hallet & Eunice Allen ware Married In Harwich ℣ ye Revd Nathl Stone

April 1st 1742 Samuel Bangs & Mary Rider ware Married in Harwich P ye Revd Nathl Stone

March 3d 1741/2 Then James Ellis & Desire Ellis both of Harwch ware Married in Harwich ℣ Judah Thacher Justice of ye Peace

March 11th 1741/ Then Isaac Chapman Jur of Yarmouth & Mary Paddock of Harwich ware Married in Harwich ℣ Judah Thacher Just Pea[ce]

Novemb 13th 1742 Then Jolley Negro & Thankfull Will both of Harwich Ware Married in Harwich ℣ Joseph Doan Justice Peace

Decembr 16th 1742 Then Theophalus Mayo of Boston & Hannah Freeman of Harwich ware Married in Harwich ℣ Joseph Doane Justice Peace

Januy 20th 1742 Then Ebanezer Mayo of Eastham & Apphia Freeman of Harwich ware Married in Harwich ℣ Joseph Doane Jus Pea[ce]

March ye 2d 1742 Then Jonathan Small Ju & Hannah Weeks both of Harwich Ware Married in Harwich ℣ Joseph Doane Justice Peace

[p. 22] John gould Son to John gould and Ruth Gould his wife was born in September the 15 day 1741

Thomas Gould Sone to John & Ruth Gould his Wife born March 26th 1743

Richard Gould Sone of John & Ruth his Wife born Decembr 9th A D 1744

Abigail Gould* Daughter to John Gould & Ruth Gould his Wife born April 22 1746

Zeruiah Winslow Daughter of Kenelm Winslow Ju & Mary his Wife born Novr 12th 1759

Kenelm Winslow Son of Kenelm Winslow Ju & Mary his wife born Augst 17th 1761

Rebeca Winslow Daughte of Kenelm Winslow Jur & Mary his Wife born Augst 9th 1763

Edmond Crosby Son to Tuley and hannah Crosby was born in June 28 day 1741

Bettey Crosby Daughter of James Crosby & Sarah his wife was Born July th 20 1776

Thomas Crosbe Son of James Crosbe & Sarah his Wife born July 20th 1753

Mark Crosbe Son of James & Sarah Crosbe born Jany 21st 1755

John Crosbe Son of Jame & Sarah Crosbe born April 4 1757

* "Abigail Rodgers" was first written, in the same hand, but was crossed out.

Eunic Crosbe Daughter of James & Sarah Crosbe May 21 1759

Elkana Crosbe born May 10th Day of May 1761

Thankfull Crosbe Daughte of James & Sarah his wife born May 25th 1763

Sarah Crosbe born March 31st 1765

James Crosbe Son of Jame & Sarah born April 19 1767

Joshua Crosbe Son of Jame & Sarah born April 15 1769

Elija Crosbe born 10th* 1771

Abial Crosbe born March 15 1773

Bette Snow Daughter of Thomas Snow Jur & Rebeca Snow his wife born June 15th 1752

Eunice Snow Daughter of Thomas Snow Jr & Rebeca hi Wif born Augst 10th 1754

Rebeca Atwood Daughter of Barnabas Atwood & Sarah his wife born ye 15th Day Novr 1773

Sarah atwood Daughter of Barnabas atwood and Sarah His wife Born augste the 13 day 1776

Tabatha atwood Daughter of Barnabas and Sarah his wife Born march th 10d: 1781

Mary atwood Daughter of Barnabas & Rebeckah his wife born august 4th 1785

Barnabas Atwood Son of Barnabas & Rebeckah his wife born May 21st 1787

[p. 23] Prisilla hopkins Daughter to Isaac hopkins and Thankfull hopkins his wife was born December the 2 day 1741

Thankfull Hopkin Daughte to Isaac Hopki & Thankfull his Wife born Augs 31st 1743

Susanah Hopkin Daught to Isaac & Thankfull Hopki his Wife born May 10th 1745

Sarah Bangs Daughter of Elkana Bangs & Susanah his wife born Octr 26th 1751

Rhode Bangs Daughter of Elkane Bangs & Susanah hi Wife born Jany 19th 1754:

Dean Son to the Same parents Born may 31: 1756

John Dillingham Son to the Same parents Born Decr 30th 1758

Bela Son to Elkanah Bangs & Susanah his wife Born Decr 19: 1763

Elkanah Son to Elkanah Bangs & Susannah his wife Born Apl 25th 1766

Susanna Daughter to Elkanah Bangs & Susanna his wife Born Janu 24: 1771

Olive Daughter to Elkanah Bangs & Susanna his wife Born august 24: 1774

Thankfull Ary Daughter of Ebanezer & Zubah Ary born Octr 10th 1764

Elizabeth Ary Daughter of Ebanezer & Zubah Ary born July 18th 1767

* The word " June " has been interlined, in different ink.

Marcy Daughter to Edward & Thankfull Nickoson his Wife was
    born Janu^y 31st 1725

Mary Daughter to Edward & Thankfull Nickoson his Wife was
    born Aug^st 10^h 1728 Died Novr 22 1736

Thankfull Daughter to Edward & Thankfull Nickoson his Wife was
    born June 10th 1731

Abigail Daughter to Edward & Thankfull Nickoson his Wife born
    Decemb^r 4th 1733

Covil Nickoson Sone to Edward & Thankfull Nickoson his Wife
    born April 19^h 1737

Edward Sone to Edward & Thankfull Nickoso his Wife was born
    Aug^st 27th 1739

Thomas Nickoson Sone to Edwd & Thankfull his Wife was born
    Feby 12^h 1743

Peter Macklough Son of Anguist Macklough [*] his wife born
    Jan^y '18^h 1773

Thankfull Atwood Daughter of Barnabas Atwood & Rebecca his
    wife Born april 21st 1791

[p. 24] Seth Dexter Sone to Seth Dexter & Eliz^a his Wife was born
    Decemb^r 26th A Dom 1743

Eunice Rodgers Daughter to Zacheus Rodgers & Eliz^a his Wife born
    July 8th A D 1745

Mercy Rodgers Daughter to Zacheus Rodger & Elizabeth his Wife
    born Aug^st 3^d 1747

Elizabeth Rodgers Daughte of Zacheus Rodger & Elizabeth his Wife
    born Jany 1st 1749

Abigail Rogers Daughter of Zacheus & Eliz^a his Wife born Feb^y
    6th 1752

John Snow Son of Jonathan Snow & Mercy his wife born Septr 6
    1764

Hannah Snow Daughter of Jonathan Snow & Mercy his wife born
    June 1st 1766

John Long Sone to Wm Long Ju^r & Sarah his wife born July 28th
    1738

Elizabeth Long Daughte to Wm Long & Sarah his Wife born May
    ye 1st 1741

William Long Ju^r Sone to William Long Ju & Sarah his Wif born
    Septr 12th 1744

Thankfull Long Daughter of W^m & Sarah his Wife born Octr 1st 1749

Susanah Long Daughte of W^m & Sarah his Wife born May 28th 1752

Mark Snow Son of Joseph Snow & Precilla his Wife born 29th
    Aug^st 1763

(To be continued)

* Space was left for the wife's name.

THE GRAVESTONE RECORDS IN THE CEMETERY BACK OF THE EPISCOPAL CHURCH AT DUXBURY, MASS.

By George Ernest Bowman

Back of the St. John's Episcopal Church, formerly the Methodist Church, on Washington St., Duxbury, Mass., is a small cemetery which contained only twenty gravestones in July, 1907. In that month two members of the Massachusetts Society of Mayflower Descendants, Mr. Stanley W. Smith, of Boston, and the late Mr. John W. Willard, made and presented to the Society careful copies of all the inscriptions in this cemetery; but we have not heretofore found an opportunity to print them, on account of the space devoted to the records in three older and more important cemeteries in that town, copied by the same gentlemen, and to the original town records, copied by myself.

In 1911, the New England Historic Genealogical Society, of Boston, published "Vital Records of Duxbury Massachusetts to the year 1850", which professed to include not only all the town and church records of births, baptisms, marriages and deaths, prior to 1850, but also all gravestone records of deaths, prior to 1850, which are not found on the town records.

That book, unfortunately, contains serious errors in names and dates, and its compilers overlooked and, therefore, failed to print several hundreds of records dated prior to 1850.

I have long known that there was a remarkable proportion of variations between the records in the cemetery back of the Episcopal church, as they were copied by Messrs. Smith and Willard, and the same records as they were printed by the N. E. H. G. Society; but I have made it an invariable rule not to publish any statement that a record has been incorrectly printed by others, until I have personally re-examined the original record, with both copies before me, and, in the present case, other work has prevented the necessary examination.

Through the courtesy of Miss Sally Freeman Dawes of Duxbury, a member of this Society, I have recently been able to visit the cemetery, and with her assistance the original manuscript copies made by Messrs. Smith and Willard were critically compared with the inscriptions on the stones, and the inscriptions as they appeared in the N. E. H. G. Society's book were also compared with those on the stones.

Of the twenty stones which were in the cemetery in 1907, we found, in 1922, all but one, which will be considered later in this article; and in justice to Messrs. Smith and Willard I wish to emphasize the fact that their copies of the remaining nineteen inscriptions were correct in every case.

There were twenty stones in 1907; one has disappeared and two bear dates after 1849. At the present time, therefore, the cemetery contains seventeen gravestones, the death records on which should have been correctly printed in the N. E. H. G. Society's book.

The deaths on two of those seventeen are not even mentioned in that book, as they were not on the town records, and the N. E. H. G. Society's copyist overlooked the two stones.

Another gravestone record is not mentioned in that book, although the date is not the same as that printed from the town records, and all variations were supposed to be printed.

One gravestone record, as printed in that book, omits valuable information found on the stone.

Six of the remaining records, as there printed, contain errors of various kinds.

And only six of the eighteen gravestone records in this small cemetery were accurately printed, without errors or omissions.

Details of the numerous errors and omissions referred to will be found at the end of this article, in connection with accurate and complete abstracts of the inscriptions, as copied and verified by Messrs. Smith and Willard, in 1907, and again verified, in 1922, by Miss Dawes and myself.

As already stated, one gravestone found by Messrs. Smith and Willard, in 1907, has since disappeared. This was the stone of Hiram Thomas Paulding, son of William and Mary Paulding, who died 14 May, 1837, aged 9 months and 9 days.

The N. E. H. G. Society's book, as will be shown, makes two very serious errors in printing this child's death in the following manner:

Polden, Hiram T., ch. William and Mary, May 14, 1837. [Hiram Thomas Paulding, May 14, 1831, a. 9y. 9d., G. R. 5.] [Hiram Thomas Paulding, May 14, 1837, P. R. 21.]

The first of these three statements was from the town records.* The second, as indicated by the reference "G. R. 5.", professed to be from the stone which has since disappeared. The third was from William Paulding's family bible, owned by his daughter, Mrs. George B. Bates of Duxbury.

As we could not find this gravestone, Miss Dawes motored me to the residence of Mrs. Bates, who was much surprised to learn that the gravestone of her brother, who died in infancy, had disappeared. She had seen this stone many times, and said that the date and age on it had agreed with the record in her father's bible. With her permission I brought the bible to Boston, and, in order to prevent the possible loss of the records in it, have had them copied by the photostat process. This bible was printed at Brattleboro, Vt., in 1833, and the earlier entries were made by William Paulding, father of Mrs. Emma Cushing (Paulding) Bates.

For convenient reference, the entries on the first of the family record pages are here printed. This page has columns for "Births" and "Deaths", but [born], or [died], will be inserted before the dates found in those spaces. In other respects the following transcripts are literal copies of the original entries.

William Paulding [born] January 12 1807 [died] 1896
Mary Southworth [born] January 25 1807 [died] Oct. 1873
William Paulding Was Maried to Mary Southworth November
    23 1828
Elisabeth Thomas [born] tuesday october 6 1829 [died] July
    8 1830
William James [born] friday June 10 1831 [died] January 7 1865
Mary Elisabeth [born] tuesday September 3 1833 [died] July
    9 1838
Hiram Thomas [born] friday August 5 1836 [died] May 14 1837
Sarah Southworth Pau† [born] tuesday April 23 1839
Mary Elen [born] friday jan 29 1841 [died] Febru 19 1842
Emma Cushing‡ [born] thur Sept 7ᵗʰ 1843

[Another child was recorded on the third page]
Julian Ellmer P† [born] tuesday March 18 1851

* From Ichabod Alden's 1851 copy.

† There was not room to finish the surname.

‡ Mrs. Emma Cushing (Paulding) Bates.

An examination of the calendar shows that, in every case, the day of the week set opposite a birth date, in this bible record, was correctly stated, confirming the accuracy of the birth dates and emphasizing the reliability of the death records.

Among the original volumes of records of births, etc., in the town of Duxbury, is one with "Births 1764 to   Deaths" on the back; and on its side is "Duxbury Record of Births No 6" . It has about 400 pages, and the first 380 pages are devoted exclusively to family records.   There are also a few records on one unnumbered page near the end.   The date 1764, on the back, is not strictly accurate, as a few earlier birth dates were entered.

This volume of original records was overlooked by the N. E. H. G. Society, and therefore was not copied for use in compiling its printed book of "Duxbury Vital Records."

On page 258 of this book we find:

" Record of William & Mary Paulding's Family
William James Paulding was born June 10, 1831.
Mary E. Paulding was born September 3, 1833.
Elisabeth Thomas Paulding was born Octr—6, 1829
Elisabeth T. Paulding died July 28—1830
Hiram T. was born Augugust 5, 1836
Hiram T. Paulding died May 14, 1837
Mary E. Paulding died July 9, 1838
Sarah S. Paulding was born [*] 23. 1839.
Mary E. Paulding was born January 29, 1841.
Mary E. Paulding died February 19, 1842.
Emma Paulding was born September 7. 1843."

All of these entries, except the birth of Emma Paulding, were written at one time.

In 1851, Ichabod Alden made for the town a copy of the old records of births, marriages and deaths. His copy, unfortunately, was very inaccurate, and in copying William Paulding's family, from the volume "Births 1764", he not only changed the spelling, but copied "Sarah S." as "Sarah H". It should be noted that he entered the page reference, 258, to the original, from which he was copying. The two records in italics were entered in a different hand. The Alden copy follows:

" 258}   Record of William and Mary Polden's Family
William James Polden born 10 June 1831 *Died 7 January 1865*[†]
Mary E Polden born 3 Septr. 1833 Died 9 July 1838

* The month was omitted.

† Entries in italics are in a different hand.

Elisabeth Thomas Polden born 6 October 1829 Died 28 July
    1830
Hiram T Polden born 5 August 1836 Died 14 May 1837
Sarah H* Polden born 23 [†] 1839
Mary E Poldin born 29 January 1841 Died 19 February 1842
Emma Poldin born 7 September 1843
Julian A‡ Polden born 8‡ March 1851.
Mary Paulding the Mother Died 5 October 1873§."

The bible records, made (with two or three exceptions) by
William Paulding, the father, show that he was married 23 November, 1828. They also show that Hiram Thomas Paulding
was the fourth child, that he was born "August 5 1836", and
that he died "May 14 1837"; and the town records of his birth
and death give the same dates as the bible. His age at death,
therefore, according to his own father's record, and also according to the town records, was only 9 *months* and 9 days.

Furthermore, the child's sister, now living, states that he died
in infancy, and that the death record on the missing gravestone
was the same as the death record in her father's bible; and
Messrs. Smith and Willard, whose copies of all other death
records in this cemetery were accurate, copied the date on the
child's stone as 14 May, *1837,* and the age as 9 *months* and 9
days; and they, as usual, marked their copy to show that it had
been compared a second time with the original stone.

We must also take into account the fact that this stone
probably was erected by the child's father; and it is inconceivable
that he should have accepted and paid for a stone bearing a date
and an age which would indicate that the child was born
before either parent was sixteen years old, that the child was
born six years before his parents were married, and that the
child died more than five years before it was born.

The child's mother did not die until 1873, and his father did
not die until 1896, and it is absurd to suppose that they would
have allowed the erection of a stone bearing such an error, or,
if erected by mistake, that they would have allowed it to remain
so many years without correction.

* Incorrectly copied by Alden.   It should be " Sarah S ".

† The month was omitted.

‡ " Julian Ellmer " and " 18 " March, in his father's bible.

§ Entries in italics are in a different hand.

The N. E. H. G. Society's book refers to William Paulding's bible records of his own birth and marriage, and of the births and deaths of his children, also to the Ichabod Alden, 1851, copy, therefore the variation in that society's copy of the gravestone of the child Hiram should have led to a re-examination of the gravestone before printing. But the remarkable proportion of errors found in their copies (as printed) of the other inscriptions in this small cemetery seems to furnish conclusive evidence that none of those copies were properly verified before printing.

I have not been able to discover a single item of evidence in support of the statement, in the N. E. H. G. Society's book, that the inscription on Hiram Thomas Paulding's gravestone gave the year of his death as *1831*, and his age as 9 *years* and 9 days; and in view of the many serious errors and omissions of that book, only a few of which have been specially mentioned, there is not the slightest doubt that their professed copy of the record on this gravestone was merely one more error, printed without verification.

Another stone in this cemetery demands especial attention. It was erected in memory of "Emily Wilder", "Mary Ann" and "Sylvanus", three "infant children" of Charles and Sally Weston; but the dates of death, and the ages, were not added.

These three names were cut on the stone in the order here given, and it would be absurd to suppose that the parents decided on this order solely for the purpose of having the names arranged alphabetically. The names were undoubtedly arranged in the order of the births of the children, and the town records* supply the proof that Charles and Sally Turner had a daughter named "Emily", born 28 March, 1840, died 4 October, 1840; and a son named "Silvanus", born 7 May, 1849, died 5 September, 1849.

Immediately following the record of Emily's birth and death, and entered at the same time, we find "Emma" born 8 April, 1842. The next entry, made at a later time, is that of the birth and death of the son "Silvanus", in 1849, seven years after the birth of Emma.

No mention of either the birth or the death of the child "Mary Ann" has been found on the town records; but the gravestone furnishes practically conclusive evidence that she was born, and probably died, also, between Emily and Sylvanus. And as "Emma" was born in April, 1842, there can be little doubt that "Mary Ann" was born between April, 1843, and May, 1849, but lived so short a time that her birth and death were not recorded.

* " Births 1764 ", page 241 ; also Ichabod Alden's 1851 copy from that book.

No account of the family of Charles and Sally Weston would be complete if it did not include "Mary Ann". But the N. E. H. G. Society's book does not mention her name, although it refers to the gravestone on which her name appears, in connection with the children Emily and Sylvanus, and, unfortunately, refers to it in a way which seriously misleads readers, who suppose that there are two separate stones (instead of only one), each with a date of death, and that it will be useless to search in this cemetery for any other record of a child of Charles and Sally Weston before 1850.

The evidence that Mary Ann Weston was born and died before 1850 is sufficient to show that her name, with the necessary explanation, should have been included in the N. E. H. G. Society's book.

Accurate and exhaustive abstracts of the inscriptions on the twenty gravestones found in the cemetery in July, 1907, with explanatory notes, are here printed.

[THE GRAVESTONE RECORDS—WITH NOTES]

Atwood, Capt. Jesse; died 6 December, 1827, aged 37. "A husband kind, a father dear" . [Although no birth, marriage or death of an Atwood, except this one, is found in the N. E. H. G. Society's book, it does not print the line showing that Capt. Jesse was married and a father. Important information was, therefore, omitted.]

Chandler, Henry, died 4 September, 1859, aged 94 years, 9 months, 7 days. [After 1849, therefore not included in N. E. H. G. Society's book.]

Chandler, Susanna, wife of Henry, died 8 June, 1850, aged 81 years, 3 months, 23 days. [After 1849, therefore not included in N. E. H. G. Society's book.]

Daman, Abigail, wife of Zachariah, died 16 May, 1836, aged 18 years.

Hyde, Mary Goodrich, youngest daughter of "Rev. Edward, & Mrs. Elizabeth N. Hyde", died 1 August, 1825, aged 5 years, 4 months. [N. E. H. G. Society's book omits "N." in the mother's name, and incorrectly prints the year as "1823".]

Josselyn, Martin B., son of Rev. Aaron and Ann, died 20 July, 1838, aged 2 years.

Paulding, Mary Elisabeth, daughter of William and Mary, died 9 July, 1838, aged 4 years, 10 months, 6 days.

Paulding, Hiram Thomas, son of William and Mary, died 14 May, 1837, aged 9 months, 9 days. [N. E. H. G. Society's book incorrectly prints the year as "1831", and the age as 9 "years", 9 days, thus making it appear that the child was born in May, 1822, before either parent was sixteen years old, and more than six years before they were married. See introductory notes.]

Peterson, Capt. George, died 18 November, 1828, aged 27 years.

Peterson, Lucy, died 22 August, 1848, aged 19 years, 3 months. [N. E. H. G. Society's book incorrectly prints the age as "13" years, "9" months.]

Peterson, Otis, died 7 October, 1820, aged 16 years.

Peterson, Sarah, died 9 October, 1849, aged 69 years, 5 months.

Sherburn, Hannah W., wife of William H., died 14 April, 1845, in her 24th year. "My husband and my children dear, I now can leave without a tear." [N. E. H. G. Society's book fails to mention this stone, although the date on it is not the same as the date printed from the town records.]

Tainter, George F., son of Ezra and Susan, died 13 December, 1837, aged 5 years, 4 months, 24 days. [No record of the death of this child was printed in the N. E. H. G. Society's book.]

Taylor, Emily S., daughter of Eben and Sophronia, died 13 December, 1848, aged 2 years, 9 months, 28 days. [N. E. H. G. Society's book incorrectly prints the year as "1849".]

Taylor, "Usula Jane", daughter of Henry and Lucy C., died 16 January, 1839, aged 1 year, 9 months, 13 days. [No record of the death of this child was printed in the N. E. H. G. Society's book.]

Waters, Martha W., died 18 January, 1835, aged 20 years, 8 months, 23 days. [N. E. H. G. Society's book incorrectly prints the year as "1833", and the days in the age as "25".]

Weston, Emily Wilder ⎫
Weston, Mary Ann   ⎬ three infant children of Charles
Weston, Sylvanus   ⎭ and Sally, on one stone, without
any dates or ages. [N. E. H. G. Society's book does not give "Mary Ann". See introductory notes.]

Winsor, John, Jr., died 6 May, 1843, aged 68 years, 9 months. [N. E. H. G. Society's book omits the months.]

Winsor, Sylvanus H., died 19 August, 1835, aged 25 years, 3 months, 26 days. [N. E. H. G. Society's book incorrectly prints the year as 1833.]

"TEN COUNTERDEMAUNDS"

By George Ernest Bowman

AMONG the books printed by Elder William Brewster, at Leyden, was: "An Answer to the Ten Counter Demands Propounded by T. Drakes, Preacher of the Word at H. and D. in the County of Essex. By Wil. Euring . . . . Printed in the yeare 1619."*

Until very recently, the "Ten Counterdemaunds", written by Thomas Drakes, Vicar of Harwich and Dovercourt, England, was known only by Euring's "Answer" to it; and the only copy known at the present time is in the Henry E. Huntington Library and Art Gallery, at San Gabriel, Cal. This copy was secured by Mr. Huntington, for the sum of one thousand and fifty dollars ($1050.00), at the auction sale, on 30 April, 1917, of the library of the late C. L. F. Robinson, of Newport, R. I.

This little tract is of especial interest to all descendants of the Pilgrims, because in its last paragraph is probably the first suggestion, in print, that the separatists "remove to Virginia, and make a plantation there" .

Through the courtesy of George Watson Cole, L.H.D., the librarian of the Huntington Library, my request for permission to reprint, in this magazine, the complete text of the "Ten Counterdemaunds" was referred to Mr. Huntington personally, and he has very generously given his consent. As the complete text has not heretofore been reprinted, we are especially grateful for this opportunity to bring it to the attention of our readers.

The "Ten Counterdemaunds" is a small quarto of only four leaves, or eight pages, and the eighth page is blank. There is no title page, and the date and place of printing are not stated; but it probably was printed about 1618, as Euring's "Answer" was printed in 1619.

At the time this tract was issued it was customary to print notes on the margin of the page, instead of at the bottom. All such notes in the "Ten Counterdemaunds" are here printed as footnotes, the reference mark indicating, as nearly as possible, the position of the note on the outer margin of the original page.

There are no page numbers in the original, but we have indicated, by footnotes, where each new page begins.

* See Mayflower Descendant, XXIII: 97–105.

The spelling and punctuation of the original text have been retained in the following copy.

[Ten Counterdemaunds]

Αντερω῾τήματα *Thomae Draks.**

TEN COUNTERDEMAUNDS Propounded to those of the Separation, (or English Donatists) to be directly, and distinctly answered.

1. Whether, that their rent, Schisme, and Separation from the Church and Congregations of England, can (in any probabilitie) bee pleasing unto God, seeing, it hath had such unhappy beginnings, the *a*† first founder of it, comming to Judas his shamefull and fearfull ende, hanging himselfe: and the *b*‡ second totally recanting it, and rejoyning himselfe to our Church, as divers of their proselites doe daily: seeing also it hath had so small encreases, and so many dismall and fatall events, and divisions: one side excommunicating the other, some of them turning Anabaptists, and *c*§ others dying and distracted, by reason of irresolution.

2. Whether, that the quintessenced profession, Religion and discipline of these Novations and In-[¶]novators, as it standeth in opposition to the Church of England, and the rest of the reformed Churches) can bee of God, or, have any approbation from God, seeing that it hath no vertue, power and efficacy in it (as the Gospell preached in our English assemblies by Gods blessing aboundantly hath) to winne, convert, and drawe unto their partie and profession, Atheists, Papists, Heretikes, rude, profane and ignorant people: The Apostles, Evangelists, and ther holy successors, converted all sorts unto God, but these refined reformers, onely seduce the sound, and pervert and estrange from us, those, that are otherwise well affected, and of some understanding and make them twofold more refractary then themselves.

* " Counter demands of Thomas Drakes."

† The "*a*" is used as a reference mark, and calls attention to " Maister Bolton." printed in the margin.

‡ The "*b*" is used as a reference mark, and calls attention to " Maister Browne." printed in the margin.

§ The "*c*" is used as a reference mark, and calls attention to " Maister Nowell, of Sheldon in Warwicke-shire, &c." printed in the margin.

¶ New page begins here.

3. Whether that (in the very separatists conscience) our reformed assemblies, (wherein the Gospell of Christ is sincerely preached and professed, and the Sacraments duly and rightly administred)* are worse then the Jewes Synagogues, in which notwithstanding Christ his Apostles preached; & our Ministers, worse then the Scribes and Pharisees, that sat in Moses Chaire, when Christ commandeth the people to heare, and observe and doe, whatsoever (according to Moses Lawe) they did bid them observe. Wherefore (to reason a minore ad maius) if our Lord Jesus, his Disciples, and the people did not separate from their Synagogues and assemblies, that were in faith and maners farre more defective then ours are, much lesse ought they to separate from our Church and assemblies, wherein, all the grounds of Christian Religion are soundly held, and professed.

[†]4. Whether that those great multitudes of people (though hitherto wanting the pretended Church-constitution of the Separatists) that even‡ fasting heard our Lord Jesus preach, and professed themselves his Disciples, (albeit many of them§ were drawen, not by doctrine but by miracles, report, & with a desire to be fed) can with any reason bee denied to bee members of the visible Church, and whither those three thousands which blessed ¶Peter at one Sermon converted (for they were baptized, continued in the Apostles doctrine, fellowship, breaking of bread and praiers.) were not, before that Presbyters and Deacons were chosen, true members of a visible Church, and this cannot bee refuted, and why are not our Church assemblies in England, (much more grounded in the truth) &c. a true visible Church? and then with what conscience, doe, or can these Separatists sequester and‖ rent themselves from them?

5. Whether, (to ascend no higher, and neerer the Apostles to me** as I might) that in Constantines the first Christian Emperours time, and ever since unto Mr. John Calvins dayes, for the space of some thirteene hundred yeares, there was no Christian Churches in Asia, Africke, Europe, because they had the same outward constitution, formal State, Bishops, Arch-bishops, Met-

---

* "Mat. 23. v. 2, 3." was here printed in the margin.

† New page begins here.

‡ "Mat. 14. 13. 14. 15. 16. 17." was here printed in the margin.

§ "Joh. 6. 5. 10. 11." was here printed in the margin.

¶ "Joh. 6. 27." was here printed in the margin.

‖ "Act. 2. 37. 38. 41." was here printed in the margin.

** "to me" probably should have been printed "time".

ropolitans, & Church-government (for substance and substance
of doctrine) that our English Church hath, and retaineth. And
if those were true visible Churches, why are not ours (also?)

6. Whether, that the reformed Churches in the [*] lower, and
higher Germany, in France, the Church of Geneva &c. (that
come neerer to their constitution and discipline, then ours doe
in England,) bee true visible Churches, or no? if they be such,
why then doe they not adjoyne themselves to some of them,
but distast them as much as they doe ours? And why doe they
not in judgment assent unto any or all of those reformed
Churches, that with a joynt consent (as may appeare by the har-
monie of Confession) acknowledge the Church of England to
be a true visible Church, and give unto it the righthand of fellowship? how dare they refuse such a cloude of witnesses? will
these μονόσοφοι put out all their eyes? is there no Church in
the world but their Platonicall Idea?

7. How can the Church, or, Church-assemblies of England,
bee false, Antichristian, bastardized, wherein the Gospell, is so
soundly and solemnly and substantially taught and professed, and
the Sacraments, so rightly administred and received, whose
Bible translations, (specially the last English translation done by
his Majesty command) are so pure, that the very Separatists rest
in them: wherein are so many thousands, yea hundred thousands
of true Converts and orthodoxe Christians, that hath bred and
brought forth so many excellent and renowned Martyrs, who
have sealed the trueth of our religion with their bloud, and died
members of the protestant Churches; wherein so many Christian
exiles are comfortably harboured, wherein so many sound,
religious and learned Pastors, Doctors, Preachers, as (for proportion) no Country in the world [*] can afford the like; and by
whose doctrine, writings, disputes, (not to speake of the Magistrates sword) the Romish Jerico hath bin more shaken, and the
second beast the Antichrist, more fatally wounded, then by any
nationall Church whatsoever: and which Church, and the members thereof, have beene so wonderfully blessed and protected,
and so strangely delivered from the rage, tumults, designes,
treasons, conspiracies of the Romish Antichrist and all his
adherents: and in which Churches (as one of the princiall Separatists I. R. in his admonition ad lectorem, in his owne name and
in the name of his faction, lately prefixed before the third booke
of M. Robert Parker, de politia ecclesi. pag. 368. confesseth, that
the grace of God by the Gospell, in respect of the cheife heads of

---

* New page begins here.

true Christian faith, by divers of the faithfull preached, doth so abound, that there are very many godly and holy men in these assemblies, both of Reformitants and Conformitants, which they acknowledge for brethren in Christ &c. We have (by their owne confession) sound faith, and holinesse, why then doe they or how dare they sunder and rent themselves from such a Church, and why will they for accidents and circumstances, denie and renounce the substance of a Church? And if they (upon better consideration) esteeme us brethren, with what warrant can they seperate from holy brethren in Christ, is it not good and pleasant for to see brethren to dwell together in unitie? Did not the converts in S. Peters dayes continue dayly with one accord in the Temple &c. And why doe not our Separatists who would be [*] accounted converted Saints imitate them. must wee† leave and forsake a goodly Cittie, for the weaknesse of the walls?

8. How can the formall state (as they call it) of the Provinciall, Diocesan, Cathedrall & Parishionall Churches of England, and the regiment thereof, be unlawfull, papall, Antichristian? And how doe, or, can the Lawes of the land, and Ecclesiasticall Cannons confirme it? seeing that the name, calling & office of B B: whether we respect ordination of ministers or power of jurisdiction, is (as hath ben, & will be proved) for substance expressed in divers places of the new Testament; seeing, it hath had a continuall succession from the Apostles time to this day, as all auncient Fathers and Counsells acknowledge: and seeing that (at least) this formall estate of Diocesan, Parishionall and Cathedrall Churches, hath bin in use, long before Antichrist was hatched, for‡ the Pope was not Antichrist before he had gotten the Title of universall Bishop, nor complete untill he had gotten into his hands both swords, that is, both Civill and Ecclesiasticall Dominion: Doth not every Bishop amongst us, every Pastor and ecclesiasticall officer, abjure the Prpes§ usurped supremacie? Doe not our statutes, and Cannons directly make againg¶ papistry and Idolafry?‖ What will Sathan expell Sathan, and will the members of Antichrist fight against Antichrist? And admitt all bee, as you pretend, doe we not (at least) kill Antichrist with his owne sword and weapons?

* New page begins here.

† " Act. 2. 46." was here printed, in the margin.

‡ " Anno 1607 " was here printed, in the margin.

§ Plainly a typographical error for " Popes ".

¶ A typographical error for " against ".

‖ Plainly a typographical error for " Idolatry ".

9. Whether, any new lawes can, or ought to be enacted, or any further reformation made without [*] the Christian Princes or Magistrates consent, or ever in a well ordered Church hath bene enacted, or made and whether, they have done well, to seperate with, out the Kings Majesties leave and licence, and consent of the state?

10. Whether, it were not the separatists best course, to returne to Gods true Church and people, from which (upon some concealed hard dealing) they have made an unlawfull rent, and therein to confer with the best learned, and if still their consciences be somewhat tender, to supplicate for some favour and liberty, or if they will not take this course, whether it were not good for them, for the avoiding of scandall, and in expectance of·some prosperous successe, by the permission of our noble King, and honourable Counsell: to remove into Virginia, and make a plantation there, in hope to convert infidels to Christianitie? FINIS.

MISCELLANEOUS DEATH RECORDS

TRANSCRIBED BY THE EDITOR

WE here present literal copies, made by the Editor, of some miscellaneous death records and notices, from gravestones, newspapers, etc., which have not heretofore been printed in these pages.

[WHITE-YOUNG]

PEREGRINE[2] WHITE. The death of Peregrine[2] White *(William[1])* of Marshfield, Mass., was noticed in "The Boston News-Letter" for "Monday July 31. 1704", as follows:

"Marshfield, July, 22 Capt. Peregrine White of this Town, Aged Eighty three years, and Eight Months; died the 20th Instant . He was vigorous and of a comly Aspect to the last; Was the Son of. Mr. William White and Susanna his Wife; born on board the Mayflower, Capt. Jones Commander, in Cape Cod Harbour, November, 1620. was the First Englishman born in New-England . Altho' he was in the former part of his Life extravagant; yet was much Reform'd in his last years; and died hopefully."

* New page begins here.

SARAH' (WHITE) YOUNG. The death of Sarah' (White) Young of Scituate, Mass., was noticed in "The Boston Weekly News-Letter" for "Friday, August 29. 1755", as follows:

"Saturday August 9th died at Scituate, in the 92d Year of her Age, Mrs. Sarah Young, the virtuous Widow of Mr. Thomas Young, and eldest Daughter of That Mr. Peregrine White of Marshfield, who was the First Born English Child in New-England: Being Son of William and Susannah White, born on board the Ship in Cape-Cod Harbour, in the latter Part of Nov: 1620, in which Governor Carver and the Rest of our Plimouth Planters came to New-England, before the Ship left said Harbour and set sail for said Plimouth. Said Peregrine White liv'd in great Health and Vigour to the 84th Year of his Age, when a Fever carried Him off on July 22. 1704 as our News-Letter soon after inform'd the Publick: And this his Eldest Daughter was Born at Marshfield in Oct. 1663, enjoy'd her Senses and Health in good measure, till towards her End, and left four Sons surviving . Two observable Instances of the Long Lives of the very first and second Race of Children born in this happy Country."

[CHIPMAN]

JOHN AND RUTH CHIPMAN. Elder John Chipman of Barnstable married, first, Hope' Howland *(John')*, who was the mother of all his children. After the death of Hope, who was buried at Barnstable, he married the widow Ruth (Sargent) (Winslow) Bourne, and removed to Sandwich, Mass. Elder John and Ruth Chipman are buried side by side in the old cemetery at Sandwich. The death records on the two stones read:

"Here Lyes Buried yᵉ Body of Elder John Chipman aged 88 years died April yᵉ 7th 1708"

"Here Lyes Buried The Body of Mʳˢ Ruth Chipman Aged 71 Years Died October yᵉ 4th 1713"

[PRENCE]

MRS. MARY PRENCE. In all autograph signatures of Governor Thomas Prence, of Plymouth Colony, known to me, he wrote his name "Prence"; and in most of the contemporary records the name is so recorded.

His fourth wife, Mary (———) (Howes) Prence, survived him, and died at Yarmouth, Mass., as shown by the following literal transcript of an entry in the third volume of the records of that town. This record, which is on the third page, with the book reversed, reads:

"mis⁸ : mary Prince late wife of governer Thomas Prince died upon the Ninth day of desember : 1695 and was Buried upon the leventh daye of yᵉ said : 1695 :"

[CHURCH]

JOSEPH CHURCH³. The death of Joseph Church³ *(Eliza-beth² Warren, Richard¹)*, of Little Compton*, was noticed in "The Boston News-Letter" for "Monday March 12 . 1710", as follows:

"Little Compton, March 8. On Monday the 5th Currant Dyed here the Honourable Joseph Church Esq; lately of Her Majesty's Council for this Province in the 73 year of his Age."

BENJAMIN CHURCH³. The death of Benjamin Church³ *(Elizabeth² Warren, Richard¹)* was noticed in "The Boston News-Letter" of "Monday February 3. 1718", as follows:

"Little-Compton, January 18. Yesterday the 17th Currant, The Honourable Col. Benjamin Church, Esq; Riding out to his Farm, his Horse stumbled and he fell, pitched upon his Head and Shoulders, was immediately taken up and carryed to the next House, but never spoke a word after, but it's thought by the motions and signs he made, that he had his Senses, and Died about six hours after, in the 78th Year of his Age. He was a true lover of his Country and approved himself so, by venturing his Life so often in it's Defence in the several Wars, & many Services he has done for it, as also in his Stedfast adherence to it's Interest in times of Temptations to the contrary; a Gentleman also that has been a great Friend and Incourager of Virtue and Religion, especially in this corner of the Province, where Providence disposed the bounds of his Habitation."

FORM FOR A BEQUEST

I GIVE and bequeath to the Society of Mayflower Descendants, a corporation organized under the laws of the Commonwealth of Massachusetts; the sum of.........................dollars.

* Little Compton, then in Massachusetts, is now in Rhode Island.

MIDDLEBOROUGH, MASS., VITAL RECORDS

(Continued from page 58)

[p. 87] april 14 1757 Bristol & Dinah Negro man & woman Ser^v to m^r Caleb Tomson of middleborough were married by Silvanus Conant

May 19 : 1757 Jesse Snow & mary Eaton both of middlebor were married by Silvanus Conant

July 18 : 1757 Nathan Wood & Betty Shaw both of middlebor were married by Silvanus Conant

August 9 1757 Nehemiah Bryant & Hannah Totman both of middleborough were marr^d by S. Con[ant]

August 23^d 1757 Ebenezer Hackit of Raynham & Abigail Thomas of middleboro were married by Silvanus [Conant]

aug^t 25 1757 abiel Cole & Ann Peirce both of middleboro were married by Silvanus Conant

Sep^t 22 1757 Josiah Vaughan & Lydia Thomas both of middleboro were married by Silvanus Conan[t]

Decr 15:1757 John Benson & Priscilla Tinkham both of middleborough were married by S: Conant*

[Decr 15 : 1757] Barzillia Thomas & Elisabeth Cox both of middleborough were married by S: Conant*

march 23:1758 Nehemiah Allen & abigail Thomas both of middleboro were married by Silvanus Conant

march 27:1758 Capt Joel Ellis & Jemima Bennet both of middleborough were married by Silvanus Conant

march 29:1758 John Thomas J^r Elisabeth Shaw both of middleboro were married by Silvanus Conant

April 13:1758 Benj^m Sawdy of Tivertown & Abigail Southworth of middleboro were married by S: Conant

april 13:1758 Phillip Negro man Ser^t to Peter Oliver Esq & Vilet Negro woman Ser^t to m^r Phinehas Pratt both of middleborough were married by Silvanus Conant

April 17th 1758 Jesse Vaughan & margeret Shaw both of middlebo were married by Silvanus Conant

Sepr 5:1758 moses Thomas & Deborah Shaw both of middlebo were married by Silvanus Conant

Octr 9:1758 m^r Seth Samson & m^rs Thankfull Bennet both of middlebo were married by S: Conant

Octr 26:1758 Ichabod Billington of middlebo & Betty Peck of Bridgwater were married by S: Conant

Jan^r 11:1759 James Willies & mary Thomas both of middleborough were married by. S: Conant

* These two marriages were bracketed, after a single date " Decr 15:1757 ".

Feby 15: 1759 abner Samson of middlebo & Hannah Drew of Hallifax
    were married by S: Cona[nt]

Jan^r 10: 1760 Joseph Darling & Huldah Thomas both of middle-
    borough were married by S: C[onant]*

[Jan^r 10: 1760] Andrew Cobb & Experaince Samson both of middle-
    borough were married by S: C[onant]*

march 11: 1760 Joseph Porter of Taunton & Martha Rider of mid-
    dleborough were married by Silvanus Con[ant]

march 20: 1760 Do^r Stephen Powers & Lydia Drew both of middle-
    borough were married by Silvanus Con[ant]

April 17: 1760 Benj^am Tucker Ju^r & mary Thomas Jur both of mid-
    dlebo were married by Silvanus Co[nant]

Octr 30th 1760 william Soul & Sarah Briggs both of middleborough
    were married by Silvanus Conan[t]

Novr 6: 1760 Samuel Tinkham J^r & Patience Simmons both of mid-
    dlebo were married by Silvanus Conant

Novr 20: 1760 Ebenezer Dunham & Patience Clap both of middle-
    boro were married by Silvanus Conant

Novr 20: 1760 Joseph Silvester of Duxbury & Lucy Samson of mid-
    dlebo were married by Silvanus Cona[nt]

Decem^r 17: 1760 Samuel Bishop of Bolton & Patience Cox of mid-
    dlebo were married by Silvanus Conant

Decr 18: 1760 Seth Thomas & mary Barrows both of middlebo were
    married by Silvanus Conant

Jany 1: 1761 John Lambart of Taunton & Lydia miller of middlebo
    were married by Silvanus Conant

Jan^r 15 : 1761 Jeremiah Thomas ju^r and Susanna Thomas 2^d both of
    middlebo were married by Silvanus Con[ant]

Jan^r 22 : 1761 William Tupper & Susanna Clap both of middlebo were
    married by Silvanus Conant

April 23^d 1761 Amos wood & mary Thomas both of middleborough
    were married by Silvanus Conant

may 12: 1761 Jonathan Porter of Taunton & Mercy Redding of mid-
    dlebo were married by S: Conant

June 18: 1761 Ephraim Hackit & Abigail Leonard both of middlebo
    were married by Silvanus Conan[t]

aug^t 27: 1761 David miller ju^r & Sarah Tomson both of middlebo
    were married by Silvanus Cona[nt]

Sepr 17: 1761 John Norris of warham & Jemimah Benson of mid-
    dlebo were married by S: Co[nant]

oct^r 29 Eben^r Samson Ju^r of Plimouth & Priscilla Pratt of middlebo
    were married by S: Conant

No^r 5 Ebenezer Thomas jun^r & Joanna Cushman both of middlebo
    were married by S: Conant

Novr 12 Gideon Cobb & mehitable Warren both of middleborough
    were married by S. Conan[t]

* These two marriages were bracketed, after a single date " Jan^r 10: 1760 ".

Novr 26 Joseph Tupper & Joanna Cole both of middleborough were
married by S: Conan[t]

Decr 3 Eliakim Barlow & mary Billington both of middlebo were
married by S: Conan[t]

Decem^r 3 Silvanus Thomas and Susanna Tomson both of middleborough were married by S: Con[ant]

(To be continued)

PLYMOUTH COLONY WILLS AND INVENTORIES

(Continued from page 73)

[JOHN WOOD'S WILL*]

[3 : 1 : 75] "The Last Will . . . . of John Wood Allies
Attwood of the Towne of Middleberry Deceased Exhibited to
the Court held att Plymouth the fift of June 1673 on the oathes
of Gorge Vaughan and Jonathan Wood; as followeth"

"Middleberry April 13, 1673 John Wood allies Atwood
the son of Henery Wood allies Atwood Deceased Did Declare
unto us . . . . as followeth; first that hee Gave the house that
hee Dwelt in, and the land and Meddow that belonged therunto
to his two youngest brothers, and to his youngest sister Mary;
and that his said brothers Abell† and James should have it for
ever provided that they payed unto theire sister Mary the prise
of her owne third p^rte"

"hee Gave unto his Mother the rent of the aforsaid house
and land During her life"

"thirdly his will was that his other lands and Moveable
estate should be sold to pay any Debts that was owing by him"

"fourthly hee Desired that Gorge Vaughan John Nelson and
Jonathan Wood Allies Atwood would be adminnestrators"

"Wee whose names are underwritten Doe Testify that the
abovesd John Wood allies Atwood; about two or three Dayes
after the abovesaid will was Declared Did att the Request of
Gorge Vaughan Give and Graunt unto the Towne of Middleberry
A sufficient hieway to be layed out upon his land that lyeth
next unto Edward Grayes land upon Namassakett River and

* See also original page 79.

† An error for " Abiel ", as shown by the settlement on original page 78, and
various other records.

to be on that syde which is next to Edward Grayes Land for the Inhabitants of the aforsaid Towne to Goe Downe to Namassakett River"

"The Testator Did Declare to the witnesses that his Desire was that what is above expressed should be made Good to the legatees and that if any thinge were not entered as it should be to assure the pticulars to them; according to the will of the Doner It should be accoumpted to arise for want of skill in the pening of it;"

[p. 76] The inventory was taken, 29 May, 1673, by "Jonathan Wood allies Atwood", and sworn to by him, 5 June, 1673. The real estate, not valued, was: "in land one hundred acrees on which his house standeth"; "25 acrees that lyeth in another place"; "more land appertaining to the said wood twenty seaven acrees".

"John Rayman" owed the estate forty shillings. John Andrews owed "one hundred of bolts and one barrell of Tarr". Thomas West owed forty shillings. Jonathan Barnes owed "two thousand and an halfe of square Marchantable Boards". David Thomas owed £4, "to be payed in Tarr or Corne". Jacob Michell owed "16 pound and a halfe of woole". "Due from Indians" £6, 16s., 6d.

[INVENTORY OF NATHANIEL BACON, SR.]

[p. 77] The "Inventory of the estate of Mr Nathaniel: Bacon seni^r: of Barnstable late Deceased exhibited to the Court held att Plymouth the 29 of October 1673 on the oath of mistris Hannah Bacon widdow" was taken by William Crocker, John Gorham, Sr., and James Lewis. The total amount was £632, 10s., 2d. "the Barke mill and fatts* and other thinges for taning" were valued at £5. The only real estate was "the lands and housing" £250.

[JOHN TILSON'S INVENTORY†]

[p. 78] The inventory of "John Tilson lately Deceased" was taken "the last of October 1673" by Jonathan Shaw and William Hoskins, and was "exhibited to the Court held att Plymouth the 29th of October 1673 on the oath of Ephraim Tilson". There was no real estate. Thomas Lucas and John Jourdaine owed the estate, and it was indebted to Edward

---

* Vats.

† See his will, original page 93.

Gray, James Cole, "the Carpenters", "Goodwife Ransom", William Clarke.

[JOHN WOOD'S ESTATE*]

[p. 79] At the court held 29 October, 1673, "In Reference unto the estate of John Wood allies Attwood Deceased this Court ordereth that Samuell Wood the eldest brother of the said John Wood shall have . . . . the said estate both of lands Goods and Chattles provided that hee Give Cecuritie . . . . to pay . . . . all Debts . . . . and likewise that hee . . . . Confeirme; the propriety of forty acrees of land unto his two youngest brothers, named Abiell Wood and James Wood allies Attwood, to each of them alike proportion of the said forty acrees; which . . . . is to be layed out to them out of the best of the uper end of the lott of Land; the said John Wood allies Atwood Died posessed off; and that hee lived and Died on;"

[THE WILL OF JOHN MORTON, SR.]

On 29 October, 1673, "The Court abovesaid Considering the Concurrent Testimonys Concerning the will Nunckupative of John Morton seni^r: Deceased; Doe . . . . Rattify these Conclusions following, which Conclusions are likewise to the satisfaction of Lettice the wife of the said John Morton; and likewise of John Morton Juni^r: his son; viz that the said John Morton Juni^r: shall have . . . . for ever all the lands hee is now posessed off; which his father Gave unto him in his lifetime . . . . And wheras it appeers likewise to be his fathers will; that hee should have the one halfe of his upland att Winnatucksett; and his Daughter Deborah the wife of Francis Combe the other halfe; This Court Doth alsoe with the Consent of the abovesaid p^{r}ties; settle the said upland unto the said John Morton Juni^r: and Deborah the wife of Francis Combe aforsaid, to each of them alike proportion therof . . . . and wheras it Doth likewise appeer to the Court; That John Morton seni^r: aforsaid hath Given all his meddow which is eight acrees of fresh meddow att Winnatucksett unto his said son John Morton; This Court Doth alsoe sette the same unto and upon him . . . . provided that his Mother shall have, the use and Improvement of the one half of it . . . . whiles shee liveth; and att her Death to be Intirely his"

* See his will, original page 75.

"And further this Court Doth . . . . Confeirme all the Rest of the Lands Remaining both upland and Meddow land of the said John Morton seni^r: with all the Remainder of the estate . . . . unto and upon Lettice, his wife To be for and towards her livelihood and subsistence, and for the bringing up of her Children; untill her Decease; and att her Death That what remains of the said estate, shall appertaine . . . . unto the foure Daughters of him the said John Morton seni^r: viz: Mary Martha Hannah and Ester; To each of them a like proportion; These Conclusions being found to be according to the mind and will of the said John Morton seni^r: were Concluded by the Court, with the Free Consent likewise of the p^rties, abovenamed whoe are therin especially Concerned: viz: Lettice Morton Widdow and John Morton Juni^r; and heer Recorded by the order of the Court"

[WILL OF JOSIAH COOKE, SR.]

[The will and inventory of Josiah Cooke, Sr., of Eastham, found on pages 90-92,* were printed in our fifteenth volume.]

[WILL OF WIDOW RICHARDEN CHAMBERS]

[p. 92] "Richarden Chambers of Scittuate . . . . widdow" made her will 18 November, 1672, and signed it by a mark. Bequests were as follows:

To "Abigaill Curtice the wife of my son Thomas Curtice all my wearing Clothes"

To "Elizabeth Curtice Daughter of my son Thomas Curtice aforesaid" £10, "in mony Goods or Cattle"

"and wheras my husband Thomas Chambers Deceased; A Day or two before hee Died; Did manifest and Declare before Leister Torrey and Sarah the wife of Abraham Suttliffe; and in my hearing, that it was his will, That his son in law John Curtice should have his house and land both upland and marshland lying and being in Scittuate and Marshfeild, Imediately after my Death; And as it was my husband will, soe I Doe heerby Declare, that it is my will, That my son John Curtice shall have and Injoy the said house and land Imediately after my Decease"

"all the Rest of my estate; my Debts and legacyes and Charges of funarall being Deducted, I Give unto John Curtis my son aforsaid; whom I . . . . appoint to be the sole executor"

* Original pages 80-89 inclusive were omitted in numbering.

The witnesses were Thomas Kinge, Elisha Besbey and Abraham Suttliffe. "Mr Thomas Kinge made oath to this will June 1673 before mee Josiah Winslow Govr:"

The "Will of Mistris Richarden Chambers Widdow of Scittuate" was proved at Plymouth, 29 October, 1673.

The inventory, taken 27 October, 1673, by Thomas Kinge, Richard Curtice and Abraham Suttliffe, was exhibited in court, and sworn to, 29 October, 1673, by John Curtis. The total was £91, 14s. No real estate was mentioned.

[Henry Rowley's Inventory]

[p. 93] "A true Invendory of the estate of Henery Rowley of Saconeesett Deceased exhibited to the Court held att Plymouth in July 1673 on the oath of Moses Rowley as followeth; Item a Debt of twenty nine pounds Due from Jonathan Hatch" £29 "upon the Repurchase of a p^rsell of land which the said hatch sold to the said Henery Rowley with that limitation provided"

[John Tilson's Will*]

"The last will and Testament of John Tilson of Scittuate late Deceased exhibited to the Court held att Plymouth the 29th of October 1673 as it is Contained in the Testimonyes following;

"I John Andrews aged about 28 yeares Doe Testify that John Tilson being sicke I asked him how hee would Dispose of his land and his answare to mee was that if hee Died without an heire; That his brother Ephraim Tilsons eldest son Edmond Tilson should Injoy his house and land;

"Taken upon oath this 30th Day of October 1673 before mee Constant Southworth Assist:

"I Samuell Savory aged 22 yeares Doe Testify That I heard John Tilson say that his brother Ephraim Tilsons son Edmond should be his heire of his house and lands and meddowes

"Taken upon oath this 30th Day of October 1673 before mee Constant Southworth assistant;

"I Abigaill Ransom aged about 36 yeares Doe witnes that I heard John Tilson say that his brother Ephraim Tilsons son should be his heire of his house and lands and meddowes

"Taken upon oath this 30th of October 1673 before mee Constant Southworth Assistant;"

(To be continued)

* See his inventory, original page 78.

EASTHAM AND ORLEANS, MASS., VITAL RECORDS

(Continued from page 91)

[p. 153] novembar ye 13 : 1747 Elezar rogers Jur of harwigh and Rebaca higgens of Eastham waare mared by Joseph Croker Clark

febuary 25 : 1747 gidean freeman and hanah freeman boath of Eastham ware mared by Mr Joseph Croker Clark

marcy Dafter of gidan freeman and hanah freeman was born in Eastham January 22 : 1748/9

Rebaca freeman Dafter of gidan and hanah freeman was Born in Eastham novembr 8 : 1750

Betty Freeman Daughter of gidean Freeman and Hannah Freeman was Born at at Eastham September 24th 1753

mary freeman daughter of gidean freeman was Born at Eastham march ye 28 : 1757

Sarah freeman Daughter of gidean and hannah freeman was Born at Eastham May ye 31th 1760 and Dide December the 25 : 1760

Sarah freeman Daughter of gidean and Hannah freeman was Born at Eastham November ye 30th 1761

Hannah freeman Daughter of gidean freeman and Hannah freeman was Born at Eastham June ye 9th 1765

Look in page 73 for the Rest of the Children

novembar 10 : 1748 then Jesse snow and loes freeman boath of Eastham ware marred in Eastham by Joseph Croker Clark   .

philip young the sun of Loes freeman was Born in Eastham march 5 : 1744

sarah snow the Dafter of Jease and Loes snow was Born in Eastham septembar 15 : 1750

Edman snow the sun of Jease and Loes snow was Born in Eastham January 6 : 1752

febuary 16 : 1748 then Joseph freeman and febe paine boath of Eastham ware marrid in Eastham by Joseph Croker Clark

febuary 23 : 1748 then Zebulon young and abigel rogers boath of Eastham ware marrid in Eastham by Joseph croker Clark

[p. 154] Aprel 15 : 1749 then Isaac higgens J^r and Rebaca mayo boath of Eastham ware marrid in Eastham by Joseph Croker Clark

Relianc higgens the Dafter of Isaac and Rebaca higgens was Born in Eastham may 3 : 1750

Rebaca higgens the Dafter of Isaac and Rebaca higgens was Born in Eastham august 30 : 1753

Isaac higgens the sun of Isaac and Rebaca higgens was Born in Eastham octobar 16 : 1755

June 8 : 1749 then James Knowles and Abigel Atwood boath of Eastham ware marrid in Eastham by Joseph croker Clark

Thomisen Knowles Daughter of James and abigail Knowles was Born in Eastham march 1749

Lucretia Knowles Daughter of James and Abigail Knowles was born in Eastham in December 1751

Siruiah Knowles Daughter of James and Abiga[il] Knowles was Born in Eastham october 1753 :

James Knowles Son of James and Abigail Knowles was Born in Eastham January 1756 :

Paul Knowles Son of James and Abigail Knowles was born in Eastham January 9 : 1758

July 20 : 1749 then James Knowles of Chatham and Ruth mayo of Eastham ware marred in Eastham by Joseph Croker Cla[rk]

septembar 7 : 1749 then mathu williams of hebron and grase smith of Eastham ware marrid in Eastham by Joseph Croker Cla[rk]

novembar 23 : 1749 then John mulford and mary mirick boath of Eastham ware marrid in Eastham by Joseph Croker Clark

January 18 : 1749 then samuel pears and mary smith boat[h] of Eastham ware marrid in Eastham by Joseph Croker Clark

John mulford Jr the sun of John and mary mulford was Born in Eastham August 14 : 1750

[p. 155] febuary 6 : 1749 then Joseph Rodgers of harwich and Abigail twining of Eastham ware marrid in Eastham by Joseph Croker Clark

hulda mayo Dafter of Benimine and Sarah mayo was born in Eastham febuary the 7th 1748* .

prisila harding Dafter of Isaac harding and Expearenc harding was Born in Eastham June ye : 9 : 1740 and Died in septembar 10 : 1741

Josiah Jr harding Jur sun of Isaac harding and Expearnc harding was Born in Eastham Desembar the 29 : 1741

prisila harding Dafter of Isaac and Expearenc harding was Born in Eastham febuary the : 9 : 1743

Isaac harding Jur sun of Isaac and Expearnc harding was born in Eastham septembar 23 : 1745 and Died octobar 17 : 1745

Abagil harding Dafter of Isaac and Expearnc harding was Born in Eastham febuary : 1 : 1747

Rebaca harding Dafter of Isaac and Expearnc harding was Born in Eastham novembar 23 : 1750

January ye : 10 : 1744 then samuel Doane the 3 and Darkes Coale ware marrid in Eastham by Mr Benimin webb minister Endrd pr Thomas Knowls Town Clark

Martha Doane the Dafter of samuel Doane the 3 and Darkes Doane was Born in Eastham January 12 : 1746

marcy Doane the Dafter of samuel and Darkes Doane was Born in Eastham novembar : ye : 12 : 1749

look in pd 120 for the rest of the Children

* The " 8 " was written over a " 9 " in different ink.

Desembar : yᵉ : 28 : 1751 then Thomas higgens : yᵉ : 3 and anna
    treet boath of Eastham ware marrid by Samuel Smith Esqr in
    Eastham
[p. 156] march : yᵉ : 11 : 1752 then samuel hopkens and sarah wile
    boath of Eastham ware marrid in Eastham by samuel smith
    Esqr
thankfull higgens Dafter of John and marsy higgens was Born in
    Eastham novembar : yᵉ : 29 : 1747
Abiezer holbrooks sun of Abiezer and hanah holbroks was Born in
    Eastham August 20 : 1741
Jesse holbrooks the sun of Abizer and hanah holbrooks was born in
    Eastham July 24 : 1743
Jonathan holbrooks the sun of Abizer and hanah holbrooks was Born
    in Eastham July : yᵉ : 21 : 1745
Elisabath holebrooks the Dafter of Abizer and hanah holbrooks was
    Born in Eastham octobar 14 : 1748
Luse holbrooks the Dafter of Abizer and hanah holbroo[ks] was
    born in Eastham Desembar 4 : 1750
marcy myrick the Dafter of Joseph and Lydia myrick w[as] Born in
    Eastham septembar 22 : 1744
Barbry myrick the Dafter of Joseph and lydia myrick was Born in
    Eastham July 21 : 1746
fear myrick the Dafter of Joseph and Lydia myrick was Born in
    Eastham Aprel 23 : 1749
Joseph myrick Jr the sun of Joseph and Lydia myrick was Born in
    Eastham June : 2 : 1751
[p. 157] Sarah Atkens the Dafter of Joseph and thankfull Atkens
    was Born in Eastham July : yᵉ : 21 : 1727
Phebe Atkens the Dafter of Joseph and thankful Atkens was Born
    in Eastham march 17 : 1729
Thankful Atkens the Dafter of Joseph and thankfl Atkins was Born
    in Eastham January : yᵉ : 24 : 1731
martha Atkens the Dafter of Joseph and thankful Atkens was Born
    in Eastham march 28 : 1733
mary Atkens the Dafter of Joseph and thankful Atkens was Born in
    Eastham febuary : yᵉ : 9 1735
anna Atkens the Dafter of Joseph and thankful Atkens was Born
    in Eastham January : yᵉ : 4 : 1736
Elisabath Atkens the Dafter of Joseph and thankful Atkens was
    Born in Eastham octobar 25 : 1738
Joseph Atkens the sun of Joseph and thankful Atkens was Born in
    Eastham June : yᵉ : 3 : 1741
hanah Atkens the Dafter of Joseph and thankful Atkens was Born
    in Eastham June 13 : 1743
Jamima Atkens the Dafter of Joseph and thankful Atkens was Born
    in Eastham septembar 15 : 1745

Juriah* Atkens the sun* of Joseph and thankful Atkens was Born in Eastham Aprel 13 : 1751

Elezear smith the sun of Levie and Jane smith was Born in Eastham January 4 : 1739

hanah Smith the Dafter of Levie and Jane smith was Born in Eastham Aprel : yᵉ : 9 : 1741

Elezabath Smith the Dafter of Levie and Jane Smith was Born in Eastham Aprel : yᵉ : 23 : 1743

[worn]eant Smith the Dafter of Levie and Jane Smith was Born in Eastham July : yᵉ : 1 : 1745

Ruth Smith the Dafter of Levie and Jane smith was Born in Eastham may : yᵉ : 6 : 1748

prissilla Smith the Dafter of Levie and Jane Smith was Born in Eastham march : yᵉ : 9 : 1752

Grace smith the Dafter of Levie and Jane Smith was Born in Eastham march : yᵉ 15 : 1754

(*To be continued*)

PROCEEDINGS OF THE MASSACHUSETTS SOCIETY OF MAYFLOWER DESCENDANTS

GIFTS FOR THE LIBRARY AND CABINET

From Mr. Arthur Winslow‡ : A Chart of the Winslow Family.

From Rev. Louis C. Cornish‡ : A piece of leaded glass from the Standish house in Duxbury; also a copy of the Cornish Genealogy.

From Mr. Reuel W. Thompson and Miss Sarah B. Thompson‡ : "A Genealogy of John Thomson . . . . By Ignatius Thomson", printed at Taunton, Mass., in 1841.

From Mrs. John Holmes Morison‡ : Four back numbers of "The Mayflower Descendant".

From Mrs. Lucy M. S. Wilson‡ : Thirteen back numbers of "The Mayflower Descendant".

From Mr. Frederick J. Simmons‡, the compiler : "Genealogy of the Simmons Family".

From Miss Fara G. Maurer‡ : Two Photostat Copies of an old Family Record.

From Mrs. Theodore C. Keller‡ : Two Indian arrow heads.

From Mr. Alfred L. Darrow‡ : The "Architectural Record" for May, 1921.

* Sic.

† This name probably was " Jean ".

‡ Member of the Massachusetts Society of Mayflower Descendants.

From **Mr.** George Henry Partridge, the compiler: "Partridge Genealogy Descendants of George Partridge of Duxbury, Massachusetts".

From Mr. Robert L. Brown: "Chipmans in Maine", 1897 edition; also "History of Machias, Me."

From Mr. George Ernest Bowman*: A framed "Family Register", in colors, of the family of Joseph Barstow, of Duxbury, Mass., who was born in 1764.

———

Mrs. Walter S. Radeker died 24 March, 1922, at Roslyn, Long Island, N. Y. She was a descendant of William Bradford, and was elected a member 13 December, 1920, her membership number being 2099.

Mrs. Clarise Sears Ramsay died 9 April, 1922, in London, Eng. She was a descendant of William Brewster, and was elected a member, 25 February, 1907, her membership number being 967.

Mrs. George H. W. Bates died 12 April, 1922, at Melrose, Mass. She was a descendant of John Howland, and was elected a member, 16 May, 1899, her membership number being 496.

Mrs. William H. Atwood died 20 April, 1922, in Brooklyn, N. Y. She was a descendant of Stephen Hopkins and Henry Samson, and was elected a member, 19 November, 1909, her membership number being 1087.

Mrs. Daniel B. Spalding died 18 May, 1922, at Stonington, Conn. She was a descendant of Francis Cooke, and was elected a member, 14 October, 1919, her membership number being 1740.

Mrs. Herbert E. Cushman died 20 May, 1922, in New Bedford, Mass. She was a descendant of Francis Cooke, and was elected a member, 14 April, 1919, her membership number being 1641.

Mrs. Joseph Watson died 26 May, 1922, in Taunton, Mass. She was a descendant of Richard Warren, and was elected a member, 4 September, 1913, her membership number being 1246.

Mr. William B. Stevens died 30 May, 1922, in Boston, Mass. He was a descendant of Richard Warren, and was elected a member, 21 November, 1901, his membership number being 689.

Mrs. James I. Hanson died 13 June, 1922, at Maumee, O. She was a descendant of John Alden, and was elected a member, 29 July, 1921, her membership number being 2305.

Miss Mary A. Mixter died 28 June, 1922, at Swampscott, Mass. She was a descendant of William Brewster, and was elected a member, 8 October, 1896, her membership number being 84.

———

* Member of the Massachusetts Society of Mayflower Descendants.

MEMBERS ELECTED

10 April, 1922.

No. 2410. Leonard William Riley, McMinnville, Or., tenth from Myles Standish.

No. 2411. Robert Alden Dawes, Commander, U. S. N., Island Creek, Mass., ninth from Myles Standish.

No. 2412. Miss Alberta Estelle Smith, Boston, Mass., tenth from Thomas[1] Rogers, ninth from Joseph[2] Rogers.

No. 2413. Mrs. Fiske Warren, Boston, Mass., ninth from Richard Warren.

No. 2414. Miss Fara Gladyce Maurer, Sleepy Eye, Minn., ninth from William Brewster.

No. 2415. William Day Allen, Evanston, Ill., eighth from John Alden.

No. 2416. Miss Anne Morton, Fall River, Mass., tenth from William[1] White, ninth from Resolved[2] White.

8 May, 1922.

No. 2417. Mrs. George Minot Baker, Concord, Mass., ninth from Francis Cooke.

No. 2418. Miss Helen Frances Smith, Boston, Mass., ninth from Richard Warren.

No. 2419. Mrs. Richard Price Davies, Richmond Hill, L. I., N. Y., eighth from Richard Warren.

12 June, 1922.

No. 2420. Thales Lucius Ames, Col., U. S. A., Springfield, Mass., ninth from Francis Cooke.

No. 2421. Jerome Carruth Smith, Newton Centre, Mass., ninth from Richard Warren.

No. 2422. William George Arthur Turner, Malden, Mass., eighth from Richard Warren.

No. 2423. Paul Dawes Turner, Malden, Mass., ninth from Richard Warren.

No. 2424. Richard Greenleaf Turner, Worcester, Mass., ninth from Richard Warren.

No. 2425. Mrs. Sidney Willis Sherman, Grand Rapids, Mich., eighth from William Bradford.

No. 2426. Miss Agnes May McNaught, Dedham, Mass., eighth from Stephen Hopkins.

No. 2427. Miss Alice Maud McNaught, Dedham, Mass., eighth from Stephen Hopkins.

No. 2428. Miss Anne Herron McNaught, Dedham, Mass., eighth from Stephen Hopkins.

No. 2429. Walter Gardner Kendall, D.D.S., Quincy, Mass., ninth from William Brewster.

No. 2430. George Kennard Wakefield, Dedham, Mass., ninth from John Alden.

No. 2431. Ralph Parkhurst Alden, Springfield, Mass., ninth from John Alden.

No. 2432. Miss Mary Smith Watson, Jersey City, N. J., ninth from William Bradford.

No. 2433. Mrs. William John Ward, Jersey City, N. J., ninth from William Bradford.

30 June, 1922.

No. 2434. Lothrop Hooper Wakefield, Dedham, Mass., ninth from John Alden.

No. 2435. Miss Orpha Inez Worcester, Conant, Fla., seventh from William Bradford.

No. 2436. Lewis Jerroldton Powers, 3d, Springfield, Mass., ninth from William Bradford.

No. 2437. Miss Josephine Judith Smith, Fort Plain, N. Y., ninth from Thomas[1] Rogers, eighth from Joseph[2] Rogers.

No. 2438. Miss Grace Hilda Smith, Auburn, N. Y., tenth from Thomas[1] Rogers, ninth from Joseph[2] Rogers.

No. 2439. Mrs. Charles Joseph Morrill, Dover, N. H., seventh from Isaac[1] Allerton, sixth from Mary[2] Allerton.

No. 2440. Mrs. James Gracey Dunseith, Mattapoisett, Mass., ninth from Thomas[1] Rogers, eighth from Joseph[2] Rogers.

No. 2441. Mrs. Margaret Child Abercrombie, Kingston, Mass., ninth from Richard Warren.

No. 2442. Mrs. Luther Warren Rugg, Sterling, Mass., eighth from John Alden.

No. 2443. Miss Bertha Ellen Sparks, Iowa City, Ia., ninth from Stephen[1] Hopkins, eighth from Gyles[2] Hopkins.

No. 2444. Mrs. Charles Sumner Norris, Brookline, Mass., tenth from Richard Warren.

No. 2445. Mrs. William White Rupp, Monmouth, Ill., seventh from John Howland.

SUPPLEMENTAL LINES ACCEPTED

[The By-Laws require an additional fee of two dollars ($2.00) for each supplemental line filed with the Society.]
May, 1922.

No. 1594. Mrs. Ira M. Beaman, eighth from Thomas Rogers.

No. 2392. Mrs. William B. Gibson, eighth from Richard Warren.

No. 2404. Mrs. John C. Bannister, ninth from Stephen Hopkins.

Attest: GEORGE ERNEST BOWMAN,
Secretary.

THE·
MAYFLOWER DESCENDANT

| Vol. XXIV | OCTOBER, 1922 | No. 4 |

JOSEPH WATERMAN'S WILL

BY THE EDITOR

JOSEPH WATERMAN of Marshfield married Sarah Snow[3], daughter of Anthony and Abigail[2] (Warren) Snow of that town, and granddaughter of Richard[1] Warren of the Mayflower; but the date of the marriage has not been found.

Joseph and Sarah (Snow) Waterman had five daughters and two sons, and literal copies of their birth records will be found in the Marshfield, Mass., Vital Records, printed in the second and third volumes of this magazine. These children, all of whom are mentioned in their father's will, were:

Sarah Waterman[4], born 4 May, 1674, married Solomon Hewitt, and left issue.

Joseph Waterman[4], born 2 or 20 January, 1676 (there are two entries on the records), married his first cousin, Lusanna Snow[4] (*Josiah*[3], *Abigail*[2] *Warren*, *Richard*[1]), and left issue.

Elizabeth Waterman[4], born 7 September, 1679, married her second cousin, Ichabod Bartlett[4] (*Benjamin*[3], *Mary*[2] *Warren*, *Richard*[1]), and died before her father, leaving issue. After · her death Ichabod Bartlett[4] married, second, Desire Arnold[5] (*Elizabeth Gray*[4], *Mary Winslow*[3], *Mary*[2] *Chilton, James*[1]), and had children by her also.

Abigail Waterman[4], born 31 December, 1681, married Kenelm Winslow, and left issue. After Abigail's death, Kenelm Winslow married, second, Ann (Winslow[4]) Taylor, widow of John Taylor and daughter of Edward Winslow[3] (*Mary*[2] *Chilton, James*[1]), but had no children by her.

Anthony Waterman[4], born 4 June, 1684, married Elizabeth Arnold[5] (*Elizabeth Gray[4], Mary Winslow[3], Mary[2] Chilton, James[1]*), and left issue. After Anthony's death, his widow Elizabeth married, second, Jonathan[3] Alden (*Jonathan[2], John[1]*), and had children by him.

Bethiah Waterman[4], born 20 August, 1687, married Samuel Doggett, and left issue.

Lydia Waterman[4], born 20 February, 1689, married John Thomas, and left issue.

On the original records of Marshfield, the death of Joseph Waterman appears as follows: "Mr Joseph Waterman Deceased January the 3:17"[*], the last two figures of the year having been worn off. His gravestone in the Winslow Cemetery, at Marshfield, states that he died in January, 1711, aged 62 years[†], but the day of the month was omitted.

Sarah (Snow) Waterman was buried in the same cemetery, and her gravestone states that she died 11 September, 1741, aged 90 years, 3 months[†].

The inscriptions on both of these stones were incorrectly printed in an article on "Marshfield Inscriptions", by Miss Marcia A. Thomas, in the New England Historical and Genealogical Register for October, 1850; and she again incorrectly printed Joseph's stone in her "Memorials of Marshfield", published in Boston, in 1854. And in the July, 1854, N. E. H. G. Register, in "Deaths and Burials from the Early Records of Marshfield", she incorrectly stated that "Mr. Joseph Waterman" died "Jan. —, 1707-8", thus putting his death more than eighteen months before he made his will.

Joseph Waterman made his will on 6 August, 1709, his inventory was taken on 16 February, 1710/11, and the will was probated on 12 March, 1710, as shown by the probate records here printed. Combining the original town and gravestone records with the probate records, there can be no doubt that he died 3 January, 1710/11, the inventory was taken 16 February, 1710/11, and the will was probated 12 March, 1710/11.

The original will is still in the files of the Plymouth County, Mass., Registry of Probate, and the accompanying illustration (facing page 145) reproduces the second page of this interesting document, with the autograph signature of Joseph Waterman. The inventory is the only other original document in the files.

* Mayflower Descendant, 8 : 177.

† Mayflower Descendant, 10 : 50.

We here print a literal copy of the entire will, also exhaustive abstracts of all records in the Plymouth County Registry, relating to the settlement of the estate.

This article is printed at the expense of Mr. Samuel Bradlee Doggett, of Boston, who is a member of the Massachusetts Society of Mayflower Descendants, through his descent from Bethiah Waterman⁴, who married Samuel Doggett.

[JOSEPH WATERMAN'S WILL]

[From original document] "The Last Will & Testament of Joseph Waterman of Marshfeild in the County of Plimouth Declared Agust yᵉ 6ᵗ 1709

"I the said Joseph Waterman being at pʳsent in health & of Sound mind & Memory Praised be God for the same Do make this my last Will & Testament in Maner & form following

"Impʳmis I Comitt my Soule to God that gave it & my body to Decent Buriall when it shall Please Almighty God to take me hence In hope of a Joyfull Resurection & Reunion to Eternall Glory through the precious Merritts of Jesus Christ my Lord & only Saviour

"And for the Disposall of my outward Estate which God hath Graciously Given me my Mind & Will is that it shall be bestowed in such maner as in this my Will is set Down

"first I give & bequeath to my welbeloved wife Sárah the one half of my Now Dwelling house outhouseing & Barne & one third part of all my lands or the Incomes & Rents therof Dureing the Terme of her Naturall Life

"Item I give & bequeath to my son Joseph the new house & Barn wher he now Dwells & the one half of all my farme both upland & Meadow as the same is allready dvided into two parts. to him & his heires for Ever.

"Item I give & bequeath to my son Anthony the one half of my now Dwelling house outhouseing & barns with the other half of all my farme as it is already Devided into two parts. to him & his heirs for Ever & also after his Mothers Decease I give him the other half of my now Dwelling house Outhouseing & Barn to him & his heires for ever

"Item I give & bequeath to Joseph Ryder my Sisters son which I have Brought up my fourth part of the sedge flatts I bought of Winter Hewett lying in Greens harbour River & the fifty acres of upland Bought of the Town and Exchanged with my sons Joseph Waterman & Kenelm Winslow to him & his heires for Ever.

"Item I give & bequeath all my husbandry utencills Tacle & furniture & all my Carpenters & other Tooles whatsoever to my two sons Joseph & Anthony to be Eaqually Devided between them.

"Item I give & bequeath my Silver Tankard to my son Joseph

"Also my mind & will is that my two sons Joseph & Anthony shall Provid their Mother sufficient firewood Cutt & brought And brought to her Door from time to time dureing her Naturall Life in Consideration wherof

"I Give & bequeath to my said two sons Joseph & Anthony all my other lands whatsoever & whersoever to them & their severall heires in Eaquall halfs.

"Item I have allready formerly Given to my Daughter Sarah Hewett the sum of one hundred Pounds

"Item I have allready formerly Given to my Daughter Elizabeth Bartlett Deceased the sum of one hundred pounds

"Item I have allready formerly Given to my Daughter Abigall Winslow the sum of one hundred pounds

"Item I give & bequeath to my Daughter Bethiah one hundred pounds to be paid her by my Executrix.

"Item I give & bequeath to my Daughter Lidia one hundred pounds to be paid her by my Executrix

"Item I give to Mary Okesman which I have brought up thirty pounds to be paid her by my Executrix

"All the aforesd Legacys to be paid them at their full age or day of Mariage which shall first hapen

"Item I give & bequeath unto my welbeloved wife Sarah all the Residue & Remaider of my moneys goods & Chattells & Estate whatsoever for her Comfort & support during her Naturall life & what shall Remaine therof at her decease to be Equally Devided amongst my Daughters that is to say my Dauters Sarah Abigall Bethiah Lidia & the Children of my Daughter Elizabeth deceased. & in Case any other of my said Daughters shall decease before their mother then their Children to have their Mothers part

"Lastly I nominate & appoint my welbeloved wife Sarah to be sole Executrix of this my last Will & Testament

Signed Sealed & Declared   Joseph waterman (seal)
by the abovsd Joseph Waterman
to be his last Will & Testament
In prsence of us
Elizabeth thomas
Samuel hills
Isaac Thomas

"Memorand That on the 12 day of March 1710 The above-named Mrs Elizabeth Thomas & Isaac Thomas made oath before me that they saw the abovenamed Joseph Waterman signe & seale & heard him declare the abovewritten Instrument to be his last Will & Testament & that he then was of a disposeing Mind & Memory to their Judgments

Nathaniel Thomas Judge of Probats"

"on ye 12 Day of March 1710 . . . . at Plymouth . . . . the will of mr Joseph Waterman of Marshfield" was probated, and administration "Committed unto Mrs Sarah Waterman Relict widow to the said Deceased & Sole Executrix". [The will and probate were also recorded, 3: 33, 34.]

[From original document] "Phebruary 16th 17$\frac{10}{11}$ An inventory of the Estat of Mr Joseph Watarman late of marshfild deseased" was taken by Nathaniel Winslow, "John watarman" and Ephraim Little. The total was £2436, 7s., 4d., with "$\frac{1}{2}$ of a Gundelo a Cano & half bushell" not valued.

The real estate was: "one share or 20s rite in ye commans" £36; "upland and medow given to Joseph Ridar by will" £50; "his housing upland and medow land given to his 2 sones Joseph & : Anthony as may appear by his will" £1800.

Other interesting items are : "mony and plate" £63, 19s., 8d. ; "mony du to ye estate by bils &: bonds" £223, 1s., 2d. ; "one third of a sloop" £30; "one silvar tankard given to his son Joseph" £13, 16s., 10d.

"Mrs Sarah Waterman" made oath to this inventory "of the estate of her late husband Joseph Waterman", but the date of the oath was not given. [The inventory was also recorded, 3:37.]

FORM FOR A BEQUEST

I GIVE and bequeath to the Society of Mayflower Descendants, a corporation organized under the laws of the Commonwealth of Massachusetts, the sum of......................dollars.

HARWICH, MASS., VITAL RECORDS

(Continued from page 114)

[p. 25] Mercy Philips Daughter to Micah & Joanah his Wife was born Feby 26th 1726

Hannah Philips Daughter to Micah & Joanah Philips his wif was born May 26^t 1729

David Philips Sone to Micah & Joanah Philips his Wif was bon July 7th 1734

Thankfull Phillips Daughtr to Micah & Joana Philips his Wife was bon March 8 1736

Rubin Philips Sone to Micah & Joannah his Wife was born May 30^t 1739

Jane Daugh to Micah & Joana Philps his Wife was born April 7th 1742

Abigail Daught to Micah & Joana Philps his Wif was born March 20th 1742/3

Samuel Hall Sone to Edward & Patiance Hall his Wife born Dcemb^r 20th 1740

Mary Pain Daughtr of Joseph Junr & Sarah Pain bon 8th of April 1763

Ebanezer Pain Son of Joseph Pain J^r & Sarah Pain his wife born Dceb^r 30^h 1765

Huldah Pain Daughter of Joseph & Sary his wife born Augst 21st 1769

Joseph Paine Son of Joseph & Sarah his wife born Augst 1st 1771

Lusea Pain Daughter of Joseph Pain & Sarah his wife Born July th 10: 1773

Rubin Pain Son of Joseph Pain & Sarah his wife Born october 22: 1776

Nathan Pain Son of Joseph and Sarah Born march th 12: 1779

Ann Murfie Daughter to Thomas & Bridget Murfie was born July 31^s A D 1743

Samuel Pain Son of Joseph Pain and Sarah Pain his wife was Born Septembr th 25 day 1781

Peter Wing Son of John Wing ye 3^{d*} born Octr 10th 1754

James Wing of John ye 3^d & Abigail his wife born Sep^t 20^t 1756

Eli Wing Son of John & Abigail his Wif born March 30th 1759

Isaiah Wing Son of John & Abigal born July 26^t 1761

Rebeca Rodgers Daughter of Joshua & Eliz^a Rodge his Wife born ye 22^d Day of May A D 1745

Joshua Rodgers Sone of Joshua & Eliz^a Rodgers his Wife born†

* " Ju " was first written, but was crossed out, and the entry completed as printed.

† The date was not entered.

Elisha Rodgers Sone of Joshua & Eiz^a Rodger his Wife born Dcemb^r 12th 1750 Dyed May . 1751

Pegga Rodgers Daughter of Joshua & Eliz^a Rodgers his Wife born May 4th 1755

[p. 26] Mary Freeman Daughter to Benj^a Freeman Junr & Sarah his wife born March 23^d 1737

Thankfull Freeman Daughter to Benj^a Freeman Ju^r & Sarah his Wife born ye 30th of Septemb^r 1741

Temperance Freeman Daughter to Benj Freeman Ju^r & Sarah his Wife born July 17th 1744

Edward Freeman Sone of Benjamin Freeman & Sarah h[is] wife born Octr 19th 1746

Lydia Freeman Daughter of Benjama Freem & Sarah his Wife born April 28th 1752

Rebeca Freeman Daughtr of Benjami & Sarah his Wife bon July 6^t 1754

Benj^a Freeman Son of Benj^a & Sarah his Wife bon Aug^st 2^d 1757

James Hopkins Sone of Samuel Hopkins & Mahitable his Wife born Sepr 23^d 1753

James Hopkins Sone of Samuel Hopkins & Mahitable his wife born April 24th 1755

Margary Robins of Heman Robins & Rebecka his Wife born Aug^st 3^d 1762

Thomas Robins Son of Heman Robins & Rebecka his Wife born Aug^st 17th 1765

Joshua Hopkin Son to Nathl Hopkin Ju^r & Abigail his Wife was born March 16th 1743

Samuel Lincoln Sone to Jeremiah & Mary Lincoln his Wife born March 27th 1747 .

Jonathan Lincoln Sone of Jeremiah & Mary born Octr 9th 1748

Temperanc Bangs Daughter of Soloman Bangs & Experianc his Wife born Jany 13th 1753

Elijah Bangs Sone of Soloman & Experianc his Wife born May 18^d 1757

Peris Bangs Son of Soloman & Experen Bangs born Jany 4th 1763

Experiance Bangs Daught of Solomn & Experan Bangs born 15th Septr 1768

[p. 27] Josiah Crosbe Sone to William Crosbe Ju^r & Phebe his Wife born April 24th 1744

Mercy Cob Daughter of Elleaser Cob & Keziah Cob his Wife bor 29th Sept 1762

Susanah Winslow Daughter of Seth Winslow & Precila his wife born June 27th 1752

William Chase Ju^r Sone of William born Octr 16th 1732

Joshua Mirick Sone to Seth Mirick & Elizabeth his Wif born 22^d Febuary 1744

Elizabeth Mirick Daughter to Seth Mirick & Elizabeth his Wif born July 23^d 1747

Isaac Pain Sone of Samuel & Sarah Pain his Wife born July 24th 1748

Samuel Pain Sone of Samuel & Sarah Pain his Wife born Feby 21st 1749

Thomas Pain Sone of Samuel Pain & Sarah his wife born April 2d 1753

David Pain Son of Samuel & Sarah Pain born Septr 2d 1755

Precilla Pain Daughter of Samuel & Sarah Pain his wife born Novr 23d 1757

[p. 28] Thomas Mayo Son of Thomas Mayo Ju & Eliza his Wife born Octr 8th 1753

Asa Mayo Son of Thoms Mayo & Eliza his Wife born Feby 7th 1755

Ebanezer Mayo Son of Thomas Mayo Jr & Eliza his Wife born March 22d 1757

Isaac Mayo Son of Thomas & Eliza his Wife born Novr 21 1758

Mariah Mayo Daughte of Thoms & Eliz his Wif bon Feby 4th 1761

[p. 29] Lidia Small Daughter of Elijah Small & Barbary Small his wif born July 15 1767

Elijah Small Son of Elijah & Barbara Small his wife born April 20th 1769

Nathaniel Small Son of Elijah & Barbry his Wife born June 23d 1771

Samuel Small Son of Elijah & Barbary his Wif born Jany 25 1774

Cathrine Burge Daughter of Ezekiel & Sarah Burge his Wife born Augst 25t 1737

Jeremiah Burge Son of Ezekiel & Sarah his Wif born Jany 25th 1738

Sarah Burge Daughter to Ezekiel & Sarah Burge born Jany 25th 1744

David Ellis Sone of Nathll Ellis & Eliza his wife born May 10th 1754

Easter Ellis Daughter of Nathl Ellis & Eliza his Wife born June 11th 1756

Nathan Ellis Son of Nathl & Elizabeth his wife born June 30th 1759

Easther Ellis Dcembr 2 1763 born

Enoch Ellis born April 29th 1766

Nathll Ellis Ju born June 20th 1771

Samuel Cole Sone of Stephen Cole Jur & Tabatha his Wife born June 30th 1749

Tabatha Cole Daughter of Stephen Cole Jur & Tabatha his Wif born March 20th 1750

Jessa Berry Son To Benjn Berry & mercy Berry His wife Born June th 6: 1782

Elisha Berry of Benjami & Mercy Berry born July 17th 1763

Benja Berry Son of Benja Berry & Mercy his Wife born 26 July 1766

Zohath Berry Son of Benja & Mercy his Wif born Jany 16 1770

Mercy Berry Daughtr of Benja & Mercy his Wife born Jny 11 1771

Theophalu Berry & Hannah Son & Daghte of Benja & Mercy his Wif born April 28 1774

Rhoda Berry Daughter of Benjan Berry & mercy his wife Born augst the 1: 1776

anna Berry Daughter of Benjan Berry & mercy his wife Born Dcember th 27: 1779 [p. 32] These Are to Enter ye Intention of Marriage between Nathl Gould Ju^r of Harwich & Jane Ary of Eastham January 1st A D 1742

These are to Enter ye Intention of Marriage between Mr Ebaneze Mayo of Eastham & Mrs Affiah Freeman of Harwich Janu^y 1st 1742

These are to Enter ye Intention of Marriage between Fortine a Negro Man of Harwich & Nancy Negro Woman of Barnstable Janu^y 1st 1742

There is an Intention of Marriage between Saml Smith Ju^r of Harwich & Mary Hatch of Truro Entred the 25th Day of Dcemb^r A D 1742

These Are to Enter the Intention of Marriage between Jonathan Smalle Ju^r & Hannah Weeks both of Harwich Janu^y 22^d A D 1742

These Are to Enter ye Intentions of Marriage between William Smith of Harwich & Annah OKilley of Yarmouth Janu^y 29th A D 1742

These Are to Enter ye Intentions of Marriage between Moses Mayo & Phebe Freeman both of Harwich Janu^y 29th 1742

These are to Enter ye Intention of Marriage between Silas Sears Junr of Yarmouth & Deberough Buck of Harwich Febru^y 5th A D 1742

These are to Enter ye Intention of Marriage between William Crosbe Junr & Phebe Mayo both of Harwich Februy 5th 1742

These are to Enter ye Intention of Marriage between Joshua Crowel of Yarmouth & Lidia Small of Harwich Feb^ry 12th 1742

These are to Enter ye Intentions of Marriage between James Gage of Harwich & Sarah Baker of Yarmouth Feby 12th 1742

[p. 33] These Are to Enter ye Intention of Marriage between Ammiel Weeks & Phebe Small both of Harwich Feb^ry 12th 1742

These are to Enter ye Intention of Marriage between Stevin OKilley of Yarmouth & Thankfull Chase of Harwich Feby 26 1742

These are to Enter ye Entention of Marriage beetween Thomas Paddock of Harwich & Mary Chapman of Yarmouth March 5th 1742

These Are to Enter ye Intention of Marriage between Seth Dexter & Elizabeth Lincoln both of Harwich March ye 11th A D 1742

These Are to Enter ye Intention of Marriage between Lott Gray Junr & Miriam Smith both of Harwich March 19th 1742

These Are to Enter ye Intentions of Marriage between Mr Hezekiah Baxter of Yarmouth & Mrs Deberough Nickoson of Harwich March 19th A D 1742

These Are to Enter ye Intention of Marriage between Rubin Nickoson of Harwich & Ruth Aary of Eastham April ye 30th A D 1743

These Are to Enter ye Intention of Marriage between Mr Nath^ll Clark & Mrs Lidia Freeman both of Harwich July 9th A D 1743

These Are to Enter ye Intention of Marriage between Saml Hall of Lebenon & Sarah Gray of Harwich July 30th 1743

These are to Enter yᵉ Intentions of Marriage between Samuel Weeber
of Yarmouth & Mary Nickoson of Harwich Augˢᵗ 6ᵗʰ 1743

These are to Enter yᵉ Intentions of Marriage between Heman Stone
& Lidia Gray both of Harwich Augˢᵗ 13ᵗʰ 1743

These Are to Enter yᵉ Intentions of Marriage between Zaccheus
Rodgers of Harwich & Elizabeth King of Eastham Octʳ 2ᵈ 1743

These Are to Enter yᵉ Intention of Marriage between Samˡˡ Crosho-
man & Darkis Wickonut both of Harwich Octʳ 2 1743

There is an Intention of Marriage between Thom Clark Esqʳ & Mʳˢ
Patiance Hall of both of Harwich Octʳ 15ᵗʰ 1743

These are to Enter yᵉ Intention of Marriag between Seth Holmes of
Rochester & Lidia Small of Harwich Oct 1743

These Are to Enter yᵉ Intention of Marriage between Seth Nichoson
of Harwich & Margaret More of Plymouth Novʳ 5ᵗʰ 1743

These Are to Enter yᵉ Intentions of Marriag between William Baker
& Elizᵃ Cowet both of Harwich Januʸ 7ᵗʰ 1743

(*To be continued*)

THE ESTATE OF WILLIAM⁴ BRADFORD, SON OF WILLIAM³ BRADFORD, OF KINGSTON, MASS.

By George Ernest Bowman

William⁴ Bradford (*William³, Maj. William², Gov.
William¹*) of Plymouth and Kingston, Mass., was born before 18
December, 1686*, and was married, at Plymouth, 18 Novem-
ber, 1712*, to Elizabeth Finney⁴, daughter of Josiah Finney and
Elizabeth³ Warren (*Joseph², Richard¹*).

William⁴ and Elizabeth Bradford had eight children. The
first four; Elizabeth, born 10 January, 1714, died 21 January,
1714; Charles, born 4 January, 1715/16; Sarah, born 15 December, 1718; Jerusha, born 20 December, 1722; were recorded at
Plymouth†. The birth record of Josiah has not been found. The
births of the other three were entered, with the death of the
father, on the original records of Kingston‡, Volume 1, page 11,
as follows:

* Mayflower Descendant, 16 : 116 and 23 : 155; and 14 : 37.

† Mayflower Descendant, 12 : 87.

‡ Kingston, formerly a part of Plymouth, became a separate town in June, 1726.

"wiliam Bradford Son of wiliam bradford and Elizabeth his
  wife born may 9 1726 and died july the 23 1726
marcy their daughter born january 15 172⅞
Elizabeth their daughter born Sep^t 15 1730 and died october 10
  1730
wiliam bradford died march 9 1729/30"

The two daughters named Elizabeth, and the son William,
died in infancy.

The daughter Sarah⁵ Bradford married Zephaniah Holmes.

The daughter Jerusha⁵ Bradford married, first, Edward
Sparrow; after his death she married, second, Josiah Carver.

The son Josiah⁵ Bradford married Hannah Rider⁶ (*Samuel⁵,
John⁴, Sarah Bartlett³, Mary² Warren, Richard¹*).

The daughter Mercy⁵ Bradford married Samuel Harlow⁶
(*William⁵, Samuel⁴, Rebecca Bartlett³, Mary² Warren, Richard¹*).

William⁴ Bradford died intestate, on 9 March, 1729/30, and
his widow, Elizabeth, was appointed administratrix, on 1 April,
1730.

We here present exhaustive abstracts of all records, and
original documents on file, in the Plymouth County, Mass., Registry of Probate, relating to the settlement of William⁴ Bradford's
estate.

In accordance with the custom at that time, the eldest son
received a double portion, and, as William⁴ Bradford left five
living children, the real estate was divided into six shares.
Charles⁵ Bradford, the eldest son, received the first and third
shares, and sold them to John Brewster and Thomas Adams.

Elizabeth (Finney) Bradford, the widow of William⁴ Bradford, survived her husband more than forty-two years, dying after
31 December, 1772, but before 15 July, 1778. We shall print the
settlement of her estate in an early issue.

The present article has been prepared at the expense of Virgil
C. Pond, D.M.D., of Boston, a member of the Massachusetts
Society of Mayflower Descendants since 1898, and a descendant
of Edward and Jerusha⁵ (Bradford) Sparrow through their son
Edward Sparrow⁶, of Middleborough, Mass., who married
Rhoda Bump.

[ESTATE OF WILLIAM⁴⁻³⁻²⁻¹ BRADFORD]

[Plym. Co. Prob., 5:665] On 1 April, 1730, "Mrs Elizabeth
Bradford of Kingston .... widow" was appointed adminis-

tratrix of "your Late Husband Willm Bradford late of Kingston
. . . . Dyed Intestate"

[From original inventory] The inventory was taken, 13 April,
1730, by Francis Adams, Samuel Foster and Seth Chipman. A
"Negro Girl" was valued at £36. The real estate was: "y^e
Dwelling house & Barn & 20 acres of Cleared Land and Meadow
on the westerly side of ye Country Road" £300; "the wood Land
adjoining to it Supposed to Be Seventy five acres" £150; "the
orchard and Land with ye Barn on the Easterly Side of the
Country Road" £110; "a peice of Cedar Swamp" £10; "an
Intrest in Land Laying near guners Exchange Pond Lying in
Plymouth" was not valued.

The inventory was acknowledged, 23 May, 1730, by Elizabeth
Bradford, administratrix, and the three appraisers. [Also
recorded, 5:714.] The files also contain an unsigned inventory.

[From unrecorded and unsigned document] A paper labelled
"Willm Bradfords movables", without date, shows a balance of
£72, 2s., 4d., of the movable estate in the hands of the administratrix, "which after the defraying the Charges of the devision and
settlement of the s^d Estate one third of the remainder to be to
the s^d widdow . . . . the other two thirds to be devided to and
amongst the Children in equall parts the eldest son to have a
double part deducting from each of s^d Children what they have
already recived"   .

[5:839] On 11 March, 1730/1, "Mr John Finney of Plymth"
was appointed guardian of "Charles Bradford the Son of William
Bradford late of Kingston . . . . deceased who is a Minor under
ye Age of twenty one Years & above the age of fourteen years"

[From unrecorded bond] On 11 March, 1730/1, John Finney,
as guardian of Charles Bradford, with Jonathan Eames of
Plymouth, as surety, gave a bond for £300. The witnesses were
Mary Winslow and Penelope Warren.

[7:249] On 29 November, 1736, "Sarah Bradford the
Daughter of William Bradford late of Kingston . . . . Deceased
who is a Minor under the age of twenty one Years & above the
age of fourteen Years" chose "Mr George Partridge of Duxborough" as her guardian.

[7:249] On 29 November, 1736, "Jerusha Bradford y^e
Daughter of William Bradford late of Kingston . . . . deceas^d
who is a Minor under . . . . Twenty one Years & above . . . .
fourteen Years" chose "m^r George Partridge of Duxborough"
as guardian.

[7:249] On 29 November, 1736, "Mr George Partridge of

Duxborough" was appointed "Guardian unto Mercy Bradford the Daughter of Wiᴴᵐ Bradford . . . . of Kingston . . . . Deceasᵈ who is a Minor under the age of fourteen Years"

[7:250] On 29 November, 1736, "Mʳ George Partridge of Duxborough" was appointed "Guardian unto Josiah Bradford the Son of Willᵐ Bradford late of Kingston . . . . deceasᵈ who is a Minor under the age of fourteen Years"

[From unrecorded bonds] On 29 November, 1736, "George Partridge House Carpenter", as guardian of Sarah, Jerusha, Mercy and Josiah, with James Arnold, gentleman, as surety, both of Duxbury, gave four bonds, of £300 each. The witnesses were Edward Winslow and Hopestill Oliver.

[7:437] On 15 December, 1737, John Wadsworth, Joseph Mitchell, Samuel Foster, Gamaliel Bradford and John Winslow made a "Division & Partition of the real Estate that William Bradford (the Son of Willᵐ Bradford) late of Kingston . . . . Yeoman died Seized of"

"First Set off to the Widow Elizabeth Bradford . . . . her Right of Dower or Thirds which is as follows viz . The Best Room in the House yᵉ Bed Room that opens into it the Cellar under the Front Room Priviledge of Baking in the oven in the Kitchin 4. Rod Square of Land afore the Door as it is Staked out About five acres of Land lying on the South Easterly Side of the Road Butting on Stony Brook as it is now Inclosed all round with Fence & a Small Barn thereon standing about one acre & quarter of Cedar Swamp Bounded beginning at a Stake Set up near a Road which is a Corner Bounds of yᵉ Cedar Swamp of Capt. Gershom Bradford and from thence to Extend Westerly by a Line of marked trees ten Rods to a maple tree marked on four Sides thence South Sixteen Rods fifteen Links to a Cedar Stake Standing in the Edge of yᵉ Meadow & from thence Easterly to a Pine Stake Standing by a Path in the Swamp that leads to Castle Hill & from thence by Capt. Bradford swamp Southerly as the Way goes to the Stake first Mentioned Which with three Cord of Wood a Year deliverᵈ at her Door as is hereafter mentioned We Esteem to be her Thirds or Right of Dower & as Such We have Set it off to her:

"After which We divided the Residue or Remainder into Six equal Parts Quantity & Quality Considerᵈ And it is in four Divisions . viz :

"The first Division containing the Clear Land,

"The first Share thereof is bounded as follows, viz: Beginning at Stony Brook and thence Extending South Westerly to

the Fence that now Stands before the Door of the Dwelling
House & from thence Northerly on a Strait Line to a Stake standing in the North Easterly Corner of the Land that of late belonged to Maj[r] John Bradford deceas[d] & from s[d] Stake North
Seven Degrees East Nineteen Rods to three Small maple trees
marked Standing by the Brook & from thence by y[e] Brook to
the Bounds first Mentioned The house is Included in this Lot.

"2[d] The Second Lot in the first Division is bounded on the
Northerly Side partly by the Widow's Dower & partly by the
first Lot to the Stake Mentioned in the first Lot & Westerly &
Southerly by the Land of y[e] s[d] John Bradford Deceas[d] to the
Road & so by y[e] Road to y[e] Widows Dower . W[th] y[e] Barn y[r]on
standing

"3[d] The third Lot in the first Division is bounded begin[g] at
the Stake which is the Corner Bounds of the first Lot and from
thence North 85 . Degrees West Seven Rod & eight Links by y[e]
Range of s[d] Maj[r] Bradfords Land & from thence South Sixty
eight Degrees West fourty Rods to a red Oak Sapling marked
Thence North twenty Six Degrees thirty minutes West nine Rod
& an half to a Stake & Stones & from thence North fifty eight
Degrees East to y[e] Brook & then by the Brook to the three maples
marked a Corner Bounds of the first Lot & thence to the Bounds
first Mentioned

"4. The fourth Lot in the first Division is bounded Begin[g]
at y[e] North Westerly Corner Bounds of the third Lot & from
thence North twenty Six & a half Degrees West fifteen Rods
to a Stake & Stones & from thence North fifty eight Degrees
East to the Brook & thence by the Brook to the third Lot & thence
by y[e] third Lot to the Bounds first mentioned

"5. The fifth Lot in the first Division is bounded Beging at
the North Westerly Corner Bounds of the fourth Lot Then
North twenty Six Degrees thirty minutes West fifteen Rods to a
Stake & Stones & from thence North fifty eight Degrees East
to the Brook & then by y[e] Brook to the fourth Lot and thence by
the fourth Lot to the Bounds first Mentioned

"6. The Sixth Lot is bounded Begin[g] at the North West
Corner of the fifth Lot Thence North twenty Six Degrees & an
half West fifteen Rods & ten Links to a Stake & Stones Standing
in the Fence, Then North fifty eight Degrees ˙East Sixty one
Rods to a maple tree marked & so on the Same Course to the
Brook then by the Brook to the fift Lot & from thence by the
fifth Lot to the Bounds first Mentioned

"The Second Division Contains Wood Land and is Bounded
as follows Viz

"The first Lot bounded begin⁸ at the Red oak Sapling which is the South Westerly Corner of the third Lot in the first Division & from thence South Sixty eight Degrees West Sixty Rods to a Spruce tree standing by yᵉ Path anciently marked & from thence North fifty nine Degrees West fourty eight Rods to a Stake & Stones & from thence North East half a Point Easterly eighty Rods to a Stake & Stones Standing on a Knowl & from thence South twenty Six Degrees & a half East five Rods & fifteen Links to a Stake & Stones being yᵉ Corner Bounds of the Sixth Lot in the first Division & from thence by the Head Line of the first Division to the Bounds first mentioned

[p. 438] "2. The Second Lot in the Second Division is bounded begin⁸ at the Stake & Stones being the North Westerly Corner Bounds of the first Lot & thence North fifty nine Degrees West to a black oak marked Thence North fifty Degrees 45 Minutes West to a Stake & Stones The whole breadth being twenty one Rod & a half, Thence North East half a Point Easterly one hundred & Sixty two Rods to a Stake Standing on a knowl & so on the Same Course to the Swamp of Capt. Bradford & then by yᵉ Swamp to a red oak Sapling Standing by yᵉ Side thereof & then South 62.D:E. twenty two Rods to a Stake Standing by yᵉ Brook & then by the Brook eight Rods to the maple tree marked which is the Corner Bounds of yᵉ Sixth Lot in the first Division & then by yᵉ sᵈ Sixth Lot to yᵉ first Lot in yᵉ Second Division then by the last mentioned Lot to the Bounds first mentioned

"3. The third Lot in the Second Division is bound⁴ Beginning at the North Westerly Corner Bounds of the Second Lot thence North fifty Degrees & fourty five minutes West twenty four Rods to a Stake & Stones and from thence North fifty Degrees 45 . minutes East to a maple tree marked in yᵉ Edge of the Swamp & then by yᵉ Swamp of Capt. Bradford to the Second Lot & yⁿ by yᵉ Second Lot to the Bounds first mentioned

"4. The fourth Lot in the Second Division is bounded Beginning at the North Westerly Corner Bounds of yᵉ Third Lot and from thence North 50 . Degrees 45 . minutes West twenty nine Rod to a Stake and Stones & from thence North 50 . Degrees 45 . minutes East one hundred & twenty five Rods to a white oak marked by the Swamp of Capt. Bradford & then by the Swamp to the third Lot & so by the third Lot to the Bounds first mentioned

"5. The fifth Lot in the Second Division is bounded Beginning at yᵉ North Westerly Corner Bounds of the fourth Lot

thence North fifty Degrees & three quarters West twenty one
Rod then North fourty five & half Degrees West fourteen Rods
to a Stake & Stones & from thence North fifty Degrees & three
quarters East to the Cedar Swamp & then by the Cedar Swamp
being markᵈ Range of Trees to yᵉ fourth Lot & then by yᵉ fourth
Lot to the Bounds first mentioned

"6. The Sixth Lot in yᵉ Second Division is bounded beginning at yᵉ North West Corner of the fifth Lot & thence North
fourty five Degrees & an half West to a Stake & Stones & from
sᵈ Stake North fifty Degrees & three quarters East one hundred
& fifteen Rods to a Cedar Stake Standing on Beaver Dam &
thence by a Range of marked Trees being yᵉ Bounds of yᵉ Cedar
Swamp to the fifth Lot & from thence by the fifth Lot to the
Bounds first mentioned

"The third Division is Cedar Swamp & the Lots therein are
bounded as follows—viz:

"1. The first Lot beginning at yᵉ Corner of the Lot Set off
yᵉ Widow & from thence to Extend Westerly by a Range of
marked trees so far as to make the Lot nine Rod in Wedth being
a Stake & from thence North Twenty three Rods to a Cedar
Stake Standing in yᵉ Edge of yᵉ meadow and thence Easterly to
the Corner of yᵉ Widows Lot & yⁿ by her Lot to the Bounds first
mentioned

"2. The Second Lot in the third Division is bounded as follows viz: Beginᵉ at the North Westerly Corner Bounds of the
first Lot & thence Westerly by a Range of marked Trees so far
as to make the Lot nine Rod wide yᵉ Corner Bounds being a
Stake in yᵉ Swamp & from thence North twenty four Rods to a
Cedar Stake in yᵉ Edge of yᵉ meadow & from thence Easterly to
the first Lot & thence to yᵉ Bounds first mentioned

"3. The third Lot in the third Division is bounded as follows
viz: Beginning at the North Westerly Corner Bounds of the Second Lot & from thence Westerly so far as to Make the Lot thirteen
Rods wide yᵉ Corner being two maple Saplings marked & from
thence North Twenty four Rods to a Stake Standing in the
meadow Line & from thence to yᵉ Second Lot & from thence by
yᵉ Second Lot to the Bounds first mentioned

"4. The fourth Lot is bounded Beginning at yᵉ North Easterly Corner of the third Lot being a Stake & from thence South
Seventy two Degrees & an half West to a large Cedar Tree
marked fifteen Rods & fifteen Links & from thence South & by
West twenty three Rods & eight Links to two maples growing
out of one Root marked & from thence by yᵉ Bounds of yᵉ Second

Division or Wood Land to the third Lot & so by the third Lot to yᵉ Bounds first mention'd

"5. The fifth Lot is bounded Beginning at the large Cedar tree mentioned in the fourth Lot & from thence North fifty Seven Degrees West to the Upland Line twelve Rods to three Small maples marked growing out of one Root & from thence by a Range of marked trees being yᵉ Range between yᵉ Wood Land & Swamp to the fourth Lot & then by yᵉ fourth Lot to the Bounds first mentioned

"6. The Sixth Lot is bounded beginnᵍ at yᵉ Cedar Stake which is the North Easterly Corner Bounds of the third & fourth Lot, & from thence South Seventy two Degrees & an half West by yᵉ fourth Lot fifteen Rods & fifteen Links to yᵉ large Cedar aforementioned & thence North fifty Seven Degrees West by yᵉ fifth Lot twelve Rods to the three maples marked a Corner of [p. 439] of the fifth Lot & from thence North Easterly by a Range of markᵈ trees yᵉ Bounds of yᵉ Wood Land to Beaver Dam and to Include a Point of Cedar on Beaver Dam & so by the meadow Line to the Bounds first mentioned

"The fourth Division is meadow & known by yᵉ name of blackwater meadow and the Lots therein are bounded as follows viz.

"1. The first Lot beginning at a Stake Standing by yᵉ Way which was the Corner Bounds of yᵉ Cedar Swamp next adjoyning Capt. Bradfromd* & from thence West three Rods to a Stake standing in the Meadow & from thence North to yᵉ Brook & so by the Brook to yᵉ Land of Capt. Bradford & by his Land to the Bounds first mentioned

"2. The Second Lot is bound from the first Lot Seven Rods in Wedth & to Hold its Wedth to the River yᵉ Corner being a Stake

"3. The third Lot is eight Rods & a half wide being a Stake &† Each Corner nex yᵉ Cedar Swamp

"4. The fourth Lot is thirteen Rods & a half wide being a Stake at Each Corner next yᵉ Swamp

"5. The fifth Lot is fourteen Rods in Wedth & there is a Stake Set up at Each Corner next yᵉ Swamp.

"6. The Sixth Lot is the Remainder of yᵉ meadow on the Westerly Side of yᵉ fifth Lot

"and further we have agreed & make the sᵈ four Divivisions into Shares as follows viz:

---

* Plainly an error of the recorder, for " Bradford ".

† Probably an error for " at ".

"1. The first Share is the first Lot in the first Division with the House all but the Widows [dow]er. The Sixth Lot in yᵉ Second Division. The Second Lot in the third Division and the first Lot in yᵉ meadow

"2. The Second Share contains the Second Lot in yᵉ first Division With the Barn thereon the fourth Lot in yᵉ Second Division. The fifth Lot in the third Division and the fourth Lot in yᵉ meadow

"3. Thirdly The third Share Contains the third Lot in the first Division the first Lot in the Second Division the fourth Lot of Cedar Swamp & the third Lot of meadow

"4. The fourth Share Contains the fourth Lot in the first Division the third Lot in yᵉ Second Division the Sixth Lot of Cedar Swamp & the fifth Lot of meadow

"5. The fifth Share Contains the fifth Share in the first Division the fifth Lot in the Second Division the first Lot in the third Division & yᵉ Sixth Lot in yᵉ meadow

"6. The Sixth Share Contains the Sixth Lot in the first Division yᵉ Second Lot in yᵉ Second Division the third Lot in the third Division & the Second Lot in the meadow .

"We have also reserved a Priviledge of a Way thro Gates & Bars thro these Lots for the Conveniencies of the Parties Interested & to the way to go by the Door of yᵉ House & so through the first Lot to the third Lot & through the Whole of the third Lot next to Majʳ Bradfords Fence to yᵉ Line that Divides the first & Second Divisions by yᵉ head of the Lots to yᵉ Second Wood Lot & so through the Whole of the Wood Lot to Beaver Damm &c And further We Determine that Each of yᵉ sᵈ Shares shall Provide for the Widow at her Door in Case She lives in the House of her late Husband half a Cord of good oak Wood. annually on yᵉ twenty fifth Day of Decembʳ so long as the sᵈ Widow Bradford shall live in & improve sᵈ House"

"Lotted for the Interests

"1 Share fell to John Brewster in yᵉ Right of Charles Bradford—3 Lot to Tho. Adams in yᵉ Right of Charles—2 Lot to Sarah Bradford—6 Lot to Jerusha Bradford—5 . Lot to Josiah Bradford—4 . Lot to mercy Bradford"

"Decembʳ the 22: 1737. The Within named John Wadsworth Joseph Michell Samˡ Foster Gamaliel Bradford & John Winslow made oath that the Within written Division by them made of the Estate of William Bradford the Son of Willᵐ Bradford late of Kingston deceased to yᵉ Widow and amongst the Children of yᵉ sᵈ Deceased is a just & equal Division . . . . Before Isaac Winslow Judge of Probate"

[7:440] On 24 March, 1737,* "The s^d Estate being divided by five good & sufficient Free holders of ye s^d County unto the Widow & among the Children of said Deceas^d & is Settled accordingly in manner following", by Isaac Winslow, Judge of Probate.

"To Mrs Elizabeth Bradford Relict Widow of ye s^d Deceased her Thirds or Right of Dower in the Housing & real Estate . . . . as follows" . [For the bounds see original page 437.] "all which is hereby Settled upon her . . . . during her Natural Life" .

"The Residue or Remainder of ye real Estate being divided in Six Equal Parts or shares for Quantity & Quality and is in four Divisions The First Division Containing the Clear Land the Second Division Containing the Wood Land the third Division Containing the Cedar Swamp the fourth Division is the Meadow Land called black water Meadow & is Settled accordingly in Manner following

"To Charles Bradford the Eldest Son of the s^d Deceased the first Share in ye first Division . . . . With the Dwelling house Excepting what is Set off to the Widow . . . . also the Sixth Lot in the Second Division . . . . also the Second Lot in the Third Division . . . . also the first Lot in the fourth Division" . [For the bounds see original pages 437–439.]

"To Sarah Bradford one of the Daughters of ye s^d deceased the Second Share and is the Second in the first Division . . . . also the fourth Lot in the Second Division . . . . also the fift Lot in the third Division . . . . also the fourth Lot in the fourth Division" . [For the bounds see original pages 437–439.]

"To Charles Bradford the Eldest Son of the s^d Deceased the third Share and is the third Lot in the first Division . . . . also the first Lot in the Second Division . . . . also the fourth Lot in the third Division . . . . also the third Lot in the fourth Division" . [For the bounds see original pages 437–439.]

"To Mercy Bradford one of the Daughters of the s^d Deceased the fourth share and is the fourth Lot in the first Division . . . . also the third Lot in the Second Division . . . . Also the Sixth Lot in the third Division . . . . Also ye fifth Lot in the fourth Division" . [For the bounds see original pages 437–439.]

"To Josiah Bradford one of the Sons of the s^d Deceased the fift Share and is the fift Lot in the first Division . . . . also the fift Lot in the Second Division . . . . also the first Lot in the third Division . . . . also the Sixth Lot in ye fourth Division" . [For the bounds see original pages 437–439.]

* This would be 4 April, 1738, in New Style dating.

"To Jerusha Bradford one of the Daughters of yᵉ sᵈ Deceased the Sixth Share being the Sixth Lot in the first Division . . . . also the Second Lot in the Second Division . . . . also the third Lot in the third Division . . . . also the Second Lot in the fourth Division" . [For the bounds see original pages 437–439.]

"And whereas there remains in yᵉ hand of yᵉ Widʷ administˣ of yᵉ moveable Estate . . . . as by her accompt the Sum of" £72, 2s., 4d., "which after yᵉ Defraying the Charge of yᵉ Division & Settlement of yᵉ sᵈ Estate one third of yᵉ Remainder to her use forever The other two Thirds to be divided to and amongst the Children in equal Parts Except the Eldest Son to have a double Part Deducting from Each of yᵉ sᵈ Children what they have already recieved:"

[From unrecorded bond] On 27 December, 1739, "John Adams of Kingston . . . . Seafareing man" gave a bond for £150, "to Deliver unto Elizabeth Bradford Widow (of William Bradford late of sᵈ Kingston deaceased) one Halfe Corde of Good Oake Wood at the Dwelling House which was the sᵈ Williamˢ in Kingston aforesᵈ once Every Year from and after the date hereof on the Twenty fifth day of December . . . . so long as the sᵈ Elizabeth Shall Live in and improve the sᵈ House and I do . . . . oblige my Selfe and My Heiars for Ever hereafter to Secure and Save Harmless Zephaniah Holmes of Plimouth . . . . Cord- wainer and Sarah his Wife from any demands from the sᵈ Elizabeth Bradford, on accᵗ of the sᵈ one Halfe Cord of Wood to be delivered anually as aforsᵈ"

The witnesses were "Aron Thomas" and James Hovey.

The bond was acknowledged by John Adams, 27 December, 1739, before Samuel Bartlett, Justice of the Peace.

[From original letter] On 21 May, 1741, "Gershom Bradford of Kingston . . . . Gentᵗ" was appointed guardian of "Josiah Bradford a minor son of willᵐ Bradford Late of Kingston aforesᵈ Yeoman Decᵈ"*. [Also recorded, 8: 342.]

[From unrecorded bond] On 21 May, 1741, "Gershom Brad- ford yeoman of Kingston", as guardian "of Josiah Bradford a Minor son of Willᵐ Bradford late of Kingston", with "Benjᵃ Loring of Duxboro Saddler" as surety, gave a bond for £600. The witnesses were Daniel Lewis, Jr., and Samuel Alden.

*The letter is endorsed "Captᵗ Bradford's Letʳ of G ship", and the bond, "Captᵗ Bradfords Bond of Gdsp".

MISCELLANEOUS DEATH RECORDS

TRANSCRIBED BY THE EDITOR

WE here present literal copies, made by the Editor, of some miscellaneous death notices, from newspapers, which have not heretofore been printed in these pages.

[LITTLE]

DR. THOMAS LITTLE[4]. The death of Dr. Thomas Little[4] *(Isaac[3], Anna[2] Warren, Richard[1])* of Plymouth, Mass., was noticed in "The Boston News-Letter" for "Monday December 29 . 1712", as follows :

"Plymouth Decemb. 25th. On the 22d. Currant, Doctor Thomas Little of this Town, Clerk of the Inferiour Court of Common Pleas, and General Sessions of the Peace for the County of Plymouth, Dyed here, Aged about 38* years."

[WINSLOW]

EDWARD WINSLOW[4]. The death of Edward Winslow[4] *(Edward[3], Mary[2] Chilton, James[1]),* of Boston, Mass., was noticed in "The Boston Post-Boy", for Monday, 3 December, 1753, as follows:

"Boston . Last Saturday Night died here in the 85th Year of his Age the Hon. Edward Winslow, Esq; one of His Majesty's Justices of the Court of Common Pleas for the County of Suffolk : He was also formerly, for many Years, Sheriff of the said County, and Colonel of the Regiment Foot in this Town."

[ALDEN]

CAPT. JOHN[4] ALDEN. The death of Capt. John[4] Alden *(John[3,2,1])* of Boston, Mass., was noticed in "The Weekly News-Letter", of Boston, for "Friday March 31. 1727", as follows:

"By Capt. Fulker from Jamaica we have the News of the Death of Capt. John Alden, Jun. of this Place."

The will of Capt. John[3] Alden, printed in our tenth volume, pages 80-82, and dated 5 May, 1727, mentions "the Children of my Son John Alden dece'd"; and in the settlement of the son's estate, printed on pages 82 and 83, "the Deceasds ffuneral Charges in Jamaico" amounted to £64, 8s., 9d.

---

* The Plymouth town records, printed in our sixteenth volume, page 64, give this death as follows : " Docter Thomas Little Deceased Desember 22ᵈ 1712 in yᵉ 38 yea of his age ". And Bradford Kingman's " Epitaphs from Burial Hill ", page 9, gives the correct date and age, from the gravestone; but in Benjamin Drew's " Burial Hill ", page 41, the age is incorrectly printed as " 58 " years.

THE MAYFLOWER PASSENGERS

THERE were only one hundred and four (104) Mayflower Passengers. Every one of them is included in the two lists following. *There were no other passengers.*

[THE 50 PASSENGERS FROM WHOM DESCENT CAN BE PROVED]

John[1] Alden
Isaac[1] Allerton
  wife Mary
  daughter Mary[2]
  daughter Remember[2]
John[1] Billington
  wife Eleanor
  son Francis[2]
William[1] Bradford
William[1] Brewster
  wife Mary
  son Love[2]
Peter[1] Brown
James[1] Chilton
  wife ———
  daughter Mary[2]
Francis[1] Cooke
  son John[2]

Edward[1] Doty
Francis[1] Eaton
  wife Sarah
  son Samuel[2]
Edward[1] Fuller
  wife ———
  son Samuel[2]
Dr. Samuel[1] Fuller
Stephen[1] Hopkins
  2d wife, Elizabeth
  son Gyles[2]
    (by 1st wife)
  daughter Constance[2]
    (by 1st wife)
John[1] Howland
Richard More

William[1] Mullins
  wife Alice
  daughter Priscilla[2]
Degory[1] Priest
Thomas[1] Rogers
  son Joseph[2]
Henry[1] Samson
George[1] Soule
Myles[1] Standish
John[1] Tilley
  wife ———
  daughter Elizabeth[2]
Richard[1] Warren
William[1] White
  wife Susanna
  son Resolved[2]
  son Peregrine[2]
Edward[1] Winslow

[THE 54 PASSENGERS FROM WHOM WE CANNOT PROVE DESCENT]

Bartholomew[2] Allerton
John Allerton
John[2] Billington
Dorothy Bradford
  (1st wife of William[1])
Wrestling[2] Brewster
Richard Britteridge
William Butten
Robert Carter
John Carver
Katharine Carver
  (wife of John)
Maid servant of the Carvers
Richard Clarke
Humility Cooper
John[1] Crakston
  son John[2]
——— Ely
Thomas English

Moses Fletcher
Richard Gardiner
John Goodman
William Holbeck
John Hooke
Damaris[2] Hopkins
Oceanus[2] Hopkins
John Langmore
William Latham
Edward Leister
Edmund Margeson
Christopher Martin
  wife ———
Desire Minter
Ellen More
Jasper More
[a boy] More
Joseph[2] Mullins
Solomon Prower

John Rigdale
  wife Alice
Rose Standish
  (1st wife of Myles[1])
Elias Story
Edward Thomson
Edward Tilley
  wife Ann
Thomas[1] Tinker
  wife ———
  son ———
William Trevore
John[1] Turner
  son ———
  son ———
Roger Wilder
Thomas Williams
Elizabeth Winslow
  (1st wife of Edward[1])
Gilbert Winslow

THE ESTATE OF JACOB TOMSON, ESQ.
OF MIDDLEBOROUGH, MASS.

By the Editor

JACOB TOMSON[3], son of Lieutenant John Tomson by his wife Mary[2] Cooke (*Francis*[1]), was born 24 April, 1662, according to the Barnstable, Mass., records, and was married, 28 December, 1693, to Abigail Wadsworth, born 25 October, 1670, daughter of Deacon John and Abigail (Andrews) Wadsworth, of Duxbury.

Jacob and Abigail (Wadsworth) Tomson had ten children, all recorded at Middleborough, Mass., as follows: Jacob Tomson[4], born 17 April, 1695; Abigail Tomson[4], born 14 February, 1696/7; Mercy Tomson[4], born 13 October, 1699; John Tomson[4], born 19 March, 1700/1; Lydia Tomson[4], born 22 April, 1703; Barnabas Tomson[4], born 28 January, 1704/5; Esther Tomson[4], born 18 February, 1706/7; Hannah Tomson[4], born 10 March, 1708/9; Mary Tomson[4], born 19 May, 1711; Caleb Tomson[4], born 4 November, 1712.

Jacob Tomson, Esq., died at Middleborough, 1 September, 1726, in his 65th year, according to the town records and his gravestone; and Abigail his widow died 15 January, 1744, in her 75th year, according to her gravestone, beside her husband's.

The foregoing births, marriages and deaths, from the original town and cemetery records, will be found in the second, third, fifth, ninth and fourteenth volumes of this magazine. Especial attention is called to these dates, because of the errors in "Descendants of John Thomson", published in Detroit, Mich., in 1890. That book, unfortunately, contains numerous serious errors in dates and names; and, with rare exceptions, neither residences, nor places of birth, marriage and death are given, in the first few generations.

Jacob Tomson[3] died intestate, and the settlement of his estate shows that his wife and all of his ten children survived him.

The widow Abigail (Wadsworth) Tomson made her will[*] on 16 April, 1739, and all of the ten children were then living.

We here print exhaustive abstracts of all records, and original documents on file, in the Plymouth County, Mass., Registry of Probate, relating to the settlement of the estate of Jacob Tomson[3].

[*] We shall print this will in an early issue of this magazine.

[ESTATE OF JACOB TOMSON³]

[Plym. Co. Prob., 5 : 140] On 22 September, 1726, "mʳ Jacob Tomson of middleboro" was appointed administrator on the estate of "your Father Jacob Tomson Esqʳ late of middleboro . . . . dyed Intestate"

[From unrecorded bond] On 22 September, 1726, Jacob Tomson, as administrator, with Thomas Tomson and Ichabod King, as sureties, all three of Middleborough, gave a bond for £2000. The witnesses were Consider Howland and Nehemiah Bennett.

[From original warrant] On 23 September, 1726, "mr Isaac Cushman mr David Bosworth both of Plimpton and mr Samuell Barrow of Middleborough" were appointed to appraise "all the Estate both Reall and Personall" [Also recorded, 5 : 299.]

[5 : 427] An inventory of "yᵉ Estate both Real & Personal" was taken, by the three appraisers, at Middleborough, 7 March, 1726/7. The personal estate was valued at £651, 19s., 7d. "Instruments belonging to Surveying & writing" were valued at £2, 3s., 9d.; "Paper & Parchment" 7s.

The real estate, amounting to £4568, 3s., was as follows:

"His two hundred acre Lotts being in Number yᵉ 12ᵗʰ & yᵉ 18ᵗʰ Lotts with yᵉ 14ᵗʰ Lott of meadow all in yᵉ 26 mens Purchase & given by Deed to His Son Jacob" £220.

"His Lott of meadow in yᵉ upper meadow in sᵈ Purchase" £20.

"His Lott of meadow Ground bought of John Haskall & Isaac Walker being yᵉ 10ᵗʰ Lott in sᵈ Purchase" £18.

"His Lott of Cedar Swamp bought of Adam Wright being yᵉ 3ᵈ Lott in Sᵈ Purchase" £60.

"His Lott in yᵉ first allottment in yᵉ Sixteen Shilling Purchase in yᵉ Right of anthony Snow being yᵉ 46ᵗʰ Lott" £55.

"His Lott in sᵈ first allottment bought of Jabez Wood being . . . . yᵉ Eleventh Lott" £30.

"His two Lotts in yᵉ third allottment in sᵈ Purchase in yᵉ Right of John Haskall being . . . . yᵉ 23ᵈ & 24ᵗʰ Lotts with 1/4 of yᵉ 18ᵗʰ Lott & 19ᵗʰ Lotts in Said 3ᵈ allottment" £33.

"His 3/4 of yᵉ 44ᵗʰ Lott in yᵉ above sᵈ first allottment" £36.

"His 169ᵗʰ Lott Bought of Samuel Barrows, His one halfe of yᵉ 173 Lott bought of Samuel Dellanoe & His 2/3 of yᵉ 156ᵗʰ & 174ᵗʰ Lotts in yᵉ Right of mʳ Samuel Fuller all in yᵉ third allottment in yᵉ Sixteen Shilling Purchase" £63.

"His 51ˢᵗ & fifty Second Lott & yᵉ Lott which He bought of Samuel Sampson all in yᵉ South Purchase: with His Sixteen acres Laid out with ye Lands of Ephraim morton in s^d Purchase with all ye Comon Land which He bought of Leiu^t Nathaniel Southworth in Said Purchase Except a Small Parcell thereof Lying on ye west side of ye black Brook" £173.

[p. 428] "His Thirty acre Lott Called ye Pine wood Lott in . . . . Snipetuit Purchase with ye 14th Lott in s^d Purchase as also His Lott of Cedar Swamp adjoyning thereto" £95.

"all His Rights in ye Little Shares in last allottment in Said South Purchase" £8.

"His 3/4 of ye 57th Lott in assawamsett neck in ye Right of Experience michell, with 3/8th of ye Saw: mill on Bartletts Brook" £42, 1s.

"His Homestead with Buildings with all His Lands meadows & Swamps whether in middleboro, Plympton, or .Pembrooke Lying on ye north side of winnatuxit River Excepting His Lott of meadow Lying on ye north Side of Colchester brook in Plympton" £1099, 5s.

"His 3/8th of ye Saw: mill near His House" £34.

"His Lott of Cedar Swamp Bought of Samuel Bennett in ye 26 mens Purchase with one third of His 21 acres of Land on ye Beach Island in S^d Purchase" £43, 6s.

"His fourty first & fourty Eight Lotts in ye South Purchase" £40.

"His 2/3^d of a Lott on assawamsett neck in ye Right of m^r Samuel Fuller" £16.

"His Lott of Cedar Swamp Bought of Nathan Howland being ye 16th Lott with one third Part of His 22 acres on ye Beach Island both in ye 26 mens Purchase" £28, 7s.

"His fifty ninth, Eighty Seventh & Eighty Eighth Lotts in ye South Purchase" £80.

"His three twenty five acre Lotts butting on ye great River with His Lott of Cedar Swamp in ye Right of Capt Mathew Fuller & one third Part of His twenty one acres of Land on ye Beach Island all Lying in ye 26 mens Purchase" £183, 7s.

"His Lott of meadow lying on ye north side of Colchester brook in Plympton with 1/8th of ye Saw : mill on Bartletts brook in middleboro" £67, 10s.

"His Lott of Land in ye original Right of John morton in ye first allottment in ye 16 Shilling Purchase His 8th 9th & tenth Lotts in ye Second allottment in ye Sixteen Shilling Purchase with His Peice of Land bought of Leiu^t Nathaniel Southworth adjoyning to ye Southerly Side of ye abovesaid tenth Lott" £118.

"His Eleventh Lott in Snipetuit Purchase with His Lott in

ye Cedar Swamp Called black brook Cedar Swamp in s^d Purchase. His two Shares & a Halfe in ye fourth allottment in ye Sixteen Shilling Purchase" £75.

"His two Lotts in ye first allottment in ye Sixteen Shilling Purchase being . . . . ye 62^d & 65th Lott with two thirds of ye 40th Lott in Said first allottment" £97.

"His Halfe Lott of Cedar Swamp bought of david Alden in ye 26 mens Purchase" £11.

[p. 429] "His Quarter of a Share of Cedar Swamp in ye Right of Experience michel in ye Sixteen Shilling Purchase with His two & a Quarter acres of meadow on baiting Brook" £3, 10s.

"His 106 acres of Land in ye five mens Purchase with ye 157th Lott in ye South Purchase given by deed to His daughter marcy Bennett" £190.

"His 4th & 20th Lotts in ye South Purchase" £60.

"His 105th & 106th Lotts in s^d South Purchase" £60.

"His 107th & 108th Lotts in s^d South Purchase" £54.

"His 114th & 168th Lotts in s^d South Purchase" £41.

"His 197th Lott in Said South Purchase" £20.

"The one halfe of His Share of Land in ye Purchase Called Lothrops & Tomsons Purchase adjoyning to Rhochester Lands" £100.

"His 58th & fifty ninth Lotts on assawamsett neck with one third Part of ye Island Called annuxanan in quitticus Pond" £40.

"His 32 acres of Land on s^d neck being Part of ye Lott which did formerly belong to Foelix ye Indian" £50.

"His one Halfe of ye Lott of Land at wopanockett in ye Right of william Bradford Junr" £11.

"His 3/4 of ye two Lotts in South Purchase in ye Right of Experience michel" £38.

"The one Halfe of His Share of Land in . . . . Lothrops & Tomsons Purchase adjoyning to Rhochester Lands" £100.

"His 30th & 37th Lotts with Halfe ye 28th Lott all Lying on assawamsett neck" £64.

"His 6th Lott in Snipetuet Purchase with His 122 acre between s^d 6th Lott & Quittagues Pond in s^d Snipetuit Purchase" £160.

"His 37 & fourty Seventh Lotts in ye South Purchase" £45.

"His Halfe Lott in ye Second allottment in ye Right of william Bradford Junr being ye 47th Lott" £15.

"His 82^d & 98th Lotts in ye third allottment in ye Sixteen Shilling Purchase" £38.

"His 106th & 117 Lotts in s^d 3^d allottment" £35.

"His 121st & 124 Lotts in s^d 3^d allottment" £48.

"His 128 & 181 Lotts in s^d 3^d allottment" £48.

"His 163^d & 164 Lotts in s^d 3^d allottment" £30.

"His 2/3^d of a Share in ye Right of m^r Samuel Fuller & 1/4 of a Share in ye Right of Experience michel in ye fourth allottment in ye 16 Shilling Purchase" £1, 18s.

"His Second Lott 69th & 70th Lotts in ye Second allottment in ye 16 Shilling Purchase" £97.

"His 45th 48th & ye 57th Lotts in ye third allotment in ye Sixteen Shilling Purchase with 16 acres at Sprouts meadow near Said Lotts" £128.

[p. 430] "His Sixty Second, 74th & 75th Lotts in Said 3^d allotment with halfe ye 63 Lott in Said allotment" £110.

"His Halfe of ye 53 Lott in s^d 3^d allotment" £18.

"His 2/3 of a Share of Cedar Swamp in ye Right of Samuel Fuller" £1, 10s.

"His 4 shares in ye Right of matthew Fuller, Peregrin White, anthony Snow, & 1 Share bought of Timothy wood in ye South allotment in S^d Purchase" £8.

"His 90 acres of Land laid out to ye westward of the Pond Called ye Elders Pond in ye 16 Shilling Purchase" £160.

"all His Interest in ye Lands Laid out on ye Easterly Side of namaskett River on ye northerly Side ye fall brook in S^d Sixteen Shilling Purchase" £17.

"His 1/4 of ye Saw: mill on ye Herring River" £30.

The inventory was sworn to by "m^r Jacob Tomson administrator", and by the three appraisers, on 9 March, 1726/7.

[5 : 230, 231] On 22 March, 1726/7, Caleb Tomson, Esther Tomson, Hannah Tomson and Mary Tomson, children of "Jacob Tomson Esqr Late of middleborough", and all minors between the ages of fourteen and twenty-one, chose "m^r Thomas Tomson of middleborough" as their guardian, and the choice was allowed.

[From unrecorded bonds] On 22 March, 1726/7, "Thomas Tomson" of Middleborough, as guardian, with "John Tomson" of Plympton, as surety, gave four bonds, of £500 each. The witnesses were Ephraim Wood and "Jacob Tomson".

[From four unrecorded receipts] "Bridgwater May ye 11th 1727 . . . . we have Received of our honered father Jacob Tomson Esqr in his Life time" £80 "in bills of Credit or the value therof p^r us Jonathan Packard Abigail packard"

"Bridgwater May ye 11th 1727 . . . . we Recev^d of our Honoured father Jacob Tomson Esqr in his Life time" £40 "in bills of Cred or the value there of p^r us John Packard Lydia Packard"

"Middleborough may 11th 1727 . . . . we have Received of our honoured father Jacob Tomson Esqr in his Life time" £40 "over and above the Land given by deed mentioned in the Inventory Nehemiah Bennett Mercy Bennett"

"Middleborough may the 26th 1727 . . . . I have Received of John Tomson a bond . . . . to pay unto Hannah Tomson" £140, 9s., 2d., "and one other bond of the Said John Tomson . . . . to pay unto Mary Tomson" £15, 17s., "to be paid to Each of them Respectively when they arrive to the age of twenty one years with Lawfull Intrest for the Same: Also I have Received of Barnabas Tomson : a bond . . . . to pay unto Esther Tomson" £39, 11s., 8d., "and one other bond of the S^d Barnabas Tomson . . . . to pay unto Hannah Tomson" £52, 4s., 6d., "to be paid to Each of them Respectively when they arrive to the age of twenty one years : with Lawfull Intrest for the Same : Also I have Received of the widow Abigail Tomson : one bond . . . . to pay unto her Daughter Mary Tomson : on her Son Caleb Tomsons account" £30, 4s., 8d., "to be paid when She arives to the age of twenty one years with Lawfull Intrest for the Same from the date of the bond". This receipt was signed, "Thomas Tomson Gardian to the above named Esther Tomson : Hannah Tomson : and Mary Tomson".

[From unrecorded papers] The files contain also an unsigned paper dated 23 May, 1727, containing memoranda of the settlement of the estate, showing the various lots assigned to the heirs, with their value. There is also a paper showing the amounts received by the various heirs, more or less than their respective shares, and the adjustment to make these shares equal. All this is incorporated in the settlement as given in original pages 430–436.

There is also a contemporary slip of paper, undated and unsigned, containing an item of a will making a bequest to "my beloved wife Abigail Tomson".

[5 : 430] "The Settlement of ye Housing & Lands of Jacob Tomson Esqr late of middleboro . . . . deceas^d Intestate", by the Judge of Probate, dated 1 July, 1728, "in manner following. The Personall Estate of ye s^d deceas^d Prized att" £632, 18s., 1d., "after ye Payment of ye Debts & ye Charge of administration was by mutuall agreement divided to ye widow & amongst the Children of ye S^d deceas^d . The S^d Housing & Lands & Reall Estate being Prised at" £4568, 3s., "which after Having Sett of to ye widdow m^{rs} Abigall Tomson . . . . as Her [p. 431] Her Dower the one third Part of ye Improvement of ye Homestead where on Her s^d Husband Last dwelt with ye use & Improvement of Halfe y^e

dwelling House Barn & out-Houses standing thereon : Said Homestead & Buildings being Prised at" £800, "it being what ye S^d widow moved for & is Content to take up with . . . . is . . . . Settled upon Her . . . . during Her natural Life".

"The Rest of ye s^d Reall Estate is Settled to & dvided among ye Children of ye Deceas^d as followeth . . . . To Jacob Tomson: John Tomson, Barnabas Tomson, Caleb Tomson, Abigall Packard; mercy Bennett : Ledia Packard; Esther Tomson, Hannah Tomson & mary Tomson"

"To Jacob Tomson ye Eldest son . . . . The two Hundred acre Lotts being in number ye 12 & ye 18 Lotts with ye 14 Lott of meadow all in ye 26 mens Purchase" £220; "The Lott of meadow in ye uper meadow in s^d Purchase" £20; "The Lott of meadow ground bought of John Haskall & Isaac Walker being ye tenth Lott in s^d Purchase" £18; "His Lott of Cedar Swamp bought of Adam Wright being ye third Lott in s^d Purchase" £60; "His Lott in ye first allotment in ye Sixteen Shilling Purchase in ye Right of anthony Snow being ye fourty Sixth Lott" £55; "His Lott in ye s^d first allotment bought of Jabez wood being in number ye Eleventh Lott" £30; "His two Lotts in ye third allotment in s^d Sixteen Shilling Purchase in ye Right of John Haskall being in Number ye twenty third & twenty fourth Lotts with a Quarter of ye Eighteenth & nineteenth Lott[s] in s^d third allottment" £33; "His three Quarters of the fourty fourth Lott in ye aboves^d first allotment" £36; "His one Hundred & Sixty ninth Lott bought of Samuel Barrow His one Halfe of ye one Hundred & Seventy third Lott bought of Samuel Dellanoe & His two thirds of ye one Hundred fifty Six & one Hundred Seventy fourth Lotts in ye Right of m^r Samuel Fuller all in ye third allotment in ye S^d Sixteen Shilling Purch[ase]" £63; "His fifty first & fifty Second Lotts & ye Lott H[e] bought of Samuel Sampson all in ye South Purchase with His Sixteen acres laid out with ye Lands of Ephraim Morton in Said Purchase with all ye Comon Lands He bought of Leiu^t Nathani[el] Southworth in s^d Purchase Except a Small Parcell thereof lying on ye west Side of ye black brooke" £173; "His thirty acre Lott Called ye Pine wood Lott in ye Purchase Called Sniptuet Purchase with ye fourteenth Lott in s^d Purchase as also His Lott of Cedar Swamp adjoyning thereto" £95; "all His Righ[t] in ye Little Shares in ye Last allotment in s^d South Purchase" £8; "His three Quarters of ye fifty Seventh Lott in assawamsett neck in ye Right of Experience mitchell wit[h] three Eights of ye Saw mill on Bartletts Brook" £42, 1s.; "The one tenth Part of His Lands laid out in ye Easterly Side of

namaskett River on ye northerly Side of ye fall brook" £1, 14;
"one third Part of the ninety acres of Land laid out to ye westward of ye Pond Called ye Elders Pond in ye Sixteen Shilling
Purchase" £53, 6, 8; "all ye s^d Land & meadows are Scittuate
in ye Townships of middleboro, Plympton & Rochester . . . .
which s^d Lands & meadow . . . . amounting to ye Sum of
£908 : 10 : 8 . which is more then His double Share or two Parts
by ye Sum of £77 : 19 : 4. which . . . . the S^d Jacob Tomson
hath Paid or given good & Sufficient Security in ye Law to Pay
to His Sister abigail Packard."

"2 To John Tomson ye one Halfe of ye Homestead with the
Buildings with one halfe of all His Lands meadows and Swamps
whether in middleboro Plympton or Pembrooke lying on ye north
Side of winnetukset River Excepting His Lott of meadow lying
on ye north Side of Colchester brook in Plympton Reserving to
ye widdow m^{rs} abigail Tomson ye use & Improvement of one halfe
of ye dwelling House Barn & out : Houses & ye Improvement or
Incomes of one third of all ye Improved Lands & meadows
belonging to ye Homestead which lye Joyning together as before
Settled upon Her during Her natural Life : Prized at
£549 : 12 : 6 . His Lott of Cedar Swamp bought of Samuel
Bennett in ye twenty Six men^s Purchase with one third of His
twenty one acres of Land in ye beach Island in s^d Purchase"
£43, 6; "His fourty first &' fourty Eight Lots in ye South Purchase" £40; "His two thirds of a Lott in assawamset neck in y^e
Right of m^r Samuel Fuller" £16; "Three Sixteenths of ye Saw :
mill near His House" £17; "one tenth Part of His Land laid out
on ye Easterly Side of namaskett River on ye northerly Side of y^e
Fall : brooke" £1, 14; "The S^d Lands & meadows . . . . with
ye Buildings thereon . . . . amounting to ye Sum of £667: 12: 6.
Which . . . . is more then His Single Part or Share of ye S^d
Reall Estate by ye Sum of £252 : 6 : 10 which s^d Sum . . . .
He Hath Paid or given good and Sufficient Security in ye Law to
Pay to His Sister abigall Packard ye Sum of £96 : 0 : 8 . To
His Sister Hannah Tomson ye Sum of £140 : 9 : 2. To His
Sister mary Tomson ye Sum of £15 : 17"

"3 To Barnabas Tomson ye one Halfe of His Homestead with
ye Buildings thereon with ye one Halfe of all His Lands
meadows & Swamps whether in middleboro Plympton or
Pembrooke lying on ye north Side of winnetukset River: Excepting His Lott of meadow lying on ye north : Side of
Colchester brooke in Plympton Reserving to ye widdow m^{rs}
abigall Tomson ye use & Improvement of ye one Halfe of y^e

dwelling House Barn & out-Houses & the Improvement & Income of one third Part of all yᵉ Improved Lands & meadows belonging to yᵉ Homestead & lye adjoyning together during Her natural Life as before is Settled upon Her" £549, 12s., 6d.; "His Lott of Cedar Swamp bought of nathan Howland being the Sixteenth Lott with one third Part of His twenty one acres on yᵉ Beach Island both in yᵉ twenty Six mens Purchase" £28, 7; "His fifty ninth, Eighty Seventh & Eighty Eight Lotts in yᵉ South Purchase" £80; "one tenth Part of His Lands laid out on the Easterly Side of namaskett River on yᵉ northerly Side of yᵉ fall Brook" £1, 14; "three Sixteenths of yᵉ Saw : mill near His House" £17; "The said Lands & meadows . . . . amounting to yᵉ Sum of £676: 13:6 . which is more then His Part or Share of yᵉ sᵈ Reall Estate by . . . . £261:7:10 . which sᵈ Sum . . . . He Hath Paid or given good & Sufficient Security in yᵉ Law to Pay to His Sister Ledia Packard yᵉ Sum of £169:11:8 . To His Esther Tomson yᵉ Sum of £39:11:8. To His Siste[r] Hannah Tomson yᵉ Sum of £52:4:6."

"4. To Caleb Tomson His three twenty five acre Lotts Lying butting on yᵉ great River with His Lott of Cedar Swamp bought of Capᵗ matthew Fuller : & one third Part of His twenty one acres of Lan[d] on yᵉ beach Island all lying in yᵉ twenty Six mens Purchase" £183, 7; "His Lott of meadow lying on yᵉ north Side of Colcheste[r] Brook in Plympton with one Eighth of yᵉ Saw mill on Bartlett Brook in middleboro" £67, 10; "His Lott of Land in yᵉ originall Right of John Morton in yᵉ first allottment in the Sixteen Shilling Purchase, His Eighth, ninth, & tenth Lotts in yᵉ Second allottment in yᵉ sᵈ Sixteen Shilling Purchase with His Peice of Land bought of Leiuᵗ Nathaniel Southward adjoyning to yᵉ Southerly Side of yᵉ abovesᵈ tenth Lott" £118; "His Eleventh Lott in Sniptuet Purchase with His Lott in yᵉ Cedar Swamp Called black brook Cedar Swamp in sᵈ Purchase" £70; "His two Shares & a Halfe in yᵉ fourth allottment in yᵉ Sixteen Shilling Purchase namely yᵉ Share in yᵉ Right of John Haskall : & yᵉ Share in yᵉ Right of John Eddy & yᵉ Halfe Share in yᵉ Right of John Irish" £5; "the one tenth Part of His Land laid out on yᵉ Easterly Side of namaskett River on yᵉ northerly Side of yᵉ fall brooke" £1, 14; "The Sᵈ Lands & meadows . . . . amounting to yᵉ Sum of £445:11:0 . which is more then His Part or Share of yᵉ Sᵈ Reall Estate by yᵉ Sum of £30:5:4 . which sᵈ Sum . . . . He Hath Paid or given good & Sufficient Security in yᵉ Law to Pay to His Sister mary Tomson".

"5 To abigall Packard yᵉ wife of Jonathan Packard of

Bridgewater . . . . one of ye Daughters of ye s^d deceas^d His two Lotts in ye first allottment in ye Sixteen Shilling Purchase being in Number ye Sixty Second & ye Sixty fith Lotts with two thirds of ye fourtieth Lott in s^d allottment" £97; "His Halfe Lott of Cedar Swamp bought of David alden in ye twenty Six mens Purchase" £11; "His Quarter of a Share of Cedar Swamp in ye Right of Experience mitchell in [p. 434] In ye Sixteen Shilling Purchase with His two acres & a Quarter of meadow on bateing brooke" £3, 10s.; "the one tenth Part of His Land Laid out on ye Easterly Side of namaskett River on ye northerly Side of ye Fall brooke" £1, 14; "the twenty fourth Part of a Saw mill on Herring River" £5; "two thirds of His ninety acres of Land laid out to ye westward of ye Pond Called ye Elders Pond in ye Sixteen Shilling Purchase" £106, 13s., 4d.; "The s^d Lands & meadows . . . . amounting to ye sum of £224 : 17 : 4 . which is less then Her Part or Share of ye s^d Reall Estate by ye Sum of £190 : 8 : 4 . which s^d Sum of £190 : 8 : 4. She hath Received or taken good & Sufficient Security in ye Law to Receive from Her Brother Jacob Tomson ye Sum of £77 : 19 : 4. from Her Sister mercy Bennett ye Sum of £16 : 8 : 4 . from Her Brother John Tomson ye Sum of £96 : 0 : 8. which makes Her full Part."

"6 : To mercy Bennett ye wife of nehemiah Bennett of middleboro afores^d one of ye daughters of ye s^d deceas^d His one Hundred & Six acres of Land in ye five mens Purchase with the one Hundred & fifty Seventh Lott in ye South Purchase" £190; "His fourth & His twentieth Lotts in ye South Purchase" £60; "His one Hundred & fifth & one Hundred & Sixth Lotts in s^d South Purchase" £60; "His one Hundred & Seventh : & one Hundred & Eigth Lotts in s^d South Purchase" £54; "His one Hundred & fourteenth & one Hundred & Sixty Eighth Lotts in s^d South Purchase" £41; "His one Hundred & ninety Seventh Lott in s^d South Purchase" £20; "The twenty fourth Part of ye Saw : mill on ye Herring River" £5; "The one tenth Part of His Lands laid out on ye Easterly Side of namaskett River on ye northerly Side of ye fall : brooke" £1, 14; "The s^d Lands aforementioned . . . . amounting to ye Sum of £431 : 14 : 0. which is more then Her Part or Share of ye s^d Reall Estate by ye Sum of £16 : 8 : 4. which s^d Sum . . . . She hath Paid or given good & Sufficient Security in ye Law to Pay unto Her Sister abigall Packard."

"7 : To Ledia Packard ye wife of John Packard of Bridgewater . . . . one of ye Daughters of ye s^d deceas^d The one Halfe of His Share of Land in ye Purchase Called Lothrops & Tomsons Pur-

chase adjoyning to Rochester Lands" £100; "His fifty Eighth &
fifty ninth Lotts on assawamsett neck with one third Part of y^e
Island Called anuxanan in quitequess Pond" £40; "His thirty
two acres of Land on s^d neck being Part of ye Lott which did
formerly belong [p. 435] Belong to Foelix ye Indian" £50; "His
one Halfe of ye Lott of Land at wopanockett in ye Right of
William Bradford Junr" £11; "His three fourths of ye two Lotts
in ye South Purchase in ye Right of Experience mitchell" £38;
"The twenty fourth Part of a Saw : mill Standing on ye Herring River" £5; "The one tenth Part of His Land laid out on y^e
Easterly Side of Namaskett River on ye northerly Side of ye fall
brooke" £1, 14; "The s^d Lands aforementioned . . . . amounting to ye Sum of £245 : 14 : 0. which is less then Her Part or Share
of ye s^d Real Estate by ye Sum of £169 : 11 : 8. which S^d Sum
. . . . She hath Received or taken good & Sufficient Security in
ye Law to Receive from Her Brother Barnabas Tomson."

"8. To Esther Tomson one of ye Daughters of ye S^d deceas^d
the one halfe of His Share of Land in ye Purchase Called
Lothrops & Tomsons Purchase adjoyning to Rochester Lands"
£100; "His thirtieth & thirty Seventh Lotts with Halfe y^e
twenty Eighth Lott all lying on assawamsett neck" £64; "His
Sixth Lott in Snippetuet Purchase with His one Hundred &
twenty two acres between S^d Sixth Lott & quitecuss Pond in S^d
Snippetuet Purchase" £160; "His thirty Seventh & fourty
Seventh Lotts in ye South Purchase" £45; "The twenty fourth
Part of a Saw : mill Standing on ye Herring River" £5; "the
one tenth Part of His Lands laid out on ye Easterly Side of
Namasket River on the northerly Side of ye fall : brooke" £1, 14;
"The s^d Lands aforementioned . . . . amounting to ye Sum of
£375 : 14 : 0. which is less then Her Part or Share of ye S^d Real
Estate by ye Sum of £39 : 11 : 8 . which s^d Sum . . . . She Hath
Received or taken good & Sufficient Security in ye Law to
Receive from Her Brother Barnabas Tomson".

"9 : To Hannah Tomson one of ye daughters of ye S^d deceas^d
His Halfe Lott in ye Second allottment in ye 16 Shilling Purchase
in the Right of william Bradford Junr being ye fourty Seventh
Lott" £15; "His Eighty Second & ninety Eighth Lotts in the
third allottment in ye Sixteen Shilling Purchase" £38; "His one
Hundred & Sixth & one Hundred & Seventeenth Lotts in ye s^d
third allottment in ye Sixteen Shilling Purchase" £35; "His one
Hundred & twenty first & one Hundred & twenty fourth Lotts in
ye S^d third allottment in ye Sixteen Shilling Purchase" £48;
"His one Hundred & twenty Eighth & one Hundred & Eighty

first Lotts in S^d third allottment in ye Sixteen Shilling Purchase"
£48; "His one Hundred & Sixty third & one Hundred & Sixty
fourth Lott in s^d third allottment in ye Sixteen Shilling Purchase" £30; "His two thirds of a Share in ye Right of m^r
Samuel Fuller & one Quarter of a Share in ye Right of Experience
mitchell in ye fourth allottment in s^d Sixteen Shilling Purchase"
£1, 18; "The twenty fourth Part [p. 436] Part of a Saw mill
Standing on Herring River" £5; "The one tenth Part of His
Land laid out on ye Easterly Side of Namaskett River on y^e
northerly Side of Fall : brooke" £1, 14; "The s^d Lands aforementioned . . . . amounting to ye Sum of £222:12:0 . which
is Less then Her Part or Share of ye s^d Reall Estate by ye Sum
of £192:13:8 . which S^d Sum . . . . She hath Received or
taken good and Sufficient Security in ye Law to Receive of Her
Brother John Tomson ye Sum of £140:9:2. of Her Brother
Barnabas Tomson the Sum of £52:4:6 . which makes Her full
Part."

"10 To mary Tomson one of ye Daughters of ye S^d deceas^d
His Second Lott also His Sixty ninth & Seventieth Lotts in y^e
Second allottment in ye Sixteen Shilling Purchase" £97:
"His fourty fifth, fourty Eighth & fifty Seventh Lotts
in ye third allottment in ye Sixteen Shilling Purchase with
Sixteen acres at Sproats meadow near s^d Lotts" £128; "His Sixty
Second, Seventy fourth & Seventy fifth Lotts in ye third allott-
ment in ye Sixteen Shilling Purchase with halfe ye Sixty third
Lott in s^d allottment" £110, 10; "His Halfe of ye fifty third Lott
in s^d third allottment in ye Sixteen Shilling Purchase" £18; "His
two thirds of a Share of Cedar Swamp in ye Right of m^r Samuel
Fuller in ye Sixteen Shilling Purchase" £1, 10; "His four Shares
in ye Right of matthew Fuller Peregrin White: anthony Snow &
one Share bought of Timothy wood in ye fourth allottment in s^d
Sixteen Shilling Purchase" £8; "The twenty fourth Part of a
Saw : mill Standing on ye Herring River" £5; "The one tenth
Part of His Lands laid out on ye Easterly Side of Namaskett
River, on ye northerly Side of ye fall brooke" £1, 14; "The S^d
Lands aforementioned . . . . amounting to ye Sum of £369:4:0 .
which is less then Her Part or Share of ye s^d Reall Estate the
Sum of £46:1:8 . which s^d Sum . . . . She hath Received or
taken good & Sufficient Security in the Law to Receive of Her
Brother John Tomson ye Sum of £15:17:0 . of Her Brother
Caleb Tomson ye Sum of £30:4:8 . which makes Her full Part"

THE ESTATES OF THOMAS HUCKENS
AND HIS SON JOHN

By the Editor

Thomas[1] Huckens of Barnstable married, first, Mary Wells, by whom he had three daughters: Lydia, died young; Mary, married Samuel Storrs; Elizabeth, died young. The wife Mary died in 1648, and, in less than four months, Thomas[1] Huckens married Rose, widow of Hugh Hyllier of Yarmouth.

Thomas and Rose Huckens had four children born at Barnstable: John[2] Huckens, born "About y[e] 2 of August 1649", married Hope Chipman[3] (*Hope[2] Howland, John[1]*); Thomas[2] Huckens, born 25 April, 1651, married, first, Hannah Chipman[3] (*Hope[2] Howland, John[1]*), and second, widow Sarah (Pope) Hinckley; Hannah[2] Huckens, born 14 October, 1653, married James Gorham[3] (*Desire[2] Howland, John[1]*); Joseph[2] Huckens, born 21 February, 1655, died 9 November, 1679, without issue, and apparently unmarried.

Literal copies of the Barnstable town records of these births, marriages and deaths will be found in our fifth, sixth, tenth and twelfth volumes.

John[2] Huckens (*Thomas[1]*) was married, at Barnstable, on 10 August, 1670, to Hope Chipman[3] (*Desire[2] Howland, John[1]*), by whom he had five children: Elizabeth, Mary, Experience, Hope and Mehitable. Four of the children were recorded at Barnstable (see our sixth volume), and the settlement of the father's estate proves that there was also a daughter Mehitable.

John[2] Huckens died at Barnstable, 10 November, 1678, and his widow married, second, on 1 March, 1682/3, Jonathan[2] Cobb (*Henry[1]*) and had children by him.

Thomas[1] Huckens and his son Joseph[2] were "cast away y[e] 9 of November 1679".

The "Jabez Serjeant" mentioned in the next to the last paragraph of the settlement of the estate of Thomas Huckens was the youngest child of John and Deborah (Hyllier) Sargeant, and the mother, Deborah, was the daughter of Hugh and Rose Hyllier. The widow. Rose Hyllier married, as his second wife, Thomas[1] Huckens, who was, therefore, the step-grandfather, not the real grandfather of "Jabez Serjeant".

We here print exhaustive abstracts of all records of the settlement of the estates of Thomas[1] Huckens and his son John[2], found in the Plymouth Colony Wills and Inventories, at Plymouth, Mass.

This article has been prepared at the expense of Mrs. Henry D. Moore, a descendant of John and Hope (Chipman) Huckens, and a member of the New Jersey Society of Mayflower Descendants.

[ESTATE OF JOHN[2] HUCKENS]

[Plym. Col. Wills, 4 : 1 : 8] "A true Inventory of . . . . the Goods Chattles and Creditts of John Huckings Deceased apprised att his house in Barnstable the 27 Day of December 1678 by Joseph Laythorp and Barnabas Laythorp". The total amount of the inventory was £154, 12s. The only real estate was: "Item in housing upland and meddow" £70, "Mr Thomas Huckengs Reserveing alwayes to himselfe the one halfe of the warehouse; with Free egresse and Regress therinto". One fourth part of a ketch was valued at £30.

"Hope the late wife of the said John Huckings made oath to the truth of this Inventory this third of March 1678 Before mee Thomas Hinckley Assistant:"

[4 : 1 : 9] "In Reference unto the settlement of the estate of John Huckings late of Barnstable (whoe died Intestate) between the mother and the Children of the said John Huckings with the Consent of Elder John Chipman and Thomas Huckings seni^r: It is ordered by the Court that Hope the Mother of the said Children and Relectt of the said John Huckings shall have the whole estate hee left; whether in house lands or other estate whatsoever To her sole Dispose for ever, Towards the support and the bringing up of the five Children which shee had by him; provided and so as shee the said Hope Doe pay or cause to be payed unto the said Thomas Huckens his executors or assignes within two yeers after the Date heerof the full sume of twenty and five pounds in Currant New England money for the use and to be Improved to and in behalfe of the said Children and the Surviver & Survivers of them whoe are Named Elizabeth Mary Experience Hope and Mehittable, To be equally Devided with the produce and Advance, which may arise by the Improvement therof as aforsaid unto the said five Children or the Surviver or Survivers of them as they or any of them shall attaine the age of twenty one yeers Respectively or the Day of Marriage which shall first happen

And the said Thomas Huckings Did apper in open Court; and Acknowlidge, his Surrender of the house and Lands in the Inventory of the said John Huckings mensioned on Record into the hands of the said Hope her heires and assignes for ever, which hee Did Intend to Bestow on the said John Huckings Deceased and which hee in his Life time had the use and Improvement off; And is Now by the said Thomas Huckings heerby ffreely and absolutely Conveyed assured and Confeirmed unto her the said Hope, And to the onely proper use and behooffe of her the said Hope The Relicte of the said John Huckinges, and to her heires and Assignes for ever in Manor and forme aforsaid, according to the true Intent and meaning of these p^rsents in Testimony wherof the said Thomas Huckings Desires the Record heerof; and for Confeirmation of the whole as aforsaid the Court have ordered the Record heerof;

Plymouth March the 7th Ann° Dom: 16⅞"

[ESTATE OF THOMAS¹ HUCKENS]

[Plym. Col. Wills, 4:1:58] "A true Inventory of . . . . the Goods Cattles and Creditts of Mr Thomas Huckens Deceased Apprised att his house in Barnstable" 10 February, 1679, "by Joseph Laythorp and Barnabas Laythorp". "2 silver spoones" were valued at £1; "Joseph Huckens his p^rsonall Estate praised to the vallue of" £14, 7s. The real estate was: "Dwelling house and barne and land belonging to it" £220; "Coopers Necke of land" £40; "the land att Cotuitt" £40; "the land att Wequoitt" £9; "the land above the meeting house" £4; "the reversion of John Coopers land" £50; "the meddow att Sandey neecke" £5. Debts amounting to £464, 15s., were due the estate. The total of the inventory was £1014, 2s.

The estate was indebted £14, 19s.

"And to Goodwife Bourne" £15 "p^r anum During her Naturall life".

[4:1:60] "Wheras Thomas Huckens seni^r late of Barnstable . . . . Deceased had not in his life time soe p^rfected his last Will . . . . as hee Intended . . . . wherby many questions and Debates were like to arise for prevension wherof; and for a finall quiett and Amicable settlement of his estate . . . . amongst those that were Concerned therin and have right to their p^rtes therof; it is Mutually and Respectively . . . . agreed and concluded by and between the said p^rties Concerned, heer unto subscribed . . . . with an eye as much as might be to what was his Declared mind and will in his lifetime, though Not fully p^rfected as aforsaid; viz:

"Imp^rs: That Thomas Huckens the onely Surviveing sonne of the said Thomas Huckens Deceased; be seized of the whole estate . . . . both Reall & p^rsonall and Adminnester upon the same . . . . paying all such Debts as are Due . . . . as alsoe to pay all such sumes and Legacyes to the p^rties heerafter Named; as theire respective p^rtes of the said estate; in such Manor and forme as is in and by these p^rsents mensioned"

"Viz . . . . the said Thomas Huckens . . . . will deliver, or cause to be Delivered unto Rose Huckens his Mother and Relict of the said Thomas Huckens Deceased, two Cowes ten sheep one Mare and four swine, to be wholly att her Dispose; and further to pay . . . . unto the said Rose yeerly . . . . During her Naturall life the full sume of six pounds in Clotheing and provisions, suitable for her; and" £3, 10s., "more in silver mony, att or before the fifteenth Day of November anually During . . . . her Naturall life . . . . att her Now Dwelling house in Barnstable" also "her late husbands best bed with the furniture belonging therunto, and three paire of sheets; and one fourth p^rte of All the rest of the houshold stuffe; whatsoever in brasse Iron pewter and wood and &c : During her Naturall life, and then to be Devided after her Decease amongst the Children shee had by said Thomas Huckens her husband, or be Desposed of by her to them or theire Children, or to such of them as shee shall see Cause; And that During her widdowhood shee have the full libertie and privilidge of the parlour and leanto against it att the westeren end of the said Dwelling house, with one third p^rte of the Garden for her use; and the said Adminnestrator alsoe to provide ffodder for her two Cowes, and ten sheep and sufficient fierwood for her use yeerly, and att all times During her said widdowhood, and this to be in full of all her Demaunds of the said estate;"

"That the said Adminnestrator Thomas Huckens his heires executors or Administrators shall and will pay or cause to be payed unto Hope Huckens the Relicte of John Huckens Deceased Eldest sonne of the said Thomas Huckens Deceased, the sume of twenty and five pounds in Currant New England Mony within one yeer after the Date heerof; and is to be Improved by the said Thomas Huckens or his Assignes for the Good and benifitt of the five Daughters shee had by the said John Huckens, or the survivers of them; To be equally Devided between them with the produce and advance therof, as they may Come of age or Day of Marriage as by agreement and order of the said Thomas Huckens Deceased, in Reference to the settlement of the estate of the said John Huckens between Hope the said mother and the Children, as by Court Record Doth appeer; This twenty five pounds aforsaid being to be in the stead of and to fulfill the said Hope Huckens her Ingagement or obligation of the twenty five pounds to be payed by her to the said Thomas Huckens Deceased his executors or assignes for the use and to be Improved for, and in behalfe of the said five Children; as in the aforsaid Court Record Doth more fully and att large appeer, att his Maties Court held in Plym March 1678: and further to pay or Cause to be payed unto the said Hope Huckens the sume of fifty pounds in Marchants pay, att prise Currant with the Marchants towards her support and the bringing up of her said Children; The one half therof to be payed to her or her Assignes att or before the fifteenth Day of November Next Insueing the Date heerof; and the other Halfe att the fifteenth of November Next following which wilbe in the yeer 1681 and alsoe to pay or Cause to be payed to the said Hope for the use and behoof of her said Children the sume of twenty and five pounds more in silver mony within two yeers after the Date heerof, or one third p^rte of what the lands of the said Thomas Huckens Deceased called Coopers Necke; and his lands att Coituitt are or shalbe sold for within these two yeers Next; [p. 61] Next coming or in Defect therof to have one third pte of all the said lands att Coopers Necke & Coituitt to be Assigned to her and the said Children to have and to hold for ever; and this to be in full for her pte and her said Childrens p^rte of the said Estate and to be paid att Barnstable;"

"the said Adminnestrator Thomas Huckens . . . . shall pay or Cause to be payed unto Samuell Stores and Mary his wife . . . . sixty six pounds in marchants pay att prise Currant . . . . viz: thirty pounds therof att or before the fifteenth of November Next Insueing & fifteen pounds within a yeer after the said November Next ensuing : and twenty and one pounds by the fifteenth of November which shalbe in the yeer 1682; and further to Deliver to them the said Samuell and Mary three Cowes; or their vallue in other Neate Cattle and a p^rsell of Marsh of late the said Thomas Huckens, Deceased in the Comittees Cove; and that p^rsell of his marsh which hee bought of Mr Linnell, since sold by the said Samuell Stores, and alsoe further to the said Samuell eight shillings, in silver Mony, and the second best suite throughout, of the said Thomas Huckens Deceased, or in liew therof three pounds in silver Mony; and this to be in full of the said Samuell and Maryes p^rte of the said estate, to be payed att Barnstable;"

"the said Adminnestrator Thomas Huckens . . . . shall pay
or cause to be payed; unto James Gorham and Hannah his wife,
the sume of Ninety pounds in Marchants pay att prise Currant
. . . . accounting that which they have alreddy Received, of the
said Thomas Huckens in his life time, to be p^{r}te therof being
vallued Att twenty and six pounds; the said sum to be payed in
three yeers time, viz : forty five pounds therof to be payed att
or before the 15th of November Next ensueing; and twenty and
two pounds and ten shillings within one twelve month after that;
and twenty and two pounds and ten shillings the Resedue therof,
within a yeer after that, Last Mensioned, viz: in November 1682,
and further to them the said James and Hannah; one bed and
furniture therto belonging and one fourth p^{r}te of all the Rest
of the houshold stuffe whatsoever as aforsaid and alsoe one Mare
and five sheep; the said twenty and six pounds, alreddy received
as aforsaid to be proportionable Deducted out of the yeerly payments; aforsaid; and this to be in full of the said James and
Hannahs p^{r}te of the said estate; the payments to be payed the
one halfe att Boston and the one halfe att Barnstable ;"

"the said Thomas Huckens . . . . shall pay or cause to be
payed unto Jabez Serjeant three pounds in like Marchants pay
as aforsaid· within two years next after the Date heerof; in full
of his Legacye Given to him by his Grandfather The said Thomas
Huckens Deceased ;"

"Finally it is Agreed and Concluded that the said Adminnestrator Thomas Huckens for the payment of the Debts sumes;
and legacyes above mensioned; shalbe seized of have and Injoy as
his owne . . . . all the rest of the said estate, both reall and
p^{r}sonall, whatsoever; In Witness wherof The p^{r}ties to these
p^{r}sents have heerto sett theire hands the fourteenth of March
Ann^o: Dom: 16$\frac{81}{82}$

In p^{r}sence of   Rose Huckens her marke
Thomas Hinckley Assistant   Thomas Huckens
Joseph Capen ;   Hope Huckens
                                              Samuell Stores
                                              James Gorham ;"

MIDDLEBOROUGH, MASS., VITAL RECORDS

((Continued from page 133)

[p. 88] Jan⸢y⸣ 21 : 1762 Jacob Soul & Sarah Shaw both of middleborough were married by S: Conant

march 4 William Cushman Ju⸢r⸣ & Susanna Pratt both of middlebo were married by S: Conant

march 18 John Thomas Ju⸢r⸣ & Faith Benson both of middlebo were married by S: Conant

[m]arch 25 Binney Cobb & Azubah Shaw both of middlebo were married by S. Conant

[Ap]ril 29 Samuel Turner & Lucy Pratt both of middleborough were married by Silvanus Conant

Jan⸢y⸣ 13: 1763 Samuel Bonney of Plimpton & Lydia Smith of middlebo were married*

[Jan⸢y⸣ 13 : 1763] James weston jun⸢r⸣ & Betty warren both of middlebo were married*

July 5: 1763 John Briggs & Abigail Morss both of middlebo were married by S: Conant

July 21⸢st⸣ Israel Smith & mary Bates both of middleborough were married by S. Conant

Sept⸢r⸣ 22⸢d⸣ moses Robbins of middlebo & Abigail Barrows of Plimpton were married by S: Conant

Oct⸢r⸣ 3⸢d⸣ 1763 Robart Tucker ju⸢r⸣ of Norton & martha Willies of middlebo were marr⸢d⸣*

[Oct⸢r⸣ 3⸢d⸣ 1763] John Eddy of Norton & Elisabeth Clap of middlebo were married*

Dece⸢r⸣ 8: 1763 Samuel Shaw & Jedidah Bumpas of middlebo were married*

[Dece⸢r⸣ 8 : 1763] Zadok Bozworth of Hallifax & Elisabeth Smith of middlebo were married*

Feb⸢y⸣ 9: 1764 Paul Pratt & Jail Bennet both of middlebo were married by S: Conant

march 8 1764 Consider Brannak & Desire Simmons both of middlebo were married by S: C

March 29: 1764 John murdoch of Plimpton & Sarah Samson of middlebo were married by S: C

June 21: 1764 John Standish of Hallifax & Rebekah Ellis of middlebo were married by S: C

Sep⸢r⸣ 6: 1764 John Miller 3⸢d⸣ & Zilpah Tinkham both of middlebo were married by S: C

[*worn*] 7: 1764 Job Alden & Lucy Spooner both of middlebo were married by me Silvanus Conant

* These marriages were bracketed in pairs, as indicated by the dates we have put in brackets; and "by S: Conant" was written at the right of each pair.

[*worn*] 25 : 1764 John Severy ju^r & Thankfull Cobb both of middlebo
    were married by me S: Conant

[*worn*] 5 : 1764 Peter Tinkham & Molly Tomson both of middlebo
    were married by me S. Conant

[*worn*] 22 : 1764 John Smith jun^r of middlebo & Bethiah Chipman
    of Hallifax were married by me*

[[*worn*] 22 : 1764] Joseph Smith & Abigail Bent both of middlebo
    were married by me*

Decr 6 : 1764 Eliakim Briggs of abington & Lois Thomas of middlebo
    were married by me S: Conant

Decem^r 10 : 1764 Abraham Vaughan of middlebo & anne Russel of
    Pembrook were marr^d by me S: Conant

Feby 7 : 1765 John Bradford of Kingston & Hannah Eddy of mid-
    dlebo were married by me S: Conant

Plimouth Ss: march 28 : 1765 this Day Nathan Barden of Freetown
    & Hannah Pratt of middleborough were married by me Joseph
    Tinkham Justic Peace

the above & foregoing marriages is on the County Records

Plimouth Ss: August 1st 1765 this Day m^r Daniel Smith & m^{rs} Han-
    nah Bates both of middleborough were Joyn^d In marriage by me
    Joseph Tinkham Justic Peace

This Certifies that John Cole of Plimpton and Elizabeth Proute of
    Middleborough were joined in Marriage on February 28th 1765
    By Isaac Backus Baptist Minister

(*To be continued*)

PROCEEDINGS OF THE MASSACHUSETTS SOCIETY
OF MAYFLOWER DESCENDANTS

GIFTS FOR THE LIBRARY AND CABINET

From Miss Janet McKay Cowing†: A Pair of very old, hand
wrought, Andirons; An old Fire Pan; Documentary History of New
York (1849), four volumes; Officers and Men of New Jersey in the
Revolutionary War; Sullivan Centennial, Seneca Co., N. Y.; "Pas-
sages from the Remembrances of Christopher Marshall"; American
Biographical Notices; A Century of Population Growth; United
States Census, 1790, Connecticut, Massachusetts, New York, Penn-
sylvania, Rhode Island.

From Mr. Nathaniel A. Shaw† : Two Historical Magazines.

---

* These two marriages were bracketed, after the date " [*worn*] 22 : 1764 ";
and were followed by " S: Conant ".

† Member of the Massachusetts Society of Mayflower Descendants.

From Mr. Summerfield Hagerty: Ninety-two (92) back numbers of "The Mayflower Descendant"; Thirty-seven (37) numbers of "Pilgrim Notes and Queries"; Twenty (20) Historical Magazines and Pamphlets.

From Miss Helen L. Church*: Ten (10) Historical Magazines.

From Mr. George Ernest Bowman*: Two Tercentenary Half Dollars (1921 issue). [The total amount authorized was not coined in 1920, and the date 1921 was put on the remainder of the issue.]

———————

Mrs. George B. Waterman died 6 January, 1922, at Williamstown, Mass. She was a descendant of William Bradford, and was elected a member, 22 March, 1916, her membership number being 1407.

Mr. Herbert Folger died 4 August, 1922, at Berkeley, Cal. He was a descendant of Degory Priest, and was elected a member, 25 March, 1907, his membership number being 969.

Mrs. Joshua Bates died 13 August, 1922, at Bridgewater, Mass. She was a descendant of Isaac Allerton, Francis Cooke and Richard Warren, and was elected a member, 2 September, 1898, her membership number being 395.

Miss Alice M. Hammond died 15 August, 1922, at Swampscott, Mass. She was a descendant of Isaac Allerton, James Chilton and Richard Warren, and was elected a member, 26 March, 1912, her membership number being 1176.

Harold C. Ernst, M.D., died 7 September, 1922, at Plymouth, Mass. He was a descendant of Richard Warren, and was elected a member, 18 June, 1920, his membership number being 1962.

Mrs. Summerfield Hagerty died 24 September, 1922, at Clifton, Mass. She was a descendant of John Howland and William White, and was elected a member, 15 December, 1897, her membership number being 296.

———————

MEMBERS ELECTED

31 July, 1922.

No. 2446. Mrs. Thomas Daniel Rhodes, Asheville, N. C., eighth from John Howland.

No. 2447. Mrs. Caleb Rochford Stetson, New York, N. Y., eighth from John Alden.

No. 2448. Robert Cushman, Boston, Mass., ninth from Isaac[1] Allerton, eighth from Mary[2] Allerton.

No. 2449. Mrs. Franklin Atwood Park, New York, N. Y., eighth from Isaac[1] Allerton, seventh from Mary[2] Allerton.

No. 2450. Dr. William Gardner, Grundy Center, Ia., tenth from William Brewster.

* Member of the Massachusetts Society of Mayflower Descendants.

No. 2451. Miss Marian Phebe Kirkland, Lexington, Mass., ninth
from John Alden.

No. 2452. Mrs. Charles Lenox, Trenton, N. J., eighth from William
Bradford.

No. 2453. Mrs. John Chauncey Van Horn, Trenton, N. J., ninth
from William Bradford.

11 September, 1922.

No. 2454. Miss Joanna White Little, Boston, Mass., seventh from
Richard Warren.

No. 2455. Samuel Peregrine White, Beverly, Mass., eighth from
William[1] White, seventh from Peregrine[2] White.

No. 2456. Samuel Bradlee Doggett, Boston, Mass., seventh from
Richard Warren.

No. 2457. Miss Eleanora Randolph Sears, Boston, Mass., tenth from
William Brewster.

No. 2458. Mrs. William Henry Brown, Boston, Mass., ninth from
John Howland.

No. 2459. Robert Longfellow Brown, Boston, Mass., tenth from
John Howland.

No. 2460. Mrs. Willard Grant Aborn, Brookline, Mass., tenth from
William Brewster.

No. 2461. Miss Louisa Williams Burgess, Boston, Mass., eighth
from William[1] Brewster, seventh from Love[2] Brewster.

No. 2462. Mrs. Walter Scott Stratton, Bismarck, N. D., tenth from
William Bradford.

SUPPLEMENTAL LINES ACCEPTED

[The By-Laws require an additional fee of two dollars ($2.00)
for each supplemental line filed with the Society.]

September, 1922.

No. 1883. Miss Sally Freeman Dawes: ninth from John Alden;
tenth from John Alden; ninth from Isaac[1] Allerton,
eighth from Mary[2] Allerton; tenth from James[1] Chilton, ninth from Mary[2] Chilton; ninth from William
Bradford; ninth from William Brewster (in two lines);
ninth from Francis Cooke; ninth from Stephen Hopkins; ninth from George Soule; ninth from Myles
Standish; ninth from Richard Warren.

No. 2029. Albert E. Hoyt: eighth from Thomas Rogers.

No. 2440. Mrs. James G. Dunseith: ninth from Stephen[1] Hopkins,
eighth from Constance[2] Hopkins; tenth from John
Howland.

Attest: GEORGE ERNEST BOWMAN,
Secretary.

EASTHAM AND ORLEANS, MASS., VITAL RECORDS

(Continued from page 141)

[p. 160*] Aprel 20 : 1753 then nathaniel paine and thankful young Boath of Eastham ware marrid in Eastham By m^r Joseph Croker Clar

John Paine Son of Nathaniel and Thankful paine was Born at Eastham August 31 : 1756

Bathsheba Paine Daughter of Nathaniel and Thankful Paine was Born at Eastham feburary 5 : 1758

Betty Paine Daughter of Nathaniel and thankful Paine was Born at Eastham Apriel 15 : 1760

Sarah Paine Daughter of Nathaniel and thankful Paine was Born at Eastham may : 8 : 1765 :

Nathaniel Paine Son of Nathaniel and thankful Paine was Born at Eastham July the 4 : 1768

may 23 1753 then william Croker of Barnstable and Lydia Knowles of Eastham was marrid in Eastham by Mr Joseph Croker Clar

the above List of mariges has Ben sent to the County Clark

Solomon Linnell Son of Jonathan and Priscilla Linnell was Born at Eastham July ye 16 : 1764

Jonathan Linnell Son of Jonathan and Priscilla Linnell was Born at Eastham may ye 29 : 1766

Goold Linnell Son of Jonathan and Priscilla Linell was Born at Eastham January ye 3 : 1768

Benjamin Linell Son of Jonathan and Priscinlla Linell was Born at Eastham June ye 12 : 1770

January 10 : 1750 then Dct nathaniel Breed and Ann Knowles Boath of Eastham ware marrid in Eastham by Edward Chever Clar Recorded pr Thomas Knowles Town Clar

nathaniel† Breed the sun of Dct nathaniel and Ann Breed was Born in Eastham June : y^e : 4 : 1753

Delivearnc Breed the Dafter of nathaniel and ann Breead was Born in Eastham may : y^e : 6 : 1755

Abigail Breed the Dafter of nathaniel and Ann Breed was Born in Eastham may y^e : 30 : 1756

John Breed the sun of nathaniel and Ann Breed was Born in Eastham octobar y^e : 14 : 1757

Ebenezer Harding the Son of John Harding & Margaret Harding was born in Eastham February the 14 1758

Hannah Harding the Daug^tr of John & margaret Harding was born in Eastham april the 20 1760

* Pages 158 and 159 follow page 161.

† "Josiah" was crossed out and "nathaniel" interlined, both above and below, in the same hand and ink.

Lattis Harding the Daug^{tr} of John & margaret Harding was born in Eastham January the 17 : 1763

Apphiah Harding the Daughter of John & Margaret Harding was born in Eastham June the 29 1765

[p. 161] Isaac Sparrow and Rebaca Knowles boath of Eastham ware marrid in Eastham January 15 : 1746/7* by Mr Joseph Crocker Clar

Richard sparrow the sun of Isaac and Rebaca sparrow was Born in Eastham Desembar 5 : 1747

Sarah Sparrow the Dafter of Isaac and Rebaca Sparrow was Born in Eastham septembr 13 : 1749

Isaac sparrow Jur the sun of Isaac and Rebaca sparrow was born in Eastham June 7 : 1752

mercy sparrow was Born the Dafter of Isaac Sparrow and Rebaca sparrow in Eastham Aprel the 25 : 1754

Rebeca Sparrow Daughter of Isaac and Rebecca Sparrow was Born in Eastham october the 2 Day 1756

Josiah Sparrow Son of Isaac and Rebekah Sparrow was Born in Eastham February the 10 Day 1759

Hannah Sparrow Daughter of Isaac Sparrow and Rebekah Sparrow was Born in Eastham December the 8 Day 1761

Elisebeth Sparrow Daughter of Isaac Sparrow and Rebekah Sparrow as born at Eastham the twelfth Day of august 1764

Elkeny smith the sun of Jaremiah and Lydia smith was Born in Eastham Desembar 8 : 1738

David smith the sun of Jaremiah and Lydiah smith was Born in Eastham June 30 : 1741

Heman smith the sun of Jaremiah and Lydiah smith was Born in Eastham march 8 : 1744

philip smith the sun of Jaremiah and Lydiah smith was Born in Eastham January 25 : 1746†

Lydiah smith the Dafter of Jaremiah and Lydiah smith was Born in Eastham Desembar : 1749‡

marcy smith the Dafter of Jaremiah and Lydiah smith was Born in Eastham march 5 : 1753

Jaremiah smith Died Aprel 2 : 1754

John gills the sun of scarlet and tabathy gills was Born in Eastham June : 15 : 1748

abiga gills the sun of scarlet gills and tabathy gills was Born in Chatham septembar : y^e : 25 : 1750

tabatha gills the wife of scarlet gills Died in Eastham January : y^e : 9 : 1753

---

* "1747/8" was altered to "1746/7" in the same ink.

† "6" was written over "8" in different ink.

‡ "9" was written over "7" in the same ink as in the preceding correction.

Abijah gills Son of Scarlet and tabatha Gills Died march the 11 Day 1772

[p. 158*] mary Brown the Dafter of gorge and Ales Brown was Born in Eastham July : yᵉ : 21 : 1741

hephzibah Brown the Dafter of gorge and Ales Brown was Born in Eastham January : yᵉ : 6 : 1744/5

Zilpha Brown the Dafter of gorge and Ales Brown was Born in Eastham febuary : yᵉ : 10 : 1747/8

samuel Brown the sun of gorge and Ales Brown was Born in East-ham June : yᵉ : 3 : 1751

gorge brown the sun of gorge and Alce Brown was Born in Eastham march 22 : 1753

phebee brown the Dafter of gorge and Alce brown was Born in East-ham may : yᵉ : 20 : 1755

Prisillah Brown Daughter George and Alce Brown was Born in Eastham march 14 Day 1759

Theoder Brown Son of George and Alice Brown was Born in East-ham april 26 Day 1761

octobar yᵉ : 18 : 1750 then Rufus Cole and Elisabath hambelton boath of Eastham ware marrid in Eastham by Mʳ Joseph Croker Clar

August 29 : 1751 then Elisha Atwood and abigel freeman boath of Eastham ware marrid in Eastham by Mʳ Joseph Crocker Clar

David Atwood the sun of Elisha and abigail atwood† was Born in Eastham may 31 : 1752

Elisha atwood Son of Elisha and abigail atwood was born July 25 : 1754

Bangs atwod Son of Elisha and abigail atwood was born auguᵗ 25 : 1756

freeman atwood son of Elisha & abigail atwood was born June 10 : 1759

Gedion Atwood Son of Elisha and abigial atwood was Born at East-ham the 10 Day of September 1761

Abigail atwood Daughter of Elisha and abigail atwood was Born at Eastham Sepᵗ yᵉ 4 : 1766

[p. 159*] octobar 3 : 1751 then Isaac taler of penbrook and Dorces higgens of Eastham ware marrid in Eastham by Mʳ Joseph Croker Clar

January : yᵉ : 9 : 1752 then Jonathan Linel : yᵉ : 3 of Eastham and priscilla gould of harwich was marrid in Eastham by Mʳ Joseph Croker Clar

Thomas Linnell the Son of Jonathan and Priscilla Linell was Born at Eastham October yᵉ 18 : 1752

Josiah Linnell Son of Jonathan and Priscilla Linell was Born at Eastham December the 19 : 1755

* See footnote on page 189.

† "freeman" was first entered, but it was crossed out and "Atwood" inter-lined, in the same hand and ink.

Thankful Linnell Daughter of Jonathan and Priscilla Linnell was
Born at Eastham february ye 17^t : 1757

Molly Linnell Daughter of Jonathan and Priscilla Linnell was Born
at Eastham febuary the 28 : 1759

Faba Linnell Daughter of Jonathan and Priscilla Linnell was Born
at Eastham may ye 15 : 1762

Look to the next page for the Rest of the Children

January 23 : 1752 then Ichabid higgens and Bethiah Knowles Boath
of Eastham ware marrid in Eastham By m^r Joseph Croker Clar

Hannah freeman Daughter of Jonathan and thankful freeman ware
Born at Eastham march ye 6 : 1764

Thankful freeman Daughter of Jonathan and thankful freeman ware
Born at Eastham may the 1 Day 1766

Mr Jonathan Freeman Died July the 2 — 1768

Loes freeman Daughter of Jonathan and thankful freeman was Born
at Eastham July ye 7 1768

march : 12 : 1752 then Jonathan freeman and thankful Linel boath
of Eastham ware marrid in Eastham By m^r Joseph Croker Clar

Edman freeman the sun of Jonathan and thankful freeman was Born
in Eastham Desembr 15 : 1752

Abner freeman the sun of Jonathan and thankful freeman was Born
in Eastham June 12 : 1755

Rebakah Freeman Daughter of Jonathan and thankful Freeman was
Born at Eastham march ye 26 — 1757

Sarah Freeman daughter of Jonathan and thankful freeman was
Born at Eastham June ye 6 : 1759

John Freeman Son of Jonathan and thankful freeman was Born at
Eastham November ye 10 — 1761

Look a Bove for the Rest of the Children

(*To be continued*)

NOTES BY THE EDITOR

"Ten Counterdemaunds." In this article, in our last issue
[Vol. 24, p. 123], I stated, on the authority of the Librarian of the
Huntington Library, that this tract had not before been reprinted;
but I have since learned that it was reprinted in "The Early
English Dissenters", published at Cambridge, Eng., in 1912.

Weston-Turner. In the twenty-eighth line on page 120 of
our last issue [Vol. 24, p. 120], "Charles and Sally Turner"
should read "Charles and Sally (Turner) Weston".

INDEX OF PLACES

33